Choice, Opportunity and Learning

Educating children and young people who are physically disabled

John Cornwall

David Fulton Publishers
London

David Fulton Publishers Ltd
2 Barbon Close, London WC1N 3JX

First published in Great Britain by
David Fulton Publishers 1996

British Library Cataloguing in Publication Data

A catalogue record for this book is available from the British Library

ISBN 1-85346-304-3

Typeset by Textype Typesetters, Cambridge
Printed in Great Britain by BPC Books and Journals, Exeter

Contents

Acknowledgements iv

Introduction 1

1 Fragmented Children: Services and Legislation 10

2 A Healthy Perspective 40

3 Disabling Schools and Colleges 64
Dr Christine Barton

4 The Challenge of Inclusion 82

5 Entitlement, Access and Differentiation 113

6 Making Partnership a Reality 140

7 Parents' Expertise and Integrity 172

8 Codes and the Sharing of Practice 194

9 Enabling Technologies for Communication and Learning 219
Mike Blamires

10 Opportunity and Change – Inclusive or Exclusive Education? 232

Bibliography 259

Index 265

Acknowledgements

- Julie, Thomas, Lucy and Sam for their patience and understanding during my mental absences while writing this book.
- Disabled and non-disabled colleagues and friends, particularly Christine and Aileen who have lent so much support to my efforts.
- Project, course members and postgraduate students of all disciplines for teaching me over the years and for their enthusiasm and interest in learning.
- Over 300 organisations and individuals who responded to my request for information and material. I look forward to being in touch again one day and I hope this book has made their trouble worthwhile.
- Over forty LEAs, schools and colleges that I have had the pleasure and privilege to work with over the past five years, since retiring as a Head.
- My colleague who persuaded me to go to Oregon, USA, and helped to make it an inspiring and confidence boosting experience.
- Simon Brisenden for his challenging and amazing poetry that has fuelled my commitment to finish this book. Your verses will live on.
- Lucy, my daughter, Liz Hirstle, CCAM (and Nick Dawes), Micheline Mason and Birkett (in Punch magazine) for their cartoons, drawings and illustrations.
- Mary for her dedicated fingers, perseverance and contribution to lay-out and presentation.

Introduction

Somewhere, over the rainbow

During the Summer and Autumn of 1994, a substantial furore built up in the country involving the attempted passage of the 'Civil Rights (Disabled Persons) Bill' through Parliament. It was alleged that the Bill had been deliberately stalled by the Government with the covert involvement of the Minister for the Disabled. They had, it seemed, used procedural mechanisms and amendments to block the passage of this Member's Bill. The result was that it did not have time to go through the House of Commons, and it was effectively lost. The same fate awaited Harry Barnes' 'Civil Rights (Disabled Persons) Bill' in 1995. The usual party political tactics seem to have been employed in the House of Commons. They have undermined belief in and understanding of the arguments surrounding this legislation.

Disability rights and other representative groups point to the American experience where tougher civil rights legislation has had a substantial impact on the behaviour of people in general and on the quality of life for many disabled people. Legislation can set a very positive agenda and stimulate action where it was previously not taking place. Laws cannot change attitudes overnight but they can influence behaviour. No government, since 1870, has ever considered merely persuading people to send their children to school. People are compelled to partake in and accept the education that is provided, unless they have the means to 'opt out' of the system: a choice available to relatively few. It is interesting to ponder what would happen if education depended on people being voluntarily convinced of its overall worth and necessity.

Collective and community responsibility on the horizon?

It would seem almost impossible at the present time, in the face of yet another rejection of the rights of disabled people in the House of Commons, to point to positive aspects. This turn of events once again legitimises prejudice against and apathy about positive change in our education system and society as a whole. Nevertheless, it is important to continue to spread the debate in diverse areas of professional practice and research. The debate must continue to allow more people who are still unaware of the depth of the issues involved and their consequences for professional behaviour, to have the opportunity to explore issues of choice and opportunity further.

The two radical pieces of legislation, in 1994 and 1995, were put aside using the excuse that they would impose an impossible financial obligation. Does this really hold water? No, because disability rights groups and disabled people themselves have been saying for a long time that they don't expect the world to change instantly or completely. There is enough realism and patience abounding to accept that changes must be introduced by first making sure that *new* buildings, projects, definitions, courses, books, articles, legislation, bye-laws, codes of conduct, guidelines, employment practices, national curricula, art, music, theatre, diplomas, degrees and almost any innovation recognises the rights of disabled people in this country. Action can follow by requiring new projects to conform and this will involve a minimal cost at the design and construction stage for facilities or in the planning stage for services. Existing facilities and services can be updated by a phased or step by step process over an appropriate and realistic period.

So, what really lies at the heart of this seemingly impossible giant step for mankind in the U.K. (the moon landing would seem like a small step in comparison)? Colin Barnes (1991) articulates a clear view about our cultural heritage:

> Behind the opposition to anti-discrimination legislation lie the assumptions of the traditional individualistic medical view of disability, which explains the difficulties faced by disabled people in their daily lives as individually-based functional limitations.

In other words, we first of all classify and perceive people according to a disability. This is a medical activity. The matron describing the ward to the consultant: 'The gall bladder is in bed 3, next to him is the peptic ulcer . . .' and so on (or something like that). There seems to be an incredible 'drive' to 'categorise' disabled people *as if they were the disability*. Warnock's proposition (1979) was to dispense, in education, with the need for categories of handicap and supplant it with the concept of special need. This was some kind of acknowledgement of a perception based on individual need and environmental change, not a category of disability. It is still, though, focusing on the individual as the source of the problem and not the environment that surrounds that individual. Can we possibly get away from this view? It is not the individual who is the 'special need'. It is a *collective choice about the way we organise our environments, community and our institutions.*

'Well, this certainly screws up our plan to conquer the Universe'

Reproduced by permission of Punch

Choice and opportunity

The title of this book contains the words 'choice' and 'opportunity'. This is a fundamental issue for teachers, educationists, psychologists and others who work in schools with young people who are disabled. For too long teachers have been pushed into accepting (or have too readily accepted) a 'medical model' of disability and applied it to teaching and learning in the area of 'special needs'. In doing so, they have been forced to step outside of or devalue the role of teacher and thus create problems of recognition of their own professional skills. Many have made a rod for their own back by accepting too much without question. This is particularly true of work alongside young people who are physically disabled. The medical ethic has ruled supreme and the roles of the context, the environment, the expectations and the organisation of experiences have been subservient. This book is an attempt to question this ethic and to review our current knowledge. It also aims to reflect the views given to us by disabled people themselves, and the groups that represent them. At the heart of the educational endeavours of all concerned, whether disabled or non-disabled, is choice, opportunity and learning. If there had been more room in the title of this book, I would have liked to include the words 'entitlement,' and 'access' since these are key elements in education to do with the quality of teaching and learning found in our schools. They are not issues that are crucial only to disabled children and adults; they are equally crucial *to all children and have an impact on the quality of our education system as a whole.*

In 1995, two more parallel Civil Rights (Disabled Persons) Bills were in Parliament. The least radical and effective seems to have proceeded. The key point about the history of this century, that has left people who are disabled without the important civil rights they have been seeking for so many years, is that financial cost is still paraded as a reason for inaction, lack of collective responsibility and denial of choice. This is a significant and important group of people who wish to contribute and participate in our society. Colin Barnes (1991) goes on to refer to:

> the experience of a growing number of disabled people and their organisations, who argue that most problems faced by disabled people are socially created and that discrimination is an everyday occurrence.

These crucial words understate the radical reality of being denied choice. There are many examples of such denials in daily life. They are all interconnected and add up to what could be deemed a hostile or uncomfortable environment to live in. Examples are:

- **Choice of courses and colleges** which suit the student's interests, abilities and career needs (Higher Education being the main offender here).
- **Choice of eating places and hotels** whilst travelling, to the point where a straightforward 'away break' becomes a 'character building' test of endurance in a selection of hostile environments.
- **Choice of transport methods and parking spaces**. The space to get in and out of your car and to be able to get to an accessible entrance. Public transport is still mostly inaccessible.
- **Choice of companions**. Companions/carers are often allocated rather than chosen. A disabled person may often have more contact with people who are paid to be there than with family, friends or their own associates.
- **Choice of entertainment**. Accessibility of clubs, pubs, theatres, cinemas, discos, not to mention attitudes in those places.
- **Entitlement to go to prison**. Many, if not most, law courts are inaccessible to wheelchairs. A disabled person cannot be tried for criminal activities. Is there a right to justice?
- **Entitlement to complain** about unsatisfactory facilities and *to be recognised as a significant 'consumer group'*. Current statutory, care and societal structures militate against disabled people being adequately, financially powerful as a lobby or pressure group.
- **Facilities**, such as those mentioned above, are still regarded as *special*, not ordinary, and schools/facilities designated for pupils with disabil-

ities are still regarded as special or designated, not ordinary.

- **Choice of learning environments** ranging from the inaccessibility to, for example, certain science facilities through to totally segregated environments where young children will have to live away from home or travel hundreds of miles a week to get the specialised resources they may need.
- **Entitlement to the same quality, amount and breadth of curricular experience** as other pupils and students in education.

The catalogue of problems imposed on people who are disabled is considerable. Until some form of executive or legislative action is taken, we are not likely to see a radical change. It is, perhaps, a tribute to our current 'hard-nosed' market-driven society that we have more children being excluded from the company of their peers in their local schools than in previous years. The above catalogue has been 'capped', in 1994, by the apparent spectacle of the Minister for the Disabled (or if not the Minister, then his Department and other back-benchers) blocking the passage of a Bill which could have radically improved the rights and lives of people who are disabled.

Ultimately it is the responsibility of those who set the political and social agenda through legislation to show positive and humanitarian leadership: to prove that they have the best interests of all the people at heart and are interested in producing a better society for all people to live in.

Learning and empowerment

The education of pupils and students who are disabled occurs within a wider social context including changing political circumstances. The effect on the lives and education of disabled people will be longer lasting. It has to be acknowledged that the attitudes of society will have considerable impact on the events and relationships within any school. Maras and Brown (1992) have investigated the attitudes of pupils towards their disabled peers in a mainstream school and found that these were often more ambiguous than appears on the surface.

In August 1990 the author was asked to design and deliver a thirty day course and joint project as a Consultant with the Spastics Society (now SCOPE) working with local education authorities to raise awareness of the different needs and abilities of pupils who are physically disabled within their school systems (special and mainstream). The wheels were set in motion and this project, which ran from 1990 to 1992, came to be known under the title 'Children with Cerebral Palsy: Exploring their

Special Educational Needs'. It was a timely initiative due to the wide range of uncoordinated support, in 1990, for children who have cerebral palsy or movement disabilities. In education, for example, children with sensory impairment or learning and behavioural difficulties had specialised support services. These services support both specialist and integrated provision in local education authorities in the general trend towards inclusion of children with special needs.

It is often children with physical or movement disabilities who are the first to be integrated (Moses, Hegarty and Jowett, 1988). Their needs were perceived as being purely physical (a few ramps and a welfare assistant). It is now realised that overcoming many, many years of segregation, on top of purely physical problems, is not as simple as it appeared then. What services there are to support children with physical disabilities are divided between health, education and social services with inevitable managerial and professional barriers or complications. This is not to blame the professionals individually but to point to the systems and the management of our statutory services in this country which do not allow these professionals to be trained together or to work together in a more meaningful way.

Since 1990, many initiatives within schools have developed to support the inclusion and integration of pupils and students who are physically disabled or have a movement disability. Some of these are exemplified in Chapter 8. There are still, though, substantial barriers to meaningful professional collaboration discussed in Chapter 6 and examined in various texts (Lacey and Lomas, 1993; Mittler, 1989). This is not a criticism of the work of colleagues in medical and paramedical work who are themselves moving away from a traditional medical model towards a more client centred and holistic approach. If anything it is a criticism of the way our statutory services are defined, organised and managed at higher levels. There is also a need to review who generates the research questions and who decides on the funding of this research.

This book questions our current, but changing, professional ethics and behaviour in the helping services and particularly in schools and colleges. The requirement under OFSTED to make visible agreed policies on equal opportunities, special needs and other areas of school and college management is a first step to holding accountable views on these matters.

References in the following chapters to a 'medical model' or a 'traditional medical model' need to be clearly qualified at the outset. There has been a tremendous amount of work done in clinical and counselling psychology, in medical and paramedical fields, which has been of benefit to children and young people who are disabled. Colleagues in the health service themselves recognise the move from the traditional 'medical model' to a more holistic approach. In the book we look at the concept of 'holistic' approaches to both learning and health, from a variety of angles.

> The terminology 'traditional medical model' relates to the precedence of professional opinion and decision over the needs and wishes of the client, learner or patient. This comes about because the definition of the disability or impairment is perceived as being centred solely within the individual. A remedy lies in doing something to the individual to put it right and the idea of treatments and cures is promoted. Decisions and choices are taken away from the client, pupil, student, parent or patient when, in fact, they should be allowed as much choice and opportunity as others. Disabled people, and their families, are particularly vulnerable to having life and learning decisions made for them all along the line thus reducing their participation and denying them basic human and civil rights.

It is espousing a view of social, health and educational facilities that are client, pupil, student or patient centred. Professionals exist to *serve* the recipients of the education service, by definition. This includes those in positions of power such as politicians, inspectors, headteachers, consultants, researchers, specialists and managers as much as those at grass roots level such as teachers, field workers, GPs or therapists.

In Chapter 8 we look at 'Methods and madness' in a search for the underlying principles for working effectively with pupils who are disabled. Some professional practice, educational strategy and empirical research in the area of physical disability is missing the fundamental principle of equal opportunity. A child or young person is not to be defined in terms of the group to which he or she is assigned by others. This is a fundamental denial of civil rights and opportunity. If we look carefully at research, theory and practice, children and young people are described as belonging to a group which is actually non-homogeneous and falsely ascribed the characteristics of that group (e.g. there is no such thing as 'the cerebral palsied child' or 'the disabled child' and spina bifida is a medical construct not a description of a person).

The social and political context has an impact on the education of *all* concerned, whether disabled or non-disabled. Schools and colleges are going to be held accountable for the general 'ethos' or, if you like, the community of the school, through whole school policies and their realisation in the daily life of the school. The OFSTED Framework does not specify how equal opportunity can be seen in the school and classroom, other than through an overall policy statement. Not everyone sees this as important but the theme of this book embraces issues of access and entitlement which are relevent to all children.

There are fundamental issues for teachers, educationists, psychologists, social work, health professionals and others who work alongside children and young people who are disabled. In short, over-prescriptive programmes (coming from medical, political or psychological quarters) for the management of learning for disabled pupils and an over-prescriptive curriculum 'for all' have deskilled teachers generally.

> The contrasting 'social model' regards the social, physical and psychological environment as being key factors in determining or defining the true extent of an individual's disability. Adopting this model means that we look at the physical environment, the organisation of surroundings and activities, the expectations of others, the choices or opportunities afforded and the attitudes of others to that individual. Disability is defined by some as nothing less than oppression of a minority group by the majority. The level of this oppression is related to the degree in which access, choice and opportunity are denied.

It is not the intention of this book to provide yet another chronicle of medical definitions of 'common physical disabilities'. In fact, it is deliberately characterised by absence of a perspective which says 'these are the educational consequences of medical diagnosis and assessment'. As a psychologist and teacher, I would like to say, 'these are the medical consequences of educational and social requirements or practices'. My own experience of nearly twenty years working in multi-disciplinary teams, teaching and working with pupils and students who are disabled and managing multi-disciplinary service provision, plays an important part in this book. I make no apologies for a fair amount of opinion and direct comment. This can, of course, be challenged and may count as a minor part of the whole debate in education. However, I also base some of the book and its findings on professional skills and understanding as a psychologist. Whilst there is opinion, there is also a degree of rigour and thought. In the academic and psychological domains we have to put philosophy, personal behaviour and principles 'on the line' in the quest for equal opportunity and inclusion of pupils and students who are currently marginalised by our social and political systems. This is not dramatic, eye-catching political radicalism but repeating messages and questions day in and day out in all kinds of everyday circumstances. Equal opportunity is more about doing than intellectualising.

> I am grateful for the generosity of friends, colleagues and people who are disabled for taking the time to help everyone understand what changes are needed. This is, in my view, on top of having to contend with a social and physical environment that is at best difficult to live in and, at worst, downright hostile.

I offer this book to you not as an academic tome or a complete philosophy nor as a 'teaching disabled pupils without tears' manual, but as an exploration into some well travelled shipping lanes with the odd, unexpected whirlpool. I hope you will enjoy reading the book and that it will stimulate thought, question current wisdom and contribute a dewdrop to the sea of knowledge.

Thrilled to bits to be here at long last . . .

CHAPTER 1

Fragmented Children: Services and Legislation

A long way back but making progress

It is something of a challenge to admit in our private moments, and even more difficult to admit in our professional capacities, that we may still be unconsciously influenced by the legacy of deeply held cultural constructs, beliefs and their consequent attitudes. Equal opportunities are not just about legislation, political correctness, positive language and social awareness. They are also about looking inwards to the sources of our own individual myths, beliefs and ideals. I hope the reader will bear with this brief journey into the recesses of our cultural heritage, some of which we would probably rather not admit could well apply to our own circumstances. This kind of introspection can sometimes be disturbing and is usually challenging. Richard Rieser expresses very clearly the role that our cultural history has played in his discourse *Disabled History or a History of the Disabled* (Rieser, 1990) and you can hardly read Colin Barnes (1990 and 1991) without becoming a little more aware of the historic and cultural influences that continue to shape our ideas, our actions, our institutions and our society.

We are challenged by disability, civil and human rights issues to become more aware of our own heritage. We cannot get away from the influence of many generations of cultural conditioning no matter how well meaning, or liberal, our actions and intentions. Equal opportunities are not only about an intellectual or academic activity but about culture, action, feelings, political and personal planning. Through the ages, from biblical times right up until earlier this century, there has been the notion that a deformed or disabled child is bad luck, a curse, possession by the devil, the outcome of evil doing or a person's just desserts (for displeasing the gods?). Disabled people and children are often described as 'victims' or 'confined' to a wheelchair. When this is done in the public domain, in the media, it adds to the general impression of passivity and helplessness.

More often than not, this is done for ulterior motives such as extracting sympathy for donation or to sway a political or resource argument. 'Help this poor child who needs special equipment and facilities which we don't have and can't provide without your generosity...'

Headline in *The Times* newspaper, 'Home News', Saturday May 15th 1993 (p. 6):
'Budapest centre's intensive therapy for cerebral palsy *victims* fails to fulfil high expectations. Psychologists attack Peto treatment for children'.

Times Educational Supplement, January 1992:
'. . . has been *confined* to a wheelchair for 30 years . . .'

This reporting is not only inaccurate (conductive education is not, strictly speaking, therapy or treatment) but it is pandering to and encouraging misleading perceptions at different levels. Nobody needs to be *confined* to a wheelchair, no matter how profound their disability. It may be that current practices and knowledge or resources keep people confined to wheelchairs. In fact, disabled people only need to *use* wheelchairs for mobility. Often this kind of emotive language is used through misguided attempts to elicit public sympathy and to identify disabled people as helpless 'charity cases'. People who are disabled do not need this kind of fuzzy pseudo-sympathetic complicity. It has formed, and continues to cultivate, deeply held cultural beliefs that lead to a perception of disability as a social burden on the non-disabled majority. It has been around for so many years that none of us can be confident of our immunity from its influence on our actions and lives, whether we are disabled or non-disabled, professional or non-professional.

Elements of our language have become so instilled through usage that we do not question their origin. The word 'handicap' derives from 'cap in hand' and carries with it all the associated baggage of charity, passivity and dependence. Associated with this use of language are subtle and perfidious forces working to undermine a person's self-respect, self-esteem and confidence to confront the 'slings and arrows' of everyday living.

'Disabled', Wilfred Owen (1893–1918)

Now he will spend a few sick years in Institutes
And do what things the rules consider wise
And take whatever pity they may dole
Tonight he noticed how the women's eyes
Passed from him to strong men that were whole
How cold and late it is! Why don't they come
And put him to bed? Why don't they come?

In contrast to Wilfred Owen's penetrating truths, subtle prejudice and social myth are communicated through vague and fuzzy words. These words are often laden with hidden messages and emotional context we do not fully understand or whose full meaning we may not wish to acknowledge.

Nevertheless, the use and misuse of words and professional jargon is part of the continuation of a collective unconscious based largely on myth and suspicion. To tell people how to speak or behave is to alienate them. To question the use of certain language and its origins is to attempt to break the cycle of ignorance, to raise our awareness of important issues and to move our understanding forward. The use and misuse of terms, in teaching practices and educational research, muddle rather than clarify the issues faced by children and young people in our education system. The 1992 Further and Higher Education Act (Cooper, 1993) and the Code of Practice (1993 Education Act) use categories and labels for artificially constructed 'groups' of people. This is in order to make sure they get their 'entitlement' to education.

Disabled children, young people and adults have a right to determine how others refer them and to question current muddled terminology used by professionals across the board.

> Extract from 'Little Gidding', T. S. Eliot (1888–1965)
> For last year's words belong to last year's language
> And next year's words await another voice . . .

Myths, suspicions and superman

These myths, suspicions, beliefs and social attitudes lurk beneath the surface in most of us. In the United Kingdom and the United States of America they have been eloquently expressed in legal, social, educational and health systems. These basic patterns that underlie present service provision continue to affect the way that services are delivered to disabled children and young adults. Ignorance, careless words and closed attitudes are the enemy of equal opportunity and disability equality in education, as they are elsewhere.

> The lack of any real medical knowledge until the middle of the 19th Century meant that people were often blamed for their disability or illness.
>
> (Stone, 1985)

The general movement towards industrialisation, in the 19th century, had a profound effect on our knowledge about our physical selves and the way social environments were organised. This, in turn, had an equally profound effect on the way in which illness and disability were perceived and treated. Industrialised communities became increasingly unable to integrate disabled people, particularly in the more sophisticated and technologically advanced countries, such as the UK and the USA. The required levels of literacy, numeracy, physical skill, co-ordination and dexterity increased rapidly as ordinary men and women were required to service more and more complex machinery. This is not to say that pre-industrial times were by any means ideal or that social inequality and disadvantage were created just by industrialisation. It did mean that there became fewer and fewer opportunities and, indeed, choices for those who were physically or movement disabled in some way. Disabled people were forced into a position of increasing helplessness and increasingly regarded as dependent.

On top of this, or perhaps as a result of this marginalisation of socially or culturally different and differently able groups, the 'Eugenics' movement in the USA, Europe and the UK regarded people (and children) with disabilities and developmental problems not only as a burden but as a positive threat. Hence the onset of new sterilisation techniques and experimentation with everything from genocide to behavioural conditioning. Many excesses and profound injustices have taken place in the name of medical and psychological sciences since the turn of the century. Some of these were the result of misguided visions of a 'Superman' stereotype coupled with incorrect, limited and unethical implementation of scientific knowledge. These were very much associated with so-called medical approaches which sought not only to make the abnormal, normal but also to make the human, superhuman. What a vain and cruel quest. It is not surprising that some current medical approaches, practices and ethics are being questioned as a backlash to treatments which have not, and do not, take into account the humanity and individuality of the person being treated:

> A Mother's joy, not shared by others . . .
> She was a young mother. It was her second child. She had given birth that day to a small boy. He was born with Down's Syndrome (a 'mongol'). Nobody had told her anything. Without asking her, the Doctor brought in a large group of medical students. He proceeded to manipulate the baby in front of the new Mother, pointing out all the symptoms of 'mongolism'. When she asked what she was to do with the child, she was told to fill the house with children. That way no-one would notice her handicapped child or think she was unable to produce normal children.
>
> (circa 1948)

There is a positive educational movement which has increasingly attempted to redefine 'special need' as a function of the context or environment in which an individual finds himself (the social perspective), as well as an individual need. The 1981 Education Act attempted to encapsulate this movement by talking about 'special needs' rather than categories of disability or handicap. In the USA, children are described as 'exceptional' if they have needs or abilities that fall outside the 'norm'. This still gives the impression that there is a dividing line between what is 'normal' and what isn't. In reality, there is no strict dividing line between mental health and mental illness, between learning disability and normal ability. It is time to stop constructing concepts and frameworks that segregate or divide and begin working on inclusive ideas and systems. The legacy of the traditional medical model reigning supreme is that many schools and colleges maintain disability and 'special need' as a problem which resides totally within the individual and one that must be 'diagnosed', even if covertly. The call for a shift from the 'medical model' of disability to a 'social model' is beginning to show signs of being understood. Changes are emerging in schools and colleges. The social model organises people into active groups and sees disability as a form of social oppression or as a problem which can be overcome by re-organising environments, structures and by changing attitudes. It has been necessary for disabled people to organise themselves into a temporary 'mini-culture' of radical protest in order to achieve some basic human and civil rights in the United Kingdom. Issues of choice and equal opportunity are ones that involve the whole of our society, they are not just the problems of a significant minority of people. Colin Barnes discusses the pervasive and comprehensive institutional discrimination prevalent in society generally and which is supported by history and culture:

> It incorporates the extreme forms of prejudice and intolerance usually associated with individual or direct discrimination, as well as the more covert and unconscious attitudes which contribute to, and maintain, indirect and/or passive discriminatory practices within contemporary organisations.
>
> (Barnes, 1991)

So, looking back over a longer perspective plays an important role in understanding the slow and often ponderous nature of institutional and legislative change. One final look at the passage of legislation in this country, which has led to the recent 'impasse' in Parliament mentioned in the introduction, illustrates the deep-seated cultural origins of general inaction. Here is a very brief summary of attempted anti-discrimination legislation since 1982, extracted from Barnes (1991) – data supplied by Peter Large and Mike Oliver:

1982: **Disablement (Prohibition of Unjustifiable Discrimination)** Bill. Introduced under the 10 minute rule. Lost at the end of the session.

1983: **Disablement (Prohibition of Unjustifiable Discrimination) – introduced as a private member's Bill**. Not enough votes for a second reading.

1983: **Chronically Sick and Disabled Persons (Amendment) Bill**. Defeated 164 for and 210 against. No second reading.

1983: **Lord Campbell's Disabled Person's Bill**. To establish a commission but no legal rights. Withdrawn by Lord Campbell after unopposed third reading.

1987: **Disabled Person's Rights Bill**. A 10 Minute Rule Bill. Unopposed but didn't get a second reading.

1989: **Employment Bill**. Mr. Wareing attempted to include a new clause to prohibit discrimination against disabled people. Its inclusion was rejected by 169 votes to 259.

1991: **Disability Discrimination Bill (Bill 78)**. Given a first reading but date for second reading not fixed. Subsequently has not been passed as legislation.

1994: **Defeated in Parliament**. Apparently by Conservative back benches with the alleged support of the Minister for the Disabled.

1995: **Civil Rights (Disabled Persons) Bill**: There are now two parallel bills in parliament. One 'watered down' version of the 1994 Bill and a more radical private member's Bill introduced by Harry Barnes, MP (for East Derbyshire). Harry Barnes has been defeated and a Bill with little legal power has got through.

Civil Rights legislation placed before Parliament in 1994 was rejected. It has been replaced by a watering down process of consultation. This has been followed (in 1995) by very much weakened legislation which is based on the needs of other minority groups (e.g. members of Parliament). At the time of writing there is a parallel Civil Rights (Disabled Persons) Bill travelling through parliament that more closely matches the kind of Civil Rights for ethnic minorities and women. It looks as though the government is set to block it (Friday 10th February 1995). It is against this backdrop of extensive and institutionalised discrimination, fuelled by individual fear and prejudice, from the industrial revolution up to the 2nd World War, that we should consider legislation from the 1944 Education Act onwards. It remains to be seen whether the second half of the 90's will produce some radical progress for the Civil Rights of disabled people.

The 1944 Education Act

This was the first major central government intervention into education in this country and contained a commitment to the current and limited view of equality of opportunity. However, the two tier system immediately restricted and directed children from the age of eleven into a land of reduced opportunity where they were labelled less able: a remarkably short sighted strategy when you consider that Albert Einstein was a very mediocre pupil and student. It wasn't until many years after school and college that his true talents and abilities came to the surface. How many talented and creative people, both disabled and non-disabled, have not realised their potential, or realised they *had* potential, until well after their school and college years?

The 1944 Education Act:

- set up a unified system of free compulsory education (5–15 years)
- included the community's need for culture and recreation and extended the concept of education to above and below school age;
- named a Minister of Education with considerable powers over LEAs, governors and the general public;
- required LEAs (in Section 34) to ascertain the needs of children for *special educational treatment* in ordinary schools, wherever possible;
- 10 categories of handicap were established;
- the term 'maladjusted' entered the educational vocabulary (as a category of handicap).

(Adapted from Tomlinson, 1985)

The 1994 Education Act recognised that some children had special educational needs and that they should be catered for in ordinary schools. In contrast to this, it defined ten categories of handicap. On the surface, and with hindsight, this looks like a far-sighted and integrative statement. So what happened? How did the education system then become one that excluded large numbers of children with significant disabilities? Once these categories had been defined then, of course, whole areas of new 'expertise' were opened up and certain people became 'specialists' in certain types of handicap. These specialists were rarely disabled themselves, they were professional 'experts'. It was then only a stone's throw to the next move which was to set up 'expert empires' where these professional experts reigned supreme and satisfied the need of the general public to see that something was being done. It must have been hard work to convince some parents and to reassure them that although their child was entering an institution, often many, many miles away, they were getting the best possible treatment or service from the 'experts'. Children with special educational needs had become the domain of specialists and other groups of more severely disabled pupils and students had also become the responsibility of medical experts. The seeds were then sown for their marginalisation and their social stigmatisation. The false and self-serving categorisation as homogeneous groups, identified by medical characteristics, had further effects on individual's life chances, self-esteem and educational opportunity.

> . . . despite a succession of legislation since the 1944 Education Act endorsing the principle that disabled children should be educated alongside their peers, the impetus towards integration has been only slight . . . While the failure to integrate is often attributable to lack of resources it is also due to lack of knowledge and understanding amongst those involved in education – educationalists, school governors, teachers and parents.
>
> (Barnes, 1992)

Circular 10/65 Organisation of Secondary Education 1965

This circular declared the Government's objective of ending selection at 11+ and introducing secondary education along comprehensive lines. It would also have had the effect of eliminating separatism in secondary education. This circular was withdrawn in 1970 and reinstated in 1974. This move to reduce the exclusivity of education through selection later became enshrined in the 1968 and 1976 Education Acts and then repealed in the 1979 Education Act. In view of this historical perspective and many other views including the current hijacking of the educational agenda by politicians, it is hard to see education in this country as anything other than a political football: a term that was coined around 1979. These ideological battles were very important to the whole of education and still have ramifications for *the culture of 'selectivity' that never died and that impacts on the lives of children and young people who are disabled.* It adds to the perception of them as a burden in a school because they are unlikely to pass exams, or will require massive amounts of resources to do so. The game in which education is the political football is that of political control and social manipulation. The 'cost accounting' and 'productivity' view of disabled people has its roots in the Industrial Revolution and legislative attitudes that have prevailed since. Special needs in schools is nowadays seen largely as a resourcing issue, which it is not. Access is too often seen in these simple terms and not in terms of positive intervention, effective teaching practices and radical changes of attitude in a school community.

The 1969 Children and Young Persons Act

Local Authorities were given powers and responsibilities for children not receiving proper education or in need of care and control. This did not apply to disabled children and young people who were not in the education system at this time.

The 1970 (Handicapped Children) Act

Responsibility for children that were then termed 'severely subnormal' was transferred from health authorities to the local education authorities. The truth of the matter was that many, many children and young people were thought of as mentally handicapped when they were severely physically disabled. Many intellectually able but physically disabled people had been cared for in hospitals where the environment was not organised to cater for personal needs or to provide access to learning (or sometimes any) activity. This was mainly due to the organisation of wards and staff numbers allocated (often two nurses all day with forty or more patients). The disabled people were seen only in terms of their medical or 'care' needs.

The following anecdote is revealing:

> I took a group of around twenty (learning disabled) adults down to the park at about 10:30 am. We walked all together in a group, some of them held hands. We sat in the park, fed the ducks and watched the people in the park. Suddenly, I realised that I had left my watch behind and that they were supposed to be back by 12:00 for their lunch. As I was considering this problem, the whole group (none had watches or could see a clock or effectively tell the time) stood up together without a word, formed themselves into a line and began to walk back towards the hospital. I asked a passer-by the time. It was 11:50 am. The time when they would, each day, begin to wander to the dining rooms and queue up for lunch.
> Story told to me by an ex-Rampton Charge Nurse (circa 1978; The event took place circa 1960).

Hence a group of passive, learning disabled people, with basic self-care abilities could be controlled by a very small number of staff because they were 'institutionalised'. This was mainly the fate of learning disabled people but also involved a great many physically disabled people (either from birth or who had become disabled) and those with debilitating, disfiguring or degenerating physical conditions.

Chronically Sick and Disabled Persons Act 1970

Section 2 listed services for people who are disabled:

- Help in the home
- Recreational facilities in the home
- Recreational facilities outside the home
- Assistance with transport to such facilities
- Aids and adaptations
- Holidays
- Meals and telephones

This act also required new educational buildings to be made accessible to disabled people, *unless this was incompatible with the efficient use of resources*. This earlier use of the 'weasel clause' (Massie, 1994) must have proved so effective that it has been used constantly since, most notably in the Children Act, 1989. It must also have provided current legislators with their perfect excuse for not requiring schools and colleges to comply with the 'access to goods and services' part of the most recent legislation, on the grounds that it has already been done. A brief tour around most primary and secondary schools and colleges of Further and Higher Education built since 1970 will show any interested party that this legislation has had little impact. It only had a patchy impact on the other areas illustrated above (e.g. recreational facilities outside the home).

National Health Service Re-organisation Act 1973

The school health service transferred from LEAs to area health authorities. It is just possible that this legislation has had far reaching effects for people who are disabled. As we examine later in almost all of the following chapters, one of the major problems for children and young people who are disabled is *the fragmentation of their personality and learning efforts at the hands of different groups of professionals*. The enormous problems created for individuals by the different management systems which health, education and social services professionals work under is becoming almost legendary. Had this legislative move not taken place in 1973, it is just possible that a system could have developed where health (speech, physio and occupational therapists, school nurses) professionals and educationists (including teachers) could well have come under *one management system*. An opportunity sadly missed, that will take many years to unravel, but one which also resounds with issues of inter-professional collaboration, practice and management considered further in Chapter 4 and Chapter 6.

The Warnock Report and the 1981 Education Act

The Warnock Report preceded and informed the 1981 Education Act which then incorporated a whole raft of legislation which had, and still has, to a great extent, defined not only special educational needs but many of the associated activities, such as assessment, that now go to make up the bureaucracy of special educational need. This legislation was mostly concerned with the *identification and assessment of special educational need*, something which has concerned the educational establishment for the past twenty years and, once more, harks back to the diagnosis model. A more appropriate emphasis for 'Code(s) of Practice' could be *monitoring pupil progress, evaluating their experience and concentrating on positive social or educational intervention*. Pinpointing deficits and problems can become an end in itself.

The 1981 Education Act was almost exclusively to do with special educational need and there were many positive outcomes. The most outstanding feature was the attempt to get away from 'categories of handicap' and develop the concept of a 'continuum of need'. This was a positive change that focused on the individual needs and abilities rather than the fixed characteristics of a category or syndrome. Paul Vevers (1992), co-author of 'Getting in on the Act' and senior manager with the Audit Commission, who analysed developments following the 1981 Act, summarises the substance of the Act:

- The most needy pupils should have the safeguard of a full assessment of their needs;
- the extra help they require should be provided with continuity for as long as necessary;
- children with special needs should generally be educated in ordinary schools, with certain provisos, as stated in the 1981 Act;
- parents' views should be taken into account;
- the pupils with the greatest needs should be subject to regular review.

(Vevers, 1992)

The use of language on that last point does illustrate an attitude which this book seeks to review. He says 'Pupils . . . should be subject to regular review.' It is not, of course, the pupils who need reviewing *but the provision and learning programmes that need reviewing* regularly. However, this is not to detract from a critically positive review of the Act which identifies specific development points:

(1) **Lack of clarity:** There is no 'working definition' of 'special educational need', only guidance on identifying special educational

need. Nor did it define levels of need or 'triggers' for multi-disciplinary assessment. Possible conflicts can also arise between parents, LEAs and schools about responsibility. There should be, based on national norms, guidelines on the level of academic and social functioning necessary to 'trigger' an assessment. It does acknowledge the impracticability of implementing rigid criteria which might exclude children who do not fit into 'categories'.

(2) **Lack of accountability:** This particular problem was highlighted with respect to assessments and statements and the development of national criteria in this area (DFE, 1992). The Audit Commission identified three main aspects to this particular problem. Lack of accountability of:

- LEAs and schools to parents;
- schools to LEAs and parents for the achievements they make with pupils experiencing SEN;
- LEAs to schools and parents for specifying resources.

(3) **Lack of incentives:** The current system has positive disincentives to making a financial commitment to a pupil or student; the LEA can benefit from delaying or withholding their commitment in a statement.

Problems of the 1981 Education Act (Vevers, 1992)
(1991 Audit Commission and recommendations)

The practical consequence of previous muddled terminology was that children who were disabled often found themselves in schools which were specifically designated for another 'type' of child (e.g. many physically disabled pupils in a school for severe learning difficulties, SLD). Current terminology could also lead to anomalies. For example, the excruciating discussions and bizarre decisions about which is the *predominant* handicap, disability or need. A child with severe visual impairment and physical disability: should he be in a SCOPE (formerly Spastics Society) School where they can provide positive mobility programmes, or a Royal National Institute for the Blind (RNIB) school where they have a specific environment for children who are visually impaired?

In a sense, these are nonsensical decisions and the discussion is not about the child or young adult at all, but about what 'expert' provision the individual should be 'slotted' into. The child is the child. He or she does not experience predominant disabilities in this way. The most suitable environment is one which is not specialised for one *type* of child and excludes catering for another but the environment in which all children can flourish. There is no such thing as a 'specific learning difficulties' child or an 'MLD child' or even an 'EBD child'. They do not exist. A child's individual need, on the other hand, can be catered for effectively either by teamwork and collaboration or by re-organising services to reduce this 'fragmentary' effect. The categories of handicap were supposedly dispensed with but in reality specialist provision was maintained. The categories of specialist provision remained and we have a patchy mixed economy of various types of provision that is now changing and identifying itself according to 'market forces' and economic necessity.

Moves towards integration: It is clear from Swann's (1985) work that the overall move towards integration that took place in the 80's is now being reversed in the 90's. More children are being marginalised and segregated than before.

Development of a continuum: There are current arguments that the so-called 'continuum' is nothing more than forcing children to conform to categories of specialist provision . The positive alternative to this type of approach is to provide proper individualised support within a child's own school and community.

Reconceptualisation and reorganisation of support: The Warnock Report and 1981 Education Act also sought to redefine the concepts and structures of special education, to take it out of the domain of specialist provision and acknowledge the fact that 18% of all children experience special educational needs at some time or other in their school career. The categories of provision in special education have remained but this reconceptualisation heralded a fundamental and long term swing towards integration. The movement still continues.

Disabled Persons (Services, Consultation and Representation)

Act 1986 This legislation had to do with early efforts to promote community care and protect the rights of disabled young people after leaving school. There may be an incorrect assumption here that perhaps there is no need to protect rights whilst at school ? It was important in bringing the concept of advocacy forward along with an assessment of need in relation to services that could be provided. Sections 1, 2 and 3 have not yet been implemented. The overall ramifications and subsequent implementation of this Act are beyond the scope of this book but, as with much education legislation, it is patchy and much of it has been altered by later legislation.

The 1986 Education Act

The central pivot of this legislation relates to governors and harmonious working relations between the so-called *major interest groups in education.*

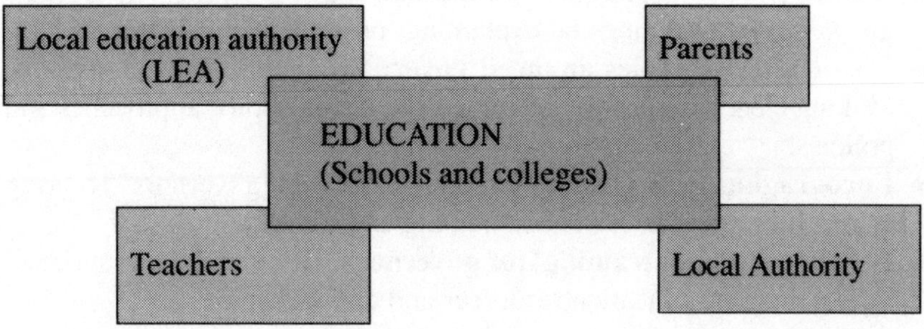

Figure 1:1 The 1986 Education Act

It heralded the preparation for local management of resources by schools. It removed the major element of responsibility and control of the curriculum from the LEA and placed it with the governing body of a school. The LEA states its own policy and the governing body states its own policy which may be a variant of the LEA policy. This Act generated contradictory feelings amongst headteachers, governors and teachers. On the one hand it gave increased local control over resources and greater participation in control of these. On the other hand, it generated considerable concern about responses to pupils in terms of behaviour and *collective responsibility*.

> On behaviour, the language of the new law is the populist political language of standards and discipline rather than disturbance, emotional difficulty or shared responsibility . . .
>
> (Sayer, 1987)

Headteachers were greatly concerned about the new definitions of standards (still, in 1995, not really defined in principle or ethic – Kelly, 1994) and more particularly about loss of control to governors and central government. The 1986 Act attempted to forge links between parents and governors and to increase community involvement. LEAs were required to make adequate training available.

John Sayer (1987) summarises the positive benefits emanating from the Act:

- **Growth of parental involvement**, through governors from learning groups directly involved with the needs of children who may be disadvantaged.

- **Opening the school to its governors** through requirements, responsibilities and involvement in curriculum, finance etc.
- **Local community resources and skills** can be mobilised, again through governors and co-option.
- **Agreed professional policy in relation to special needs** with teacher-governors representing and explaining 'professional insights'.
- Distributing **key roles amongst governors of mainstream schools**. Making clear responsibilities for special needs pupils, approaches and policies.
- **Encouraging local clusters** of schools, through governors. To bring in specific expertise or outside training and support.
- **Better 'corporate training' for governors**. To assist them in successfully managing education resources and opportunities.

Whilst a positive view is encouraging, it could not, in 1987, have foreseen the massive impact that a *politically and centrally defined curriculum* would later have. Nor could Sayer have possibly imagined the effect that competitive and market-based systems would have after 1990. It was almost as if the legislation was preparing for the imposition of a national curriculum by taking control away from headteachers and LEAs of both finance (resources) and the curriculum itself. If our society generally was more equitable *and there were more disabled governors*, this could have had a substantial impact on the accessibility of schools and education.

The 1988 Education Reform Act (ERA)

A national curriculum for all? Or, moving goal-posts for all?

The national curriculum was a further development of the ground prepared in the 1986 Act where control and power was radically shifted. It was a further response to the 'standards' debate. Special schools and units up and down the country did not use the 'modification' and 'disapplication' procedures and make an exception of pupils who are disabled or have severe learning disabilities. The actual legislation would, if it had been applied strictly, have disenfranchised large groups of pupils in the country. The general feeling was that pupils should be included despite the fact that the 1988 Act *made no provision for pupils experiencing special educational needs and none for disabled pupils and students*. The national curriculum and testing arrangements were drawn up and subsequently modified by the political process with no reference to the diversity of ability and need present in our schools and colleges.

Professor Paul Black (1992) provides an erudite reflection on the initiation and early development of the national curriculum and its assessment procedures. He did this from his vantage point as chair of the Task Group on Assessment and Testing (TGAT), reporting to Kenneth Baker in 1988, and from his place on the National Curriculum Council (NCC). His address to the Education Section of the British Association Science Festival (1992) condemned the 'sweeping and hurried change'. This pales into insignificance when compared with his statements relating to the manipulation and perversion of extensive professional advice to the government. Many years of work on curriculum development and delivery, on sensitive, appropriate but rigorous assessment were, it seems, sacrificed on the altar of political expediency and social manipulation through national curriculum 'orders'.

Entitlement without access? A house without a door

The philosophy and the practice of the 1988 Education Reform Act (ERA) seem to be totally at loggerheads with each other. Whether this was because there really was little (educational or curricular) philosophy behind much of the Orders and Regulations, or whether there was a deliberate attempt to marginalise children and young people whose needs make them unable to conform to a 'standardised' view of achievement and attainment, is difficult to say. If Professor Paul Black is to be believed, then it looks more like the latter, or a combination of ignorance and half-baked philosophy. It is interesting that the terms 'access', 'differentiation' and 'entitlement' emerged from the 1988 Act as key points, despite the fact that the Act itself was particularly lacking in any real consideration of diversity in the education system. It was a bit like designing a house without a door for significant portions of the school and college population. The idea of disapplication in itself is an exclusive, not inclusive, approach and would marginalise pupils with diverse needs even more than was already the case. Thankfully, the concept of disapplication was largely ignored by heads, teachers and other professionals. It was specifically stated in the original orders of the Act that modification and disapplication would be considered, on the whole, more appropriate to certain schools or provision rather than for any individual needs. There were only three ways in which pupils with diverse individual needs were recognised:

- by Orders or Regulations;
- in a statement of special educational needs made under the 1981 Act;

- by Regulations for modification or disapplication.

It was also the only system in the world that gave such comprehensive control over the curriculum to central government through a closely controlled system of national assessment (Black, 1992). In a sense, children and young people who are disabled have been battling and jumping through hoops with their teachers for the past six or seven years to negotiate and remove the hurdles placed in their way. A great deal of teacher, pupil and student time has been wasted since 1988 in trying to make a rigidly imposed, prescriptive and exclusive system workable, not just for disabled learners but for a far larger proportion of diverse learners within our education system. Thankfully, this rigid kind of education system was not imposed on further and higher education through colleges although there were undoubtedly 'knock on' effects.

Breadth, balance and the spirit of learning

Despite the bitter but absolutely justified criticism that followed the original national curriculum 'Orders' and 'Regulations', there were some good points that could be described as the 'spirit' of parts of the Act rather than the 'letter of the law'. The concept of breadth and balance is a very worthy one. Many pupils with disabilities, particularly those with severe learning disabilities, had become so set apart that their whole curriculum and learning experience was thought to be something completely different from the experience of the rest of humanity. The consequence was narrowly defined learning experiences with an almost slavish adherence to the narrowest definitions of behavioural psychology or programmed learning; narrower and narrower 'targets' or objectives until the child was going round in ever decreasing circles, learning more and more 'skill steps' that were less and less use to them. One reason that this happened was that it looked good on paper. It gave plenty of apparently objective records and adults were able to 'measure' (on paper, in pseudo-scientific terms) the minute amounts of progress that some children were making. What about the consequences of this approach for the learner? It took some time before it began to dawn on professionals that the more narrowly and closely defined 'progress' is, the more opportunity is denied to the learner, the less motivated they will become (necessitating complicated and artificial reward systems) and the more meaningless will be their skills in terms of their real life events. This is a legacy that has been left by blindly applying and promoting limited 'behavioural' techniques. It was somewhat ironic that, at the time when many educationists and practitioners working with children and young people who were severely disabled came to realise that they were depriving learners of life experiences and breadth of learning, the rest of the educational world was being pushed down the pathway of a limiting and objectives-based curriculum by the implementation of the national curriculum. Kelly makes this point:

> again, therefore, we are left to divine for ourselves the definition of 'balanced and broadly based' which the Act has adopted or assumed. And again we can only do this by interpreting the concrete proposals which follow and which have subsequently emerged. These make it clear that the concept of balance within the National Curriculum is the simplistic concept of a balance of subjects and subject content. We must note too, however, the difficulty of recognising the coherence of any notion of 'breadth' or 'balance', even one framed in terms of subjects, within a curriculum which devotes the majority of curriculum time at primary level . . . to the [three] core subjects (DES, 1987).
>
> (Kelly, 1994)

There are one or two key questions that need addressing in relation to pupils and students who are disabled.

- How does the concept of breadth and balance of learning experience work within a subject-based curriculum which narrowly defines all the available time?
- Is this subject-based approach broad enough in its conception to encompass the additional needs of pupils and students who are physically disabled? Or even the additional needs of all learners?

Assessment at 7 and 11

The Government's objectives for assessment were to 'raise standards in schools' (DFE, 1993). In a little more detail its purposes were to:

- set higher standards in English, Maths and Science;
- ensure that pupils' attainments are rigorously assessed through standard national tests at 7, 11 and 14 years;
- focus curriculum requirements on the core essentials and give teachers more time to concentrate on the basics;
- increase the flexibility at Key Stage 4 to provide a well-informed choice of vocational and academic options for 14–16 year olds.

The problem with all this is that none of these high sounding statements about 'standards', 'rigour', 'standard tests', 'core essentials' or 'basics' are properly evidenced, defined or understood. According to Black (1992) the results of implementation and assessments of the core curriculum should be treated with concern and suspicion. They have little to do with the business of curriculum development, teaching or learning. They are confused in their appreciation of the difference between external accountability and rigorous, but practical and ongoing, monitoring and evaluation of an individual pupil's progress. A more detailed discussion of the problems, opportunities and definitions of diagnosis, assessment, identification and monitoring can be found in Chapters 2 and 5.

Black's words in 1992, from our current perspective, after Dearing's radical changes (new Orders in January 1995), ring true:

> No other country in the world has a system which gives such comprehensive control to its government over the curriculum with such a frequent and closely controlled system of national assessment.
>
> . . . comprehensive programmes for monitoring were cut back by ministers, who have retained to themselves direct control over any research or evaluation activities of that (NCC) council.
>
> (Black, 1992)

So, how do the details of this imposed curriculum relate to those pupils and students who are disabled? The galling fact is that teachers and pupils up and down the country are still jumping through hoops to 'evidence' things that were not properly defined in the first place.

Access and entitlement: The concept of these as individual rights of every child does not sit easily with the reality of local management, opting out to become grant-maintained and the need to maintain 'standards' evidenced by exam results. A child has the right of access and entitlement to a broad and balanced curriculum in a mainstream school, providing he or she lives in an area where the school is willing and able to provide such a thing. This is not, by any means, universal and is contradicted by a 'standardising' and 'selective' ethos promoted by other aspects of the Act.

Opting out: This was part of the general package that has given many schools greater autonomy, given other schools reason to question their existence and has increased the general air of competition and selectivity.

Heightening of governance role and responsibility: The combination of delegating a 'set' or formularised budget and giving Governors the responsibility for that budget has enabled central government to maintain a tighter financial grip on education. At the same time, local education authorities have been severely curtailed. They do maintain a budget for pupils who are disabled and can now act as the 'purchaser' of services for each pupil. However, this is always on the basis that any school wishes to act as the 'provider' of such services. As a financial accounting activity it has been most successful. As an exercise in people management and educational progress it has been less successful.

Local management of schools (LMS): Has the potential to adversely affect educational opportunities for pupils with special educational needs and particularly those who are physically disabled and seen, by some, as expensive. In brief, the characteristics and effects of LMS and LMSS have been to polarise views of pupils with disabilities as a burden or an asset according to the financial resources attached to them.The Audit Commission, focused on the 1981 Education Act, looked at the statementing process, took evidence from schools and services and made recommendations and changes which now come within the 1988 ERA. In the context of purchaser/provider relationships between LEAs and schools:

> LMS and the pressures it brings to schools have decreased the capability of mainstream schools to respond to pupils with special educational needs.
>
> (Evans and Lunt, 1993).

One positive development of LMS has been an increased degree of definition of the allocation of funds to pupils with special needs, particularly those in mainstream. Pupils who are physically disabled sometimes require extensive additional resources or aids and it is important that these are clearly defined as 'access' issues. The specific allocation of funds to pupils who are disabled has become something of an issue. Should the resources be targetted at individual pupils (as in the Statement of Educational Need)? Or, should a school be additionally resourced in order to provide a diverse range of pupils or a specified group of pupils? This debate and its practical implications are still being rehearsed up and down the country.

The replacement of LEAs by Funding Agencies for Schools (FAS) once 10 per cent of pupils are in Grant Maintained (GM) schools has not taken place. It was also intended that LEAs would cease to be involved at all, once 75 per cent of all LEAs pupils were in 'opted out' GM schools. It doesn't appear that this will take place either as the government's target of 5,000+ GM schools has now been revised to below 1,500.

The Canadian experience provides an illuminative mirror and contrast to what has happened in this country since the late 60's. It seems from the initiative, in Alberta, of 'Programme Unit Grants' (PUG), that the allocation of funding to purchase the expertise needed, across professional and management boundaries, had a profound 'inclusive' effect for disabled children and young people.

> ...there was a financial benefit for individual solutions in regular

programmes. News of innovation spread through the provincially sponsored curriculum development committees and through university courses preparing the early teachers.

(Marlett and Buchner, 1987).

This 'granting' (PUG) system facilitated an appropriate and sensitive response to pupils with severe disabilities and the percentage of children with profound and multiple disabilities who remained within their own communities shot up from 8.3 per cent (age 6–10 years) in 1975 to 56.1 per cent in 1978 and from 12.8 per cent (age 0–5 years) in 1975 to 81.1 per cent in 1978. When economic recession struck, there were cutbacks and a new system of funding was introduced in 1984, a block funding policy. This was a formula funding approach and all programmes had to be paid within that block grant, per 'head' of disabled pupils. So what are the lessons for our own systems? Table 1.1 illustrates.

FUNDING/SUPPORT BASIS	
Money allocated to individual needs (e.g. statement in UK or PUG in Alberta, Canada) on a 'grant' basis.	Formulae (or category based) funded or allocation to *provision* not individuals. Or, money controlled by centre quality assurance criteria
• Increased inclusion in mainsteam school/college.	• Increased tendency to set up segregated units to maximise ease of administration.
• Increased choices for individuals (and their parents).	• Decreased choice for the individual, increased power to professionals concerned.
• Innovation shared through professional networks to secure funding for new pupils with particular needs.	• Innovation held within school/unit – set up as a centre of 'excellence' (a competitive model induced).
• Pressure to remove professional barriers and prejudices centring purchasing power around individual need.	• Increased bureaucracy to deal with initial allocation criteria, moderation of opinions and arguments about levels of disability.
• Requirement on single funding authority to clarify criteria for allocation of funds.	• Reduced equality as those who can campaign most vociferously get the *provision* they want.

Table 1.1 Allocation of funding – lessons to be learnt from English and Canadian experience.

The Children Act, 1989

This Act was designed to have some impact on the families of 'children in need', some of whom are disabled, and it is, therefore, important. The Children Act, though, was riddled with the usual 'let out' clauses that have characterised much legislation aimed at supporting those 'in need'. For example, the 'Duty to provide' does not stipulate amount of provision or the means. Unfortunately, the Children Act did not give any statutory powers or additional, specific resource allocation so the words 'duty to provide' may well prove to be hollow if anyone expected provision over and above that which already exists. Parts II, IV and V relate to the status of the child, mostly giving some rights to the child, outlining parental responsibility as well as rights and attempts to deal sensitively with family, legal, care and supervision procedures. Unfortunately, Part III relating to 'children in need', including disabled children and their families appears, with hindsight, to have been the weakest part of the Act.

PART III: Local Authority Support for Children and Families.
(1) Provision of services for 'children in need', their families and others . . .

Schedule 2 – Part I Provision of Services for Families:

- Identification of 'children in need' and provision of information
- Maintenance of a register of disabled children
- Provision of accommodation to protect the child
- Provision for disabled children
- Provision to reduce need for care proceedings
- Family centres
- Maintenance of the family home etc. etc. . . .

(2) Day care for preschool and other children; (3) Accommodation;
(4) Advice and assistance; (5) Review; (6) Co-operation between authorities;
(7) Re: component of cost.

Once again the concept of bureaucracy and maintenance of registers is seen as 'action' in terms of providing for 'children in need'. Whilst it is undoubtedly necessary to have 'registers' and to 'identify' children and young people who are disabled, this is only part of the problem-solving process.

Once again, the statutory services, in this case Social Services, are stuck in these early stages of the problem-solving process. They have become increasingly *aware of the problems* – identifying children at risk, or children with physical disabilities who are 'in need', at the same time becoming increasingly unable to act due to restriction of resources and provision. The main restrictions in Social Services are lack of ability to train enough social workers in enough depth to handle the situations that arise.

This following outline of significant parts of the Children Act is adapted from Herbert (1993):

Identification of 'children in need' and provision of information
Children are assessed in terms of:

- Physical well-being and physical care
- Mental health
- Social and intellectual development
- Emotional development
- Behaviour

'Each professional should refer to their own practice tools and guidance' (Children Act, 1989) in assessing health and development. One of the problems for social workers is that the development of children is seen in terms of 'normal' development. If we accept that a child with a significant movement disability will have its own particular version of developmental stages, then the concern over the so-called normal developmental stages disappears. There may be alternative 'developmental stages' for a child with movement disabilities which can chart progress measured against a whole different set of objectives. Isn't it worth trying these, rather than assuming that everyone has to be 'measured' according to these 'normally' defined (and often limited) stages of development?

> *Reasonable standard of health and development means that their conduct, presentation or care sets them apart*;
> What is meant by 'normal' development ? Here are some examples . . .
> - 12 months – beginning to develop bowel control
> - 14 months – begin to messily feed themselves
> - 15–18 months – begin to build bricks
> - 18–20 months – learn to kick or throw a ball

To reiterate the points made above about this kind of 'normal' developmental checklist: it might be more useful if it helped to identify alternative activities to 'enrich' the child's experience. It does not even identify a child's loss of experience but simply measures their 'deficits'. This is the remedial assumption that underpins much professional activity and should be re-considered as less efficient and not child-centred.

Significant impairment – indicated by objective evidence (developmental

> checklists, child protection events...) where a child's development is adversely affected . . .
>
> (The Children Act, 1989)

The significance of the impairment lies not in its relation to normal development but in the effect it has upon the life of the child or young person. These are two different things. 'Normal development' defines targets and aspirations that professional groups become concerned with. Being able to get on, live and learn, socialise, play, make relationships, access experience and control some events in your surroundings are of greater importance to the individual. In putting forward developmental checklists we are measuring children against these 'norms'. How far is this relevant for a teenager who has great difficulty in holding and controlling a spoon? Is it expedient to continue 'training' a person for what might be years to hold a spoon or are there alternative ways of looking at it ? We regard the person as 'dependent' because they cannot feed themselves in a normal way. Do we regard astronauts in the Apollo capsules and Lunar modules developmentally backward because they had to exist within an environment, in space, that makes them dependent? Is dependence the only thing to be measured and stigmatised? These are complex questions for those who work with children who are physically disabled. It raises questions of larger dimensions for many areas of early development.

> *Disability* defined as visual impairment, learning impairment, serious communication difficulties, substantial handicap from illness, injury or congenital conditions . . .
>
> (The Children Act, 1989)

The World Heath Organisation defines disability in terms of loss of functional ability or the effect that impairment, injury or illness has upon an individual's ability to function in daily life. The Children Act description, for social workers, is confused, limiting and ambiguous. More importantly, it defines disability in terms of the label or the impairment and not necessarily in terms of functional ability. In certain circumstances, a relatively minor impairment can cause serious disability. Conversely, relatively major disability can have limited impact with an appropriate use of technology and aids.

The Children Act was intended to be implemented in positive and promotional ways for disabled youngsters. It places a clear and separate duty on Local Authorities, mainly Social Service Departments, to provide services to:

- minimise the effect on children with disabilities in the area of their disability;

and
- give such children the chance to lead lives which are as normal as possible. (Herbert, 1993)

Martin Herbert (1993) goes on to view the Children Act, the 1981 and 1988 Education Acts as combining an 'active search' for children who need extra services. This has always been, ever since the 1944 Education Act, an attempt to define and make clear what 'children in need' actually means and, furthermore, what constitutes a 'special case'. Unfortunately, in terms of legislation, this 'active search' still largely involves a search to categorise into one or another group of perceived problems, such as dyslexia, or physical disability or medical conditions. Again, the whole process is geared to assessment and categorisation. Evidence of disability is one thing. *Evidence of a positive response to it is another matter entirely*. It conveniently stops short of going further into some kind of affirmative or supportive action. There has been a tradition of lumping children together according to (medical) diagnosis and hence emphasising perceived problems rather than pointing to different abilities, personal resources or individual differences.

The Children Act also points up some further suggestions for direct service requirements:

- **Direct help for the child**: e.g. speech/language cards, special toys, diet, recreational activities etc.
- **Parenting skills**: specialist help in responding to the adult's (special) needs.
- **Parenting resources**: includes practical equipment, financial resources, support networks, extended family, shared care etc.

There are also more subtle effects in the social sphere, pointed to by Warnock (1987). Children who are disabled, as compared with their non-disabled peers, are more likely to:

- play alone;
- spend more time alone with an adult;
- engage in passive or receptive activity (listening to or watching others);
- communicate less with other children;
- have one-way rather than two-way speech patterns.

They are equally or *less likely* to:

- communicate with peers rather than adults;
- engage in imaginative play.

The consequences, both socially and educationally of just this short list, at an early stage of development, are considerable. The interesting thing about the list is that these are consequences of, if you like, social and inter-personal discrimination. It is understandable that children who have difficulty communicating will spend more time communicating with adults, who are sometimes better placed to extend meaning to their attempts at communicating. Nevertheless, all of the above could be interpreted as effects of the environment. A small scale postgraduate diploma study in 1992 found that disabled primary school pupils are communicated with or have social interaction with their peers substantially less than their non-disabled peers. Communication is a two-way process and a child cannot communicate, particularly if he or she is disabled, if the environment does not allow time and space for it, and if there are *not enough willing partners to communication efforts*.

The 1992 Further and Higher Education Acts

There are two Acts associated with Further and Higher Education, one covers England and Wales and the other covers Scotland. Along with the Acts there were, in 1992 and 1993, a number of circulars and regulations issued by Government departments and the new funding bodies set up to implement the Acts. The definition of students with learning difficulties continues as from previous legislation, based on:

- difficulties with others in comparison with others in the same age group;
- difficulties in using provision or accessing general and appropriate courses.

The term 'special educational needs' is not used anywhere in the legislation but the term 'learning difficulties' seems to cover the whole range including students with physical and sensory disabilities.

Previous legislation has also had an effect on Further and Higher Education provision. The Disabled Persons (Services, Consultation and Representation) Act 1986 is carried over into the new further education structure.

Funding

The FEFC's document called 'Recurrent Funding Methodology' provides guidance on funding arrangements for 1994/1995 and indicates a major change in the funding arrangements from previous years. This new arrangement provides for six bands of additional funding for students with learning difficulties and disabilities, with methods for calculating these bands.

LEAs still have responsibility for determining where they will allocate funding for students who are disabled in pursuance of their responsibilities towards these students.

Higher Education

The differences between Universities and Polytechnics have now been reduced and new 'Higher Education Funding Councils' have been set up in England and Wales. In 1993/94, £3 million was distributed for special initiatives in 38 universities and colleges by the HEFCE.

Quality in Higher education

'Quality Assessment Committees' (Section 79 of the Act) will look at issues and monitor quality at three levels:

1. **Quality Control**: institutions' own QA mechanisms;
2. **Quality Audit**: by Higher Education Quality Council (HEQC) looking at quality control of provision for students with disabilities where institutions make claims to such provision;
3. **Quality Assessment**: external judgment of delivery at subject level.

Much of the material in this section has come from SKILL, the National Bureau for Students with Disabilities (formerly the National Bureau for Handicapped Students). Readers who wish to get more information about current legislation and initiatives should contact SKILL (address found under Cooper, 1994) who are active in many ways alongside students who are disabled.

It is interesting to note that, whilst in FE and HE teachers take their responsibilities for providing appropriate and relevant courses very seriously, they have not had a massively prescriptive curriculum dropped on them from a great height. Rather, their frameworks, whether competency based (as in NVQ's) or dealing with broader academic conceptual issues in HE, for example, allow for more creative course development and for flexible learning approaches and for environmental change (HEFCE, 1995).

The 1993 Education Act and the Code of Practice

The Code of Practice is contained within the 1993 Education Act. Leaving aside arguments about the ethics and practice of 'labelling', this chapter merely summarises the main framework. Components of the Code of Practice are discussed in more detailed later in the book. The

Code of Practice expresses its fundamental principles in relation to pupils with special educational needs (SEN):

- Needs of pupils who have SEN must be addressed.
- There is a continuum of both provision and needs (variety . . .)
- Children with SEN require special provision to access educational experiences.
- Needs of most pupils can be met in mainstream without SEN provision.
- Pupils with SEN's should, taking into account the wishes of parents, be educated in mainstream, alongside their peers.
- A child may have SENs even before starting school.
- Knowledge, views and experience of parents are vital to securing effective assessment and provision in partnership with LEA's and other agencies.
- All pupils with SEN should be identified and assessed as quickly as is consistent with thoroughness.
- In most cases no statutory assessment will be necessary.
- LEA assessments must:
  - be within prescribed time limits
  - be clear and thorough
  - set out educational and non-educational needs
  - clarify the objectives to be secured
  - describe the provision to be made and monitoring arrangements
  - ensure the Annual Review and updating targets
- The ascertainable views of the pupil should be considered wherever possible to make SEN provision effective.
- There must be co-operation between all agencies concerned and a multi-disciplinary approach to resolution of issues.

Unfortunately, the ethic of assessment, labelling and accountability in the 1993 Education Act have once again dominated. The need for more training and development to 'skill' teachers and lecturers has been submerged by a mounting bureaucracy that is hard to parallel. It seems that mountains of paperwork can compensate for serious, in-depth understanding of issues of access, choice and opportunity. The quality of teaching and learning is less important than assessment and allocation of resources. Teachers are once again being de-skilled and de-professionalised by being reduced to the level of clerks and recorders in a complex accounting system which, at the end of the day, is designed to stigmatise and marginalise children and young people who are different. We have yet to see whether the legal requirements of the Code of Practice for resources and for professional services actually come about, or whether the proposed legal and independent tribunals have a significant effect.

It remains to be seen whether the 1993 Act and Code of Practice is really the most radical piece of education legislation this century, as claimed by Eric Forth. Will it become yet another unwieldy edifice to the bureaucracy of accountability, a battlefield for scarce resources or will it sink into the quicksand of labelling and identification as an end in itself, without the ensuing support for pupils, students and teachers? It has, though, energised a debate about acknowledging diverse learning needs in mainstream education.

Legislation by definition of 'Special Needs' – an outdated concept?

For educationists there are often two main problems with legislation. Firstly, there is legislation which is largely positive and is drawn up after a gradual and open process with those who are involved in, or recipients of, that legislation ('bottom up' model). Its intentions may well be honourable and appropriate but the problems arise when it is incorporated or generalised without real understanding of the underlying principle(s) involved. Then trouble comes in its implementation in a day to day practical sense. There is many a slip 'twixt cup and lip and many factors (e.g. resources, opportunity, vested interests, lack of understanding or training) which may militate against new developments having the impact intended.

Secondly, there is the 'top down' model or being legislated on from a great height. Someone, somewhere, perhaps on a selected panel, has an 'expert' idea which then has to be tried and tested. There will be generated an inherent resistance whilst the recipients and planners digest the ramifications of legislative requirements. It may then become part of practice, albeit modified to suit local circumstances, or it may be rejected, or it may become the subject of an extended war of attrition, often with no notable changes or growth and a lot of time wasted. Perhaps you recognise these scenarios? Legislation from the mid 80's onwards has been very much the 'top down' variety with only hurried and politically biased consultation (Kelly, 1994 and Black, 1992).

Comprehensive and detailed discussion of the historical and social effects of legislation, including the 1944, 1981 and 1988 Education Acts can be found in Colin Barnes (1991); Sally Tomlinson (1981; 1982; 1985) whose work has informed and has explored the social implications of legislation and provision in a number of books and texts tracing the history of special educational provision. Deborah Cooper of SKILL (National Bureau of Students with Disabilities) has also written commentary and analysis of the Further and Higher Education Acts

1992. Richard Rieser and Micheline Mason (1990) explore and challenge the legacy of individual and institutionalised discrimination that currently exists in the education system, schools and the classroom. If the reader wishes to delve more deeply into the complex social and political milieu from which our current provision has developed then these authors can be recommended.

Educate the best and ditch the rest?

So, here was a digest of policy and legislation picked out as being relevant to the education of young people who are disabled. You may have different views and I can recommend that you read the 'Disability Manifesto for the 90s' and also read Colin Barnes' book *Disabled People in Britain and Discrimination* (1991).

Discrimination and social attitudes start at an early age in the home and at school. Our beliefs as adults can either reinforce prejudice and discriminatory attitudes, or they can reinforce positive, open attitudes that accept difference and diversity in all spheres of human endeavour including learning and education. There is much work to be done in the political sphere by disabled and non-disabled groups or allies to their work. In the meantime, the least we can do is to educate our young people about discrimination and about choice and opportunity. This must be done to redress the balance of negative knowledge and attitudes, or just plain ignorance.

The choice about the kind of society we want to live in and create in the next twenty years is down to all of us – a collective responsibility. The old order and the out of date language is that of 'exclusivity' in standards, perfection and unreal stereotypes. Educate the best and ditch the rest, with its consequent fragmentation of the individual, has had its day. A society that accepts diversity, change and can incorporate many different responses to the problems of learning, is an inclusive one. The choice of an 'exclusive' or an 'inclusive' society, over the next twenty years, is ours to take.

CHAPTER 2

A Healthy Perspective?

The research tradition – problems and opportunities

This chapter looks at the influence of traditional empirical and scientific research on the perception of the educational needs of physically disabled individuals. Historically it has had a negative impact on social attitudes which continue to influence educational provision and practice. This chapter proposes an alternative. Through equal partnership with disabled people, an alternative set of research and academic questions could be (and is being) drawn up that has greater allegiance to choice, opportunity and access to learning. Many text books for teachers, social workers and psychologists have been based on the acceptance of research questions that are aligned with institutionalised political, economic, traditional and scientific methodologies rather than a personalised and more subjective view. Too much of what has happened to young people who are disabled has been done *to* them and *for* them without due regard to their own perceived and more recently expressed views. Their needs have been perceived for them by non-disabled professionals rather than constructed from views arising from the experience of disability. This has led to what has been described as 'learned helplessness', discrimination and even oppression.

Scientific or empirical research seems to have difficulty with a psychology that is to do with subjective data and individual human experience. So much so that this has almost become a separate branch known as humanistic psychology where the so-called 'rigour' of empiricism or objectivity cannot be applied in the traditional reductionist manner. George Kelly in the 50's called his ideas a new psychology because the engine wheels of reductionism, standardisation and selection were rolling at that time. His 'Personal Construct Psychology' proposed a new way of looking at individual psychology that gave credence to an individual's unique way of perceiving the world around him or her. This was an alternative to a medical and psychological view that applied traditional scientific methodologies to the study of groups and group characteristics. In effect, these approaches put people into categories, some of which were medically useful but less relevant to the immediate purposes of teaching and learning. Every learner is an individual, there is no such thing as a 'disabled learner' nor such a thing as a 'special needs child'. Every individual assimilates new concepts and ideas into their own individual or personal framework. In using statistics that describe mean differences and deviations, many individual differences are lost.

> One definition of discrimination has to do with judging an individual on the basis of some ill-defined, or inappropriately defined, set of group characteristics and then treating them in this way regardless of their individual humanity, their rights or their unique characteristics.

Let us now take the example of 'Cerebral palsy' a label used to describe this medically constructed 'group' of people, the condition being characteristically defined as 'motor disorders which are due to non-progressive abnormalities of the brain' (Pimm, 1992). Unfortunately, the main purpose of diagnostic tests in disability terms is to 'recognise' the problem in the eyes of others or those who hold the key to resources. In personal and social terms the 'labelling' (Quicke and Winter, 1994) can have a disastrous effect by placing and treating each labelled person within a non-homogeneous group. People often unconsciously 'live up to' their labels and their behaviour can become subservient to the perception of their group stereotype. This often involves loss of individuality, control and self-esteem.

> Cerebral Palsy is therefore a complex condition. Whilst the common feature is lack of voluntary muscle control, there is little else that two people with cerebral palsy will have in common.
>
> (Pimm, 1992)

This is all very well and if you are in the business of 'body mechanics' then there is some use to describing groups of people according to physical or bodily characteristics. The problem comes when, having invented these grouped and labelled physical symptoms (e.g. 'the cerebral palsied', the 'physically disabled', the 'motor impaired child') we then have to invent a whole series of procedures and characteristics that go hand in hand with this definition of the group. Research questions are then created, serving to legitimise the use of this group terminology based on a set of physical characteristics (e.g. Down's Syndrome when it was first labelled). When these 'physical or medical characteristics' or statements about physical characteristics become over-emphasised, they can radically change and even dictate a general perception of that person's whole functioning or personality. It would be farcical to invent a 'special needs' category of people who are over seven feet tall, or children who have small feet or children who have freckles, or blue eyes. There could be a correlation between the colour of eyes and certain types of learning difficulty. Or worse still, there could be correlational statistics between psychological disorder or maladjustment and being over seven feet tall. It could be assumed that people over seven feet tall have problems of adjustment because of their physical structure. Or could it be because they can never find clothes that fit in their regular high street store?

The problem with research

Traditional scientific research methods were supposed to have no 'culture', being purely a quest for the truth or for fundamental principles. This is ignoring the 'King Kong Factor'. Scientists, doctors, educationists and practitioners have pursued their research projects, usually with good intentions and subject to the current ethical codes of their institutions but with scant regard for the actual views and feelings of the 'subjects'. There are still wider ethical problems in the system of generating research questions.

- Questions for research are generated and selected by the sponsors, therefore they are particularly biased.
- Methodologies and styles are referenced by academics who need to get 'respectable' research published.
- 'Generalisable' findings are applauded as they inform policy: individual differences are not recognised by this process.

Firstly, most research is undertaken through Higher Education Institutions. These are academically 'authoritarian' in nature (Heron, 1994). Thus the ethics and the definition of what actually constitutes 'new knowledge' is controlled. Secondly, once this 'new knowledge' has left its institutional base it then becomes subject to interpretation and selective perception, particularly by those who have vested interests and political agendas and who will not only select research findings that suit their overall purposes but will select specific aspects of one piece of research. The debate about reading methods, history curricula, the teaching of music and the effectiveness of conductive education for disabled young children are examples. Research is always tentative, it can only support principles and laws, it is never absolute. It is, therefore, open to (mis)interpretation and abuse. The reality is that research is usually biased by the social and political milieu in which it is undertaken. The agenda for eugenics and the uses subsequently of 'standardised assessment' in IQ testing of 'subnormals' was, with hindsight, most political. It had more to do with social control and manipulation than with human beings as individuals. It has also influenced a deeper cultural view (see Chapter 1) of the groups that it defined. A group of people, described by their physical characteristics or some other less obvious facet of their person, then becomes the subject of discrimination. It becomes necessary to construct special rooms, transport, equipment, leisure facilities, social areas, living accommodation and even literary culture specifically for that group. If individuals in that group say 'it does not fit me', they are exceptions to the norm and thus maladjusted. The 'norm' does not exist, like developmental milestones, and are abstracted from group characteristics and research with large numbers of 'subjects'.

Who decides what to test?

Standardised attainment targets, IQ tests, developmental checklists, reading tests, motor skill tests are designed to measure a level of skill, knowledge or understanding against what is regarded as the 'norm'. This is called normative assessment and can yield figures or results that are useful in specific ways. The kind of statistics produced will enable judgments on whole populations or large groups. This will then lead to *manipulation of resources and planning of provision according to the criteria by which the populations were originally judged.* To deal with this, 'criterion referenced' tests were developed. They do not need to show a 'normative' trend and can be set up to measure any group or set of criteria, factors or skills. *This is still subject to the problem of who draws up the questions, what they are and why it was done.*

If we now turn our attention to the actual content of such measures, again in the context of assessment tests applied to children who are disabled, we find that there are further problems. A test or measure is valid if it measures what it purports to measure or test. In other words, a paper and pencil test first and foremost measures the ability to use a pencil. It is not valid if the subject is unable to hold a pencil. This is an obvious example but, given this ability, the test probably claims only to measure things like spelling ability, comprehension, addition, subtraction and the like. The key problem here is that assumptions are often made, or conclusions drawn, about the subject's abilities in areas other than that actually tested. The subject may have a very low, or even zero score on the spelling test whereas given the chance to undertake such a test in a different way (e.g. orally or with a keyboard) that child may well show a completely different score.

Even with 'criterion referenced' tests, that are not based on norms, there is a problem. First of all, they tend to masquerade as being purely descriptive but in fact the criteria have been selected. Who decides, and on what basis, what these criteria should be? By whose agenda are they worked out? More often than not they are also related to what is described as 'normal development'. This can be as vague and inappropriate as purely normative or standardised tests. To whom are the test criteria important? *Standardisation is perceived as legitimising and adding power to the results of assessment and diagnostic tests. This is the basis for too many assumptions.*

The TES printed an article 'Enough is Enough' in January 1995:

> The natural curiosity of children must be crushed so that 'Learning how to learn gives way to learning how to be taught'. A 'national' curriculum – 'a mishmash of adult hang-ups selected according to various national prejudices' – only compounds this oppression with its recurrent testing – 'Do children really get taller by being measured?'
>
> R. Meighan

An individual may be unable to access the test properly. This does not *invalidate the individual concerned but it does invalidate the test.* Global conclusions about a child's general developmental level or intellectual functioning have, on many occasions, been made simply because the individual is unable to co-ordinate movement to dress him or herself. This is ignoring the movement disability and drawing invalid conclusions from test observations. Performance measures test individuals and make judgments on the evidence of ability which is limited to that defined by a particular group of professionals in a situation which may bear little relationship to reality for any given individual. This is equally true of both criterion referenced (e.g. diagnostic, skill based) and 'norm' referenced (e.g. IQ, ability) testing. It is particularly true where any kind of movement or co-ordination disability is experienced by the person under test or assessment, or where a child is experiencing pain or discomfort as a result of a medical condition.

> Although individuals may not speak with the same voice on some particular issue, each speaks from a unique and subjective viewpoint. Taking seriously the subjective perspectives of teachers and pupils is a considerable departure from an educational psychology which portrays teachers as understanding pupils in terms of measurable individual differences of personality and attainment. It centres on the individuality of persons rather than attributes on which they may differ. It asserts the importance of the self, the self which projects a voice expressing uniqueness of thought and feeling in terms of a particular developmental history within a particular social world.
>
> (Professor Hazel Francis, 1993)

The legacy of medical research – a healthy perspective?

There has been, over the past ten years, considerable national debate about the educational needs of children with movement disabilities and about the most effective way of meeting those needs. A common factor is that professionals seem to be debating *their own* preferred methods, whether they be educationists, teachers, physiotherapists or other professionals. It is significant that the views of those groups representing disabled people, to whom these methods are applied, are not felt to be influential in changing professional practice. The diagnostic process has tended to identify symptoms (label) and prescribe treatment for a whole group. This is sometimes erroneously applied to, or called, education, but education does not consist of remedies for symptoms. A symptomatic approach leading to marketable packages or treatment can be either swift to apply with a minimum of fuss, or can involve a panoply of technical or human resources which give the impression of great activity surrounding the problem. Whether they have a beneficial effect for the disabled child or young person is often difficult to prove or disprove. They are sometimes characterised by set strategies, calculated steps and prescribed outcomes for dealing with defined groups or situations and can sometimes add to discriminatory practices on the part of professionals.

Even in so-called educational books or guidelines, special needs are reduced to an impersonal description of disease or condition characteristics, the simplistic interpretation being that anyone falling into that category is likely to exhibit all these symptoms. On the face of it they look ever so useful as if it helps to 'know what you are doing'. In reality, knowing symptoms does not create an educational programme. The educational work is still to be done in planning and delivering meaningful experiences to the pupil or student. There are also many assumptions very often made, if not by the writer then certainly by readers, about the range and consequences of those symptoms.

There has grown up in special needs generally a culture of looking for the symptoms, say, of dyspraxia, epilepsy, Aspberger's or dyscalculia (inability to do maths). The way in which the medical aspects of disability or 'special need' are presented often has the effect of imposing unnecessary limitations on teachers' creativity; what we can, or wish to do, with children in school or on what disabled students and adults can, and should, undertake. Furthermore, it increases the worry that teachers have when they are already concerned about all the children in their care. There is a constant stream of literature and 'helpful' articles which are communicating hidden, subtle messages saying 'Watch out, watch out! There's a "special needs" child about'. The 'specialisation' of special needs teaching in the past has left a legacy of concern, fear and lack of confidence in working with children who are perceived to be other than average. The truth of the matter, and most teachers already recognise it, is that all children have a variety of needs. Disabled children are no different, and education is about accepting and working with diversity not about categorisation and diagnosis.

This debate about methods and approaches in the area of disability research and professional practice has been characterised by partisan drum beating ('my method is better than yours'), by political interventions, even by such things as international monetary exchange considerations and by a significant lack of broader appraisal or partnership between the professional researcher and the subjects. The whole debate about 'methods' has been injected with a form of madness (Chapter 8). It has been kept within specific groups of professionals and set up as the domain of either 'experts' as individuals or 'expert knowledge'. It has become the plaything of (sometimes very powerful) groups who claim intellectual ownership of methods often based on current available or shared knowledge and sometimes just common sense. Is it any wonder then that schools, colleges and teachers, when faced with the possibility of receiving a child or young person who is physically disabled or has a medical condition, tend to panic somewhat?

Many groups of parents and professionals work hard to overcome these obstacles to genuine progress and understanding. There are many positive initiatives where professionals, parents and disabled people are beginning to form partnerships and strategies that bring together some fundamental and underlying principles in offering positive learning experiences. There are fundamental questions such as: 'Who decides what the research priorities are with respect to disability?', and 'Where is the common base of knowledge and research that supports work in health, education and social services, to do with disability?'

A little knowledge is . . . better than ignorance and fear?

In the spirit of equal opportunities and in the 'entitlement for all' mode, the inclusion of a child with 'brittle bones', in all lessons including physical education, should no longer be a matter for 'special consideration', but a matter of course. It should happen without all the concern, fear and lack of confidence that still exists today. This is because we have not yet questioned enough the fundamental impact that the spreading of superficial 'medical or expert knowledge' has had on teachers and schools, on the child and on their family. The 'professionalisation' of disability and the supremacy of medical expertise over other professional groups has encouraged a passive or hesitant attitude. It has defined who is seen to be capable of taking positive and effective action in educating disabled children and young adults. It has the effect of relegating the rest of us to 'fund raisers' or 'an extra pair of hands' but with little acknowledged ability to make a difference to the physical difficulties or problems encountered. This may sound a little extreme but it is evident in the way that carers, helpers and classroom assistants are treated and is a result of profound institutionalisation of the knowledge and expertise surrounding learning, disability and medical conditions generally.

On a recent working visit to a 'designated' primary school (1995) the following was heard:

> The physiotherapist will not work in the classroom but prefers to withdraw individual children for specific periods of treatment. We don't know exactly what happens in these sessions and there is no sharing of progress. She is employed by the health authority with separate managers and it is a difficult situation with the amount of time she can spare being under scrutiny.

Is this an exception? It is more common than is acceptable and it raises issues of professional probity, power and collaboration (dealt with in more detail in Chapters 4, 7 and 8). This is not to say that, in general, individuals or specific groups are at fault. Many therapists now work much more closely in the classroom with teachers and withdrawal is becoming rarer. A different set of research questions is beginning to remove disability and associated endeavours from the hands of professional practitioners alone and place it firmly back into the community and with disabled people where it belongs. This is gradually increasing the accountability of professionals to their clients and increasing the power of disabled people generally to have greater control over their lives. It will eventually enable children and parents to have greater choices than they currently have. Services could be made available for disabled people (including children, their parents or advocates) to *access as they need* or choose, not to be controlled and directed into specific channels that suit others and lump people together in meaningless (but nevertheless highly defined) groups in order to fulfil someone else's expectations.

Supported education is characterised by:

- An appreciation of diversity.
- Alignment of practices and beliefs.
- Education is more than academic achievement *or physical performance*.

This list comes from Oregon, U.S.A. (Author's addition in italics).

Much research is produced for a limited audience and often judged by academic criteria within limited professional boundaries or parameters. Researchers and practitioners, who are busy trying to get their research projects funded, more often than not target their papers to a specific audience of similar professionals, once the original submission has been agreed. These specific audiences can become either elitist ('I have the knowledge, you don't') or professionally arrogant ('You are not trained, wouldn't understand') or even openly exclusive ('This is my job, not yours'). The impetus and direction for research into disability and education could be more firmly based on the comments and views of adults, students and pupils who are disabled. Indeed it is possible that the needs of disabled people, as identified by themselves, could be the framework and driving force for future inter-disciplinary research projects. It would be interesting to see how many disabled professionals and lay people are on the panels that distribute money for research or for projects.

It would be particularly interesting if the whole process of allocation of funds by the national lottery, trusts, marathon fund raising projects and charities was altogether more transparent. It is not really apparent at the moment whether disabled people are involved in these decision making committees. We need to be much more creative in forming partnerships between parents, disabled groups, medical, paramedical, psychological, educational and social science practitioners. In this way it may be possible to build a body of knowledge more directly defined by adults and children who are physically disabled. Hopefully, a greater involvement of disabled individuals and groups and willingness to listen would then provide a more coherent and appropriate base for research, education and training.

> *Don't impose labels and definitions on disabled people. Ask what their own preferences are*, urges Michael Bishop who works for the British Council of Organisations of Disabled People . . .
> Most people look on disability as a 'personal tragedy'. It is an attitude that sees the problem as springing directly from the individual's condition. Not surprisingly, it shifts the responsibility for change onto the shoulders of the 'victim'.
> This myopic view has been propagated by countless swarms of able bodied professionals who have come to dominate the lives of disabled people and who reinforce this theory at almost every turn – doctors and nurses, occupational therapists and physiotherapists, social workers and teachers, even social contacts in daily life.
> The media mirrors the popular view. Disabled people are portrayed as passive recipients who long for able bodiedness...Any who dare to make the slightest complaint about the way society treats them have clearly not yet adjusted to their disability.
>
> (Michael Bishop, 1987)

Who defines Mr. Average?

Educational psychology continues to play into the hands of those who wish to define and measure us according to more and more limiting and limited criteria. Who sets these criteria? Who decides what children need to know and how they should go about learning? Who says that this subject content is more important than that for a child or young person to make the best of their lives after school? In the past, IQ tests were used to select children for special education (Ministry of Education, 1946) although this was not the original purpose of such tests.

> What intelligence tests measure, what we hope they measure is...the capacity of an individual to understand the world about him, and his resourcefulness to cope with the challenge.
>
> (Wechsler, 1958)

Tests also have a cultural and contextual invalidity built in. Sternberg (1984) argued that any definition of intelligence must recognise the cultural context in which it is applied. A lot of people show greater ability to recognise and solve problems when they are couched in familiar contextual terms. If we then add emotional pressure or anxiety to this equation, performance suffers even more (Yerkes and Dodson, 1908; Broadhurst, 1957, and Martens 1987). If we again add an unknown hindrance of a physical or movement variety or underlying discomfort or pain, we get added pressure on top of the discomfort. If no-one wishes to acknowledge the feelings or discomfort or fatigue associated with performing in certain ways, then we have additional emotional pressure and lowering of self-esteem.

> Emphasis on the subjective and the social individual also departs from other psychological perspectives on the learner. There is good reason for doing this for an educational psychology which aims to assist teachers, the reason being that while psychologists serving their own discipline may legitimately suspend belief in aspects of human nature in order to look at them afresh, teachers may not. They must engage directly with learners in their full humanity. Just as Pope in his time argued that the proper study of mankind is not theology but man . . . the proper study of learners is not psychology but the learner . . . it follows that psychologists might do well to try to work with teachers to develop that perspective.
>
> (Professor Hazel Francis, 1993)

The debate about structure and function

In the introduction and in Chapter 1, the 'medical' and 'social' models of disability were presented. These are intertwined with the search for a structural answer to functional disabilities. They are also very much related to ways of describing the phenomena we are talking about, summarised in the many definitions of disability currently used. Reindal (1995) discusses a framework that seeks to balance the disabling structures and practices in our society with an acknowledgement of biological variety and diverse ability. Medical and clinical psychology researchers are very much concerned with finding a structural cause to explain the natural biological variety in humans. This has led to assumed links between structure and function that are not proven or patently do not exist. Where function is said to be impaired, although seemingly logical, it is an assumption that there must be a structural cause. Wrong conclusions are then drawn about the nature of the problem (as can happen in 'dyslexia' or 'dyspraxia'). Diagnostic tests have been set up with a fixed range of 'symptoms' indicating that you are 'dyslexic' or 'dyspraxic'. These are constructed for certain uses and can lead teachers to the conclusion that some form of special treatment will correct the assumed structural problem in the child's psyche.

The following extract is from The Guardian, Sept, 1994:

> As a young child, Nicky could not walk or talk and had severe feeding problems. 'We were told he would be a cabbage and live on a beanbag', said Mr. Crane, a bank clerk. 'We were advised to send him to an institution and get on with the rest of our lives. The thought of him going to school was beyond our wildest dreams'.
>
> But the head of the local primary agreed to take Nicky if resources were made available, and the Cranes regard his progress there as miraculous. He cannot read or write but has an extensive vocabulary, likes stories and sings along to records.
>
> 'He learns by copying, and he has learned normal behaviour by staying with mainstream pupils', said Mrs. Crane. 'We want him to remain with them'.
>
> (Ward, 1994)

It could be environmental factors that will help the child's development and, in some cases, these may even be the cause of the problem. It is also forgotten that the so-called problem may just be a part of normal development *for that child.*

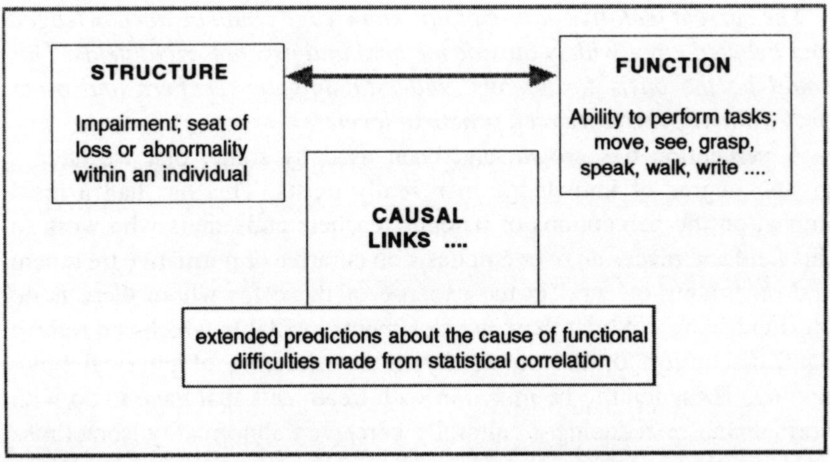

Figure 2.1 Assumptions can lead to wrong predictions about ability

The implication of the label is that a teacher may assume that a child cannot perform a task or action because he or she has some structural impairment when there is no direct comparison (Shallice, 1988; Caplan, 1981) for this. Another assumption, and more common, is that the child is 'normal' and has no impairment (that can be seen or has been recognised) and therefore is lazy, disruptive or unwilling to try or to comply with the demands of the school, task or activity underway. A child may choose not to walk, or be unable to control a pencil properly, because of a number of other reasons (e.g. it is too painful, too difficult, too much effort for little obvious benefit, not enjoyable in relation to the effort involved, cannot see the point . . .) The existence of assessment tests in the neuropsychological domain have the implication that we can make predictions about structural (e.g. brain or nerve) impairment from an assessment of functional abilities and behaviour. These connections are not proven and do not acknowledge the complexity of choice, control, expression and other personal or social influences. Yet some remedial programmes are based on the assumption that there is an underlying physical impairment or structural problem which can be put right or changed by *direct* and limited 'remedial' action. There may be no structural problem at all, it may simply be a matter of experience and development. On the other hand, if there is a structural problem, unless there is a specific and proven medical cure, it does little good to use it as the basis for an educational programme. The usefulness of the 'structure = functional behaviour' equation needs to be questioned in relation to educational programmes.

The current tentative nature of this knowledge could be acknowledged and debated more widely outside medical and psychological fields. This could be the basis for greater understanding by teachers and other professionals who work on a practical level.

A perception has grown, and been used by some, that we have a greater degree of knowledge than really exists. This has had a great impact on the perceptions of parents, teachers and others who work in this field and places an over emphasis on curative or normative treatment and on finding a 'cure' at the expense of those for whom there is no apparent 'cure'. Whilst there are treatments available which can relieve pain, discomfort or the possibility of deterioration of physical functioning. These tend to be mixed in with treatments that have to do with normalising or reducing a culturally perceived abnormality, sometimes only cosmetic in nature.

We live in a society where plastic surgery is available for cosmetic reasons. Who could deny any individual the possibility of improving their physical appearance when it means so much to them? Images of almost impossible physical perfection (or at least the appearance of it) are constantly promoted in the popular visual media. It is sufficient to point out the profound effects on a person's image of themselves of the linking of physical 'perfection' with acceptance, success, sexuality and power.

Here we perceive:

(a) a striving for the illusion of physical perfection, put into practice by doctors (through cosmetic and some other types of surgery) and by the media through selling images (in films and advertising mainly but also in publications ranging from soft pornography to pulp fiction);

(b) the real fear of those who appear different, or are made to feel inadequate, that they will be socially isolated and marginalised because of some physical or mental characteristic(s);

(c) the influence on professional practice and research to pursue strategies and lines of enquiry that will 'normalise' rather than recognise uniqueness, creative individuality and diversity;

(d) a common assumption or message that the problem for a child or young person lies entirely within that individual and not in the way the social environment around them is organised.

So we seem to have a context that generates a need for medical treatment, magical cures or promising remedies. This context has a profound effect on the way in which we build up (and feel about) our physical 'image' of ourselves.

Ourselves in the eyes of others

Kurt Lewin investigated the existence of variable and internal subjective processes affecting the way in which we process and understand events around us, including the actions of others. He explored, in social problem solving, how these perceptions affect our ability to respond to problems we encounter or to develop ways to deal with our circumstances (Lewin, 1981). The recurrent theme of the historical and contemporary 'images of disability' arose in Chapter 1 and appears in current writing. Why is this so important? From an activist point of view, it is useful to develop slogans to enhance positive attitudes in a similar vein to 'black is beautiful . . . bald is beautiful . . . fat is beautiful'. For practitioners in education, therapy and social services, there are fundamentally important principles relating to disabled children and young people. These have to do with self-esteem, which is a constructed but useful measure of processes that have to do with how we see ourselves and how we feel about ourselves. As such, it is a measurable variable in the learning process. Self-esteem has a *considerable effect* on performance, motivation, persistence, co-operation and general learning (Lawrence, 1987, see figure 2.2). Self-esteem is a measure based on the relationship between self-image and ideal self. Our overall and consistent understanding of ourself, in relation to what others tell us, is our self-concept. These are complex constructs but some understanding of their importance gives a degree of insight into the global and specific effects that our social environment and relationships *can* have on our self-esteem.

An important part of our understanding of ourselves as individuals arises from the way in which others see us. A constructed measure of this is called self-esteem. Self-esteem is understood as a measure of the feeling we have about our self and the platform from which we launch ourselves at life. It is a crucial factor in our functioning as a social animal and in enabling us to make the most of the living and learning experiences that life has to offer. Sadly, there are many parts of our culture which undermine an individual's self-esteem and these are not limited to an accepted view of disabled or able bodied. They are more in the realms of normal and abnormal or human and superhuman. We mere mortals with our imperfect bodies are constantly undermined by those who make money from flesh. We still accept the most outrageous and apparently perfect physical and sexual stereotypes paraded day after day in our media (television, magazines, newspapers) and in advertising. It has moved from the realms of fantasy and myth (e.g. angels and mermaids) to soft pornography and into a grinding and unsubtle, day to day conditioning process which wears us all down. It changes our appreciation of each other as real, though imperfect, human beings. Have we really moved very far from the primitive cultural constructs and ideas that motivated our ancestors to kill sickly, deformed or unusual babies?

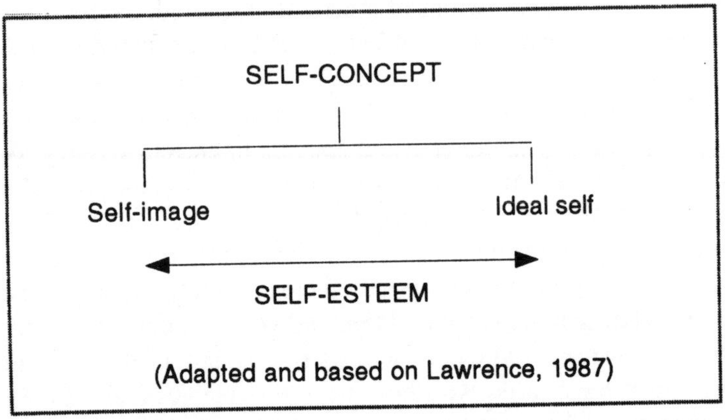

Figure 2.2 Self-esteem

It is difficult to evaluate the 'global' effect of stereotypes and negative images of disability on children and young people. Conversations with young people who are disabled and the voice of those who are active in civil rights for disabled people clearly indicates the profound effect of deep-seated personal, professional and scientific attitudes on disabled individuals. This groundswell of opinion, articulated by Colin Barnes (1991), Michael Bishop (1987), Richard Rieser and Micheline Mason (1990), Jenny Morris (1992) and many others, should leave us in no doubt about this. Self-esteem, like intelligence, is a psychological construct with a proven impact on learning and academic performance.

The author's interpretation of Lawrence's terminology would be as follows:

GLOBAL: images propounded by media and structures within which we live and work.

SPECIFIC: those images communicated from one individual to another about them as a person.

Once again, it is clear that the problem has less to do with any internal impairment but more to do with the impact of others and social or cultural factors.

SELF-IMAGE: The image we create within ourselves based on what we pick up from those (significant others) around us. We can, of course, reject or accept what others communicate to (not necessarily tell) us. The more significant to us another person is, the more likely we are to accept or be affected by their view.

IDEAL SELF: our own personal aspirations and visions of what we would like to be in intellectual and physical terms. Also, in terms of our social position. This is 'stoked up' by media hype and ongoing, subtle stereotypes. Disabled youngsters need their own role models and images to give them aspirations that are real and possible. Impossible aspirations lead to lowered self-esteem.

SELF-ESTEEM: a constructed measure of how we feel, on an ongoing basis, about ourself, based on the relationship between our own aspirations (ideal self) and what our circumstances and significant others tell us (self-image). Disabled people constantly have to come to terms with the difference between their own aspirations and the circumstances in which they find themselves.

SELF-CONCEPT: our ability to understand or represent the different facets *of ourselves* (including our self-esteem) *to ourselves*. It requires a degree of abstract thinking and problem-solving to understand our own reactions based on preserving a reasonable level of self-esteem. It is a facet of maturity and ability to represent our 'self' in abstract terms. In the absence of this – many reactions are based purely on feelings and are not mediated by conscious thought. Often a necessary human response!

Equal opportunity in education is not about striving to get into a 'grammar' type school to reach other people's 'standards', or even to get to the best University. It is about:

- **choices** (for teachers as professionals and for pupils and students of all ages);
- **educational opportunity** (entitlement to satisfactory and appropriate teaching in a high quality learning environment, both subject and non-subject based);
- **access** (relating to the skills and qualities of the teachers and the resources available to the school or college).

The practice of measuring and the political use of standardised testing has left us with a legacy of discrimination, exclusion and marginalisation and of promoting the myth of academic attainment as against broad and utilitarian education. In other words, what is the real purpose of an incredibly complex and bureaucratic system of testing, assessment, diagnosis and remediation in education? It has been seized on by those who would continue to engage in a process of social manipulation and engineering with the sole purpose of preserving the myth that there are those who are clever and academically gifted and those who are not. There are those who are able, economically and socially productive and there are those who are not. This is very important for children and young people who are disabled or experience movement disabilities or medical conditions. Without access to appropriate and satisfactory teaching, to quality learning environments and to a range of ordinary educational facilities, at all ages, with their peers, the presence of disabled children and young people in the education system is devalued right from the start.

The illustration figure 2.3 is a common 'equal opportunities' model and frame of reference. It has advantages as a model for sharing expertise in that it is very strong on the social and educational factors. Before disabled children and young adults can truly benefit from any remedial programme they must have suitable environments in which they can live and work. What is needed first and foremost is not a 'system' at all, but a way of life. This type of approach involves everybody and not just specialised bunches of professional experts who do their thing in specialised circumstances and then send the child or young person out into the 'real world' to survive, or not. The cruelty is not that people are

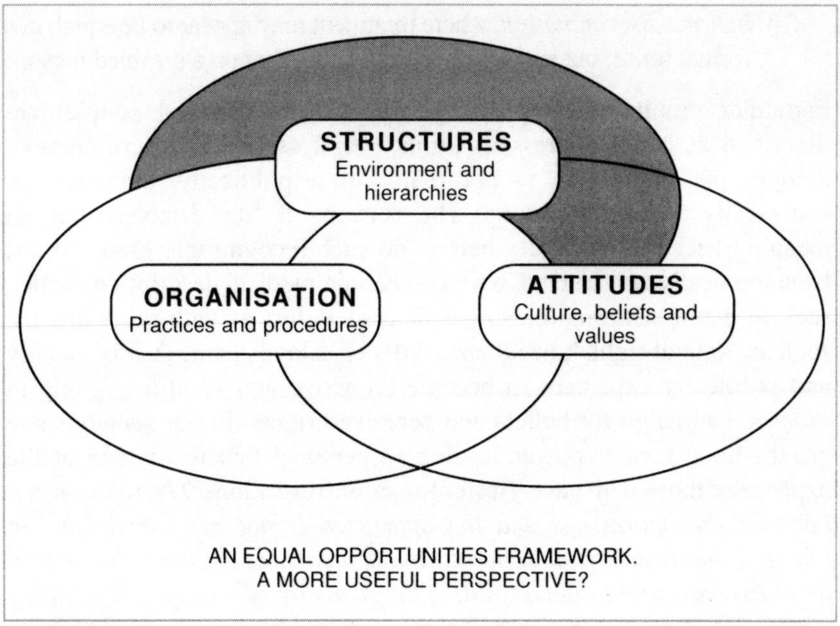

Figure 2.3

born disabled or less than perfect. We are all less than perfect to some degree. The cruelty really lies in the covert messages sent out, all the time from non-disabled professionals, that disabled children and young people must be changed into something else. They must become 'whole' and 'normal'. Children and young people particularly have reduced choice in these matters. They are sometimes exposed to prolonged treatments which have as much to do with the aspirations of the professionals (and sometimes parents) than to do with the aspirations of the child or young person (Anthony Clare, 1990).

Equal Opportunities describes policies and practices which provide equal access and rights, and seek to remove discrimination against people on the basis of disability (or race, class, gender, age or sexual orientation).

Discrimination refers to individual or general practices which, by default or intent, put individuals or groups of people at a disadvantage because of their disability. The Sex Discrimination Act (1975) describes two kinds and these can be usefully adapted to look at issues for disabled people:

(a) *direct discrimination*, where a disabled person, intentionally or not, is treated less favourably than any other member of the non-disabled community;

(b) *indirect discrimination*, where treatment may appear to be equal, in a formal sense, but is discriminatory in its effect on a disabled person.

Particular groups of people (e.g. women and disabled people) are described as being oppressed. Unlike racial or gender discrimination, though, the oppression is not really of a politically, culturally or historically recognised group. The concept of 'the disabled' has no meaning because, in effect, there is no such recognisable group. It has been medically constructed, based on certain medical descriptions which seek to define abnormalities or deficiencies. Just as with other groups, such as 'animal rights', backbench MPs or 'Lloyds names', it is socially and politically expedient to become an active and identified group in order to campaign for beliefs and perceived rights. In our society some groups have greater power leading to personal benefit or gain at the expense of those who have greater losses or frustrations. *The relationship between the oppressors and the oppressed is not necessarily one of intention but results from a perception of weakness as being the fault of an individual rather than a result of the structure of society.* Overcoming oppression depends on the willingness of those who are oppressors to work towards changing this structure. It is useful to consider the basic tenets of equal opportunity in the context of schools, classrooms and the process of learning. Of necessity, these concepts also involve understanding who holds power over whom in both personal and political terms. It is not possible to consider choice and opportunity without considering where the power lies and how attitudes have changed over the years.

The following account by a teacher illustrates the changing definition of integration over the years.

> A 'special' unit within a mainstream school was set up in mid-70's. Integration then meant 'coming into assemblies'. It then became possible to integrate one or two less disabled children with sympathetic teachers. Integration moved on from there. One class in each year group would be smaller. Children then moved out of the unit building. Overall school management made three or four classes smaller and all physically disabled children would be in these classes. Access improved gradually, for example, by ramping, exits, and accessible play areas. Moved from larger groups of physically disabled pupils to a more integrated approach where pupils were more 'scattered' throughout the school. SSA's still do not have enough time for in-class support. Buildings still need changing.

Inevitably any consideration of equal opportunities in both education and research necessitates a good hard look at the way in which educational and associated structures and systems have been set up in relation to their impact on individuals. For example, the school and college system as a whole reflects the general discrimination against women in a number of ways. Women comprise the majority of the teaching force and yet hold relatively fewer of the positions of influence and power in education. Although this is changing, there is still an imbalance brought about by society's structures (child rearing practices, conditions of employment, selection practices preserving the status quo, (unconscious) prejudice, peer pressure, cultural habits) that have been set up according to previous cultural 'norms'.

Self-image and esteem: Recognition of exclusive behaviour and social 'norms'. Improved learning environment through affirmative action and positive strategies.

Stereotypes and role models: The preservation of cultural 'norms' fed by 'blinkered research', hierarchical and competitive environments, existing prejudice, narrow performance or attainment testing and inability to provide flexibility in learning (inc. situations and environments). Introduction of positive and individual role models through employment and the curriculum.

Life changes: Open sharing of issues of diversity and change. Early personal and social education. Increased emphasis on personal, social and health education

ATTITUDES
Culture, beliefs and values

Peer Culture: Children and young people encouraged to examine their (learned) beliefs) and values. Acceptance of diversity and difference.

Stress & Culture: Disassemble stereotypes and unrealistic expectation of physical perfection. Good health and PSE programmes. Accept diversity in human physical attributes.

Dependence and learned helplessness: Reduction of over and under protectiveness. Undermine the supremacy of the traditional medical expertise in disability. Positive but supportive and realistic social and educational expectations.

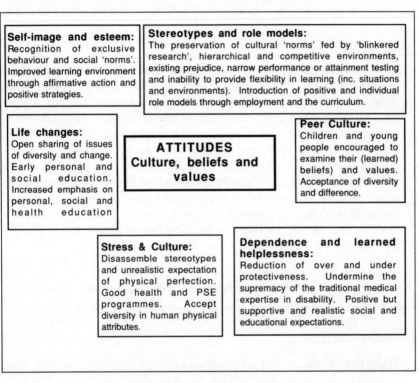

Figure 2.4 Attitudes and their impact on educational opportunity

Jenny Morris writes:

> Other changes in attitudes are required . . . .
> To get back to people's attitudes to me. Generally, I find there is a combination of total insensitivity to the difficulties which I experience and paradoxically, at the same time, a classification of me as 'unable'; there is a failure to see that being unable to walk means exactly that, and not 'unable' generally. I am handicapped by various physical obstacles, but these obstacles can be got round given the willingness of people to help.
> (Jenny Morris in Booth and Swann, 1987)

Phil Jones (1992) describes the effect that a non-developmental approach has had on the provision of services to disabled people. When these developments are viewed in terms of their social (and psychological, if you like) consequences, it has led to a range of disabling strategies and institutions. This, in turn, has produced certain behaviour from those who are the recipients of these strategies. Often further labelling or assumptions are made about the response of people who are disabled to their surroundings, placing them in the non-normal category. In reality, any non-disabled person would probably behave in a variety of extreme ways if they were subjected to the basic obstacles to functioning that our society unwittingly creates.

> Well-meaning paternalism from other people, including caring professions and professionals. 'You poor thing, what can we do to help?' 'Don't worry about a thing, it will all be taken care of' 'No, no, you mustn't do that, it is not good for you'. Avoiding this feature of 'normal' behaviour can be labelled as abnormal. Classic ways of doing this are declining help offered or missing appointments made. Both these can cause annoyance to the person proffering the help without any understanding of the fact that disabled people who have self-respect do not like to be patronised or made to feel helpless. Let us take a salutary look at how we educate or place-children in the constant position of having to do things '...because it is good for you...'. If all the decisions are made by the adults (or the one who, basically has the power), then it disables the child.
>
> (P. Jones, 1992)

Attitudes, beliefs and values underpin our behaviour in all arenas. When it comes to including disabled children and students into schools and colleges, there seem to be two polarised attitudes, typified by the following examples:

> **We'd like to but** . . . Many schools and colleges currently say this. They look at the physical facilities and rule out wheelchairs etc. It is true that there are resource implications but basically, this kind of argument nearly always marks the negative attitude to including disabled students: 'It's too much trouble!'
>
> **We will and we have** . . . Almost as many schools and colleges, through a variety of reasons, have included pupils who are disabled, even before they had the full resources. In these cases, the problems have been considerable but were never seen as overwhelming; the end result has justified the action.

The institution reflects prevailing attitudes within the staff. They may prevail because they are the attitudes of those 'in power', or they may prevail because they are the attitudes of the majority. There will always be individual variation. Figure 2.5 shows appropriate procedures and practices.

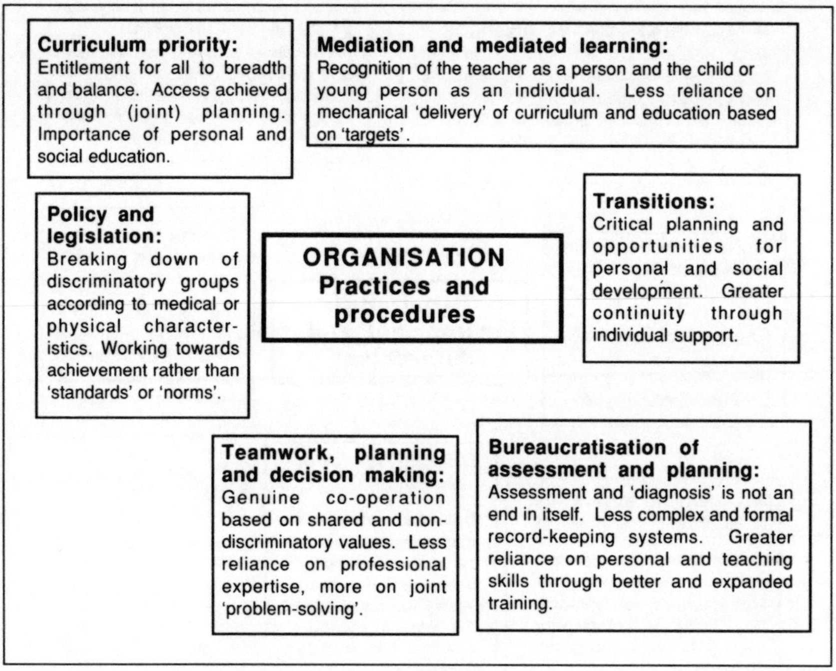

Figure 2.5 Procedures and customary practises

One of the most obvious factors that emerges from this is the way in which mass education has become 'mechanised' in schools and colleges. The relationship between teacher and learner has been progressively eroded by the emphasis on 'targets', attainment and delivery of curriculum chunks (of knowledge). The bureaucracy of formalised accountability and endless record-keeping has undermined the positive effect of a well-trained educator who can form relationships with learners. Teachers and other associated professionals have been pushed towards distant and mechanical practices by an overwhelming need to deny diversity and professional autonomy. To let teachers be the judge of the efficacy of their approaches, to rely on their training and ability, and to use their skills sensitively, it seems, cannot be trusted. This devaluing of individual interaction in schools and colleges has a knock-on effect as people begin to be measured or judged solely by their ability to perform. Children and young people who are disabled are thus further disadvantaged, along with their teachers, and marginalised. Figure 2.6 shows hazards and problems.

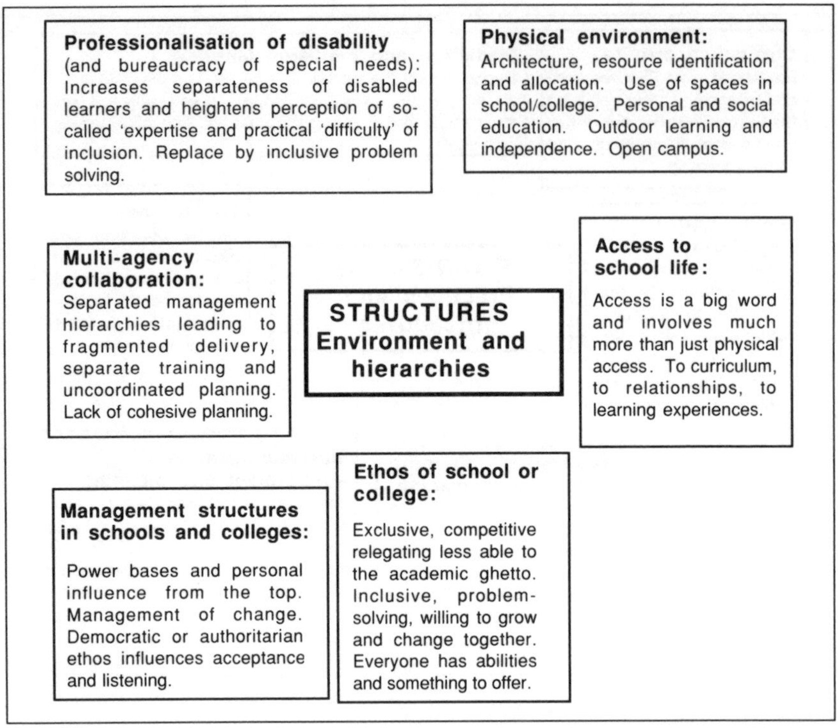
Professionalisation of disability (and bureaucracy of special needs): Increases separateness of disabled learners and heightens perception of so-called 'expertise and practical 'difficulty' of inclusion. Replace by inclusive problem solving.
Physical environment: Architecture, resource identification and allocation. Use of spaces in school/college. Personal and social education. Outdoor learning and independence. Open campus.
Multi-agency collaboration: Separated management hierarchies leading to fragmented delivery, separate training and uncoordinated planning. Lack of cohesive planning.
STRUCTURES Environment and hierarchies
Access to school life: Access is a big word and involves much more than just physical access. To curriculum, to relationships, to learning experiences.
Management structures in schools and colleges: Power bases and personal influence from the top. Management of change. Democratic or authoritarian ethos influences acceptance and listening.
Ethos of school or college: Exclusive, competitive relegating less able to the academic ghetto. Inclusive, problem-solving, willing to grow and change together. Everyone has abilities and something to offer.

Figure 2.6 Provision of choice through collective responsibility

Many of our public institutions, including schools and medical services, do not offer choice to their clients. The doctor's view is the one that holds sway. It is his professional opinion which dictates what happens next. The teacher (or more recently, the Government) dictates what children are to learn in school. The element of choice has become more limited. Both teachers and doctors, given a different cultural and political context, could offer a lot more choice. Their whole professional expertise could be about offering choice to their clients. Teachers could plan and lay out a range of learning options for children and young people and they could then choose not only *what* they want to learn but *how* they want to learn it. Doctors could lay out the health problems and opportunities for their patients; their patients could then choose what particular path they choose to follow, including ignoring all advice and going their own way. Of course, we wish to be healthy and we wish to be educated, but on whose terms?

The broad consequence of the 'professionalisation' of support and the bureaucratisation of assessment in special needs is that it is maintained as a *domain for action by professionals and experts only*. Action support for children and young people involves the whole community, as well as the individuals themselves. It is only by defining and re-defining the whole construct of disability that it can be shared between the experts and choices placed back into the hands of disabled people themselves and their local communities. When this is achieved, the professional services will really become services *for* disabled people, from which they can choose and to which they can contribute. Only a radical shift of attitudes and power, with consequences for organisation and structures, could achieve this.

Extract from Strange Mystique
(by Simon Brisenden)

They say
that every person is unique
but some of us
have a strange mystique

can he walk or talk or screw?
what exactly can he do?
I suppose it shows
society cares
that I'm a public subject
destined to tick boxes
in eternal questionnaires . . . .

It is vital that research and training begins to break down the barriers to inclusion in education and to reduce the 'fragmentation' both of the pupil, client or patient and the bodies of knowledge that underpin teaching and learning. An holistic approach is integral to building on a research movement based on a socially creative model of disability (Reindal, 1995) which takes the views of the disabled individual as a starting point. This is not easy as it means rejecting the simple 'categorisation' type approaches and re-defining both research and training priorities away from the technical, limited and pseudo-scientific (objectivity assumed) and towards the qualitative, humanistic and subjective domains. In short, education and social research could ask different questions and reconstruct the definitions of disability into personal and social rather than medical or purely academic domains.

CHAPTER 3

Disabling Schools and Colleges

Dr. Christine Barton

Equality of opportunity or special need?

> All individuals should have an equal right to develop and achieve their full potential through our education system.
>
> (Leeds City Council, Department of Education, Equal Opportunities Policy, 1991)

Such a statement, or one very similar, is likely to be found as part of the documentation of many schools and colleges and Local Education Authorities (LEAs) throughout the United Kingdom. Few would be prepared to argue with the principle and in the last few years far reaching, fundamental changes have been made to state education in the pursuit of equality. Despite the number of initiatives which have now become an integral part of many schools and colleges, including mixed class lists and careful monitoring of curriculum materials, the reality of equality has yet to be established. It beckons from the distance, a tantalising ideal, in sight, but always out of reach.

Nearly twenty years ago Downey and Kelly (1975) offered one explanation:

> The main reason for this discrepancy and confusion is that the notion of equality in education, and even the apparently more precise notion of equality of educational opportunity, are too general and vague to provide any clear directives as to how education should be organised to achieve them.
>
> (Downey and Kelly, 1975)

Since then we have seen the appearance of numerous legislative acts including the Sex Discrimination Act (1975 and 1986), the Race Relations Act (1976), the Public Order Act (1986), the 1981 Education Act (based on the Warnock Report) and the Education Reform Act (1988), plus a multitude of school policies and procedures, all working towards the goal of equality. However, its achievement in education continues to be elusive. Even if we accept how difficult it is to identify and initiate appropriate procedures and practices, there still remains the essential question. Just who are 'all' the individuals who have an 'equal right'?

At one level the answer is obvious, it means what it says. However, some organisations, particularly LEAs, go on to identify groups who are likely to experience discrimination, usually ending up with a list including women, minority ethnic groups, people who are disabled, the young or the old, gays or lesbians, working class people and those who follow particular religions. This identification of categories of people moves the focus of attention away from individuals. Although it supports the argument that injustice stems just as much from treating unequals equally as from treating equals unequally, it also suggests that there is equality within a group; what is effective for one member of an identified group will work just as well for any other person with a similar label.

Many of the excellent initiatives currently taking place in schools and colleges attempt to address issues of equality through ensuring equal treatment where it is appropriate, e.g. equal coverage in the curriculum for men and women, and different treatment where it is thought to increase equality of opportunity, e.g. differentiated teaching materials. However, despite this emphasis on equality, one particular category, which is usually included within equal opportunities statements, is then treated differently from all the others. Special needs is seen as being exceptional and is treated as a separate issue at almost every level in education today.

Centrally, both in the Department for Education and LEAs, there are structures and people differently charged with responsibility for equality of opportunity and special needs. The Framework for Inspection of Schools (1992) describes different criteria and procedures for each area. At the local level, the majority of schools and colleges have different policies, different departments/working groups and different people concerned with implementing very different procedures.

Students who are physically disabled are usually identified and treated as students with special needs. It will be argued that this categorisation works against equality, exacerbating rather than breaking down the barriers that society erects and maintains. Instead of recognising and celebrating difference, it effectively reduces the 'equal rights' of a large number of individuals and renders them outside the framework designed to promote equality and remove discrimination. Viewed in this way it becomes apparent that equality of opportunity is the ultimate goal for some, but not for the 'all' who might expect to achieve it. To paraphrase Orwell in *Animal Farm*, some will always be more equal than others.

Special needs – a label for life

Why are the educational rights of those defined as having special needs, Warnock's 20 per cent, viewed as being so different from the rights of 'all' individuals described in equal opportunities policies? The root of the problem lies in social perceptions of what is normal and desirable, and what is labelled as an individual weakness and, therefore, undesirable and needing to be changed. Much evidence exists that the education system is part of a sexist and racist society. Nevertheless, in Western culture, the birth of a female child is not a cause for sorrow, neither is the birth of a black child to black parents. On the other hand, the birth of a disabled child may be seen as a tragedy. Pity and sympathy are offered in abundance as the medical professions seek to put right that which is seen as being wrong.

This negative image of disability is reinforced through the identification of children who have 'special' needs. Usually, it is only individuals who are seen as being flawed who are also seen as being special. This view is not limited to schools and colleges but permeates all of society and is by no means a recent phenomenon. Detailed accounts of the damaging historical view of disability are provided elsewhere (Rieser and Mason, 1992; Barnes, 1991). Despite a softening of attitude towards people who are disabled, with the growth of the welfare state and the vociferous demands for civil rights, the image of 'special' people has little to do with reality and is very slow to change. The polarisation of disabled people into the tragic but brave superperson, or helpless, embittered dependant, was clearly described by Weinberg and Sanatana (1978) following a study of the way that disability was depicted in comic books.

> The physically disabled were represented as either good or evil . . . This continued misrepresentation of the disabled only makes it more difficult for the disabled to be accepted as ordinary persons who happen to be disabled, rather than as special persons who have a trait that overshadows and influences every aspect of their being.
>
> (Weinberg and Sanatana, 1978)

Sue Ralph (1989) argues that while provision for people who are disabled is described as being special, for instance, special toilets, special parking, special tickets, special guides, special education, society will continue to see the disability first and the person second, if at all.

For some, the labelling process begins at, or even before, birth. Tom Shakespeare (1994), a university lecturer, gives a vivid description of the lengthy, painful, and in his view unnecessary, attempts made to alter his physical state to conform to a majority view of what a person should look like. He did not consider his needs to be special, but normal for him. For others, the process begins at school when they are identified as having special needs because they do not conform to an accepted view of the way in which people learn, or they fail to demonstrate the academic outcomes of education. These outcomes are inextricably linked to the high status of knowledge described by Young (1979) and are greatly valued by those with status and power, often to the exclusion of other forms of achievement.

Through this labelling process, some children stop having the same rights as other individuals, but now become part of a sub-culture. For them, equality of opportunity depends first of all on being returned to a nebulous and non-specific state of normality. To this end, massive resources are allocated to the sub-culture in an endeavour which must inevitably fail, and which creates and maintains a group who will be seen as being dependent on, and inferior to, those who are not special.

Does the name fit?

The meaning now given to the use of the term 'special' reinforces a negative image of the children it encompasses. Other children may have individual needs which are referred to with pride; these children may be described as gifted and they are valued for their exceptional talents in music, sport, maths, or whatever their field of achievement might be. Rarely are they included in the category of special needs and equally rarely does a child, parent or teacher speak with enthusiasm or pride of belonging to the special needs group. Many children resent the way in which they have been labelled within a school and the following is typical of the comments made to Hodgkinson (1992) in a survey of the views of year 10 and 11 who had been taught as a group of special needs students in a designated part of the school.

> .... cos this room and the one above is known. Everyone else calls it 'dummies room' .... When they see you walking in it, it's embarrassing.
>
> (Hodgkinson, 1992)

In the search for equality of opportunity, the notion of equal value for all individuals despite their differences has largely been ignored. The school community reflects and reinforces the values of society as a whole. The curriculum is aimed mainly at those few who will go on to Higher Education and ultimately high status employment. They will be rewarded by the acquisition of power and financial gain. Inevitably this situation results in schools and colleges which produce individual failure, and also fail to meet the demands of a highly technological society. It creates a culture where value lies not in the individual, but in wealth and status. In a political climate where schools and colleges are obliged to compete for scarce resources and are judged mainly on their examination results, more and more children are described as having special needs.

They are condemned as individual failures and, in some cases, selected out in order not to hold back their 'less special' peers.

Closer investigation reveals just how diverse are the children lumped together as having special needs. They include children who are blind, children who are deaf, children who are physically disabled, children who have learning difficulties and children who have emotional or behaviour difficulties. The provision made for special needs children will also vary considerably, but the variation in provision is based not on individual difference, but on difference in policy between LEAs and between schools and colleges and the ways in which resources are allocated. Children with very similar needs may or may not have a statement, may attend special school, a resourced school, special unit or be the responsibility of a special needs department. They may be integrated with mainstream peers, with or without additional teacher or non-teacher support, or they may be segregated for all of their time at school or withdrawn for some subjects. The possible variations are endless, but have little to do with the infinite variety of learners.

The issues were highlighted by HMI and the Audit Commission (1992) who identify some fundamental causes for concern. These include:

- no practical definition of what constitutes special education needs (SEN) in schools and colleges and no clear LEA guidelines;
- fear of demand which exceeds resources;
- lack of clarity concerning school and LEA responsibilities and in interpreting the 1981 Act, leading to an open ended commitment for LEAs which is incompatible with devolution of monetary responsibility to schools and colleges;
- lack of consistency between and within LEAs in provision for children with SEN.

(Audit Commission, 1992)

These and very similar serious concerns still focus on a deficit model of provision and do little to address issues of equality.

The problems that arise from the special needs label are experienced by any child who is identified as being in this category, but the remainder of this chapter will focus on children who are physically disabled and the way in which school or college education, far from seeking to develop equality of opportunity, reinforces and perpetuates disability and dependence.

Who owns disability?

Disability has no fixed or absolute definition; the definition varies throughout history and within particular societies or social contexts. At any one time it may also vary depending on the perspective or experience of those whose lives are most affected by the prevailing ideology. The greatest influences on the policies and beliefs which structure special educational needs systems for those children who are physically disabled, are the result of the application of an individual model of disability, mainly by those who are not themselves disabled.

Traditionally, disabled children are identified by their medical condition and the emphasis of intervention is on treatment and remaking the child in society's image of normality. A child who is disabled is not seen as being able to learn in the same way as her peers. She is a 'tragic' individual who may be very brave and determined or she may not have accepted her disability and is aggressive in her efforts to join in with her peers. If a cure is not possible she must be cared for by special workers. In the school situation the image is of a child who has a physical problem which means that she cannot, and should not be expected to, achieve the same standards or take part in the same activities as her peers.

The disability is the fault of an individual weakness, and is owned entirely by the child. The child can be changed, but the education system cannot. The implications of this model are illustrated in Figure 3.1.

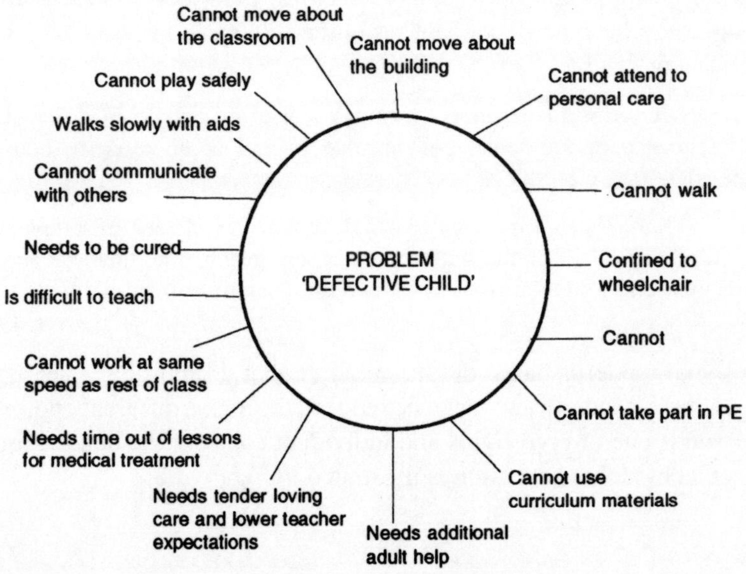

Figure 3.1: The Individual (or Medical) Model

Barnes (1991) argues that institutional discrimination, resulting from this model of disability, is deeply embedded in the present education system.

> .... educational provision for disabled children and students .... is dominated by traditional medically-influenced attitudes .... As a result, rather than equipping disabled children and young people with the appropriate skills and opportunities to live a full and active adult life, it largely conditions them into accepting a much devalued social role and in doing so condemns them to a lifetime of dependence and subordination. (page 28)
>
> (Barnes, 1991)

This model of the ownership of disability has been challenged by people who are disabled. While not denying the implications and restrictions placed on an individual by a particular impairment, they argue that a person with such a condition is disabled by the society in which she or he lives. Disablement occurs because little, or no, provision is made for people whose needs are different and they are then unable to play a full productive role in the community. A simple example can be seen in the need to travel quickly and easily from one place to another for work, shopping, leisure etc. Not everyone owns or has access to private transport, but, in an industrial society, there is a public transport system available. However, this system is public only for those who have access; for others, special arrangements must be made or they are unable to take part in activities which the majority take for granted. Because people who are disabled are often denied access to the systems structured by society, they become dependent on others for basic necessities. Oliver (1989) suggests that:

> .... the creation of dependency amongst disabled people is an inevitable consequence of the social policies that prevail in all modern industrial societies.
>
> .... welfare states have created whole groups or classes of people who become dependent on the state for education, health care, financial support and indeed any other provision the state is prepared to offer.
>
> (Oliver, 1989)

The social model is based on the principle that disability is constructed and owned by society and it can be reduced through a different approach- the issue is one of civil rights and individual control. The application of the social model to education is illustrated in Figure 3.2.

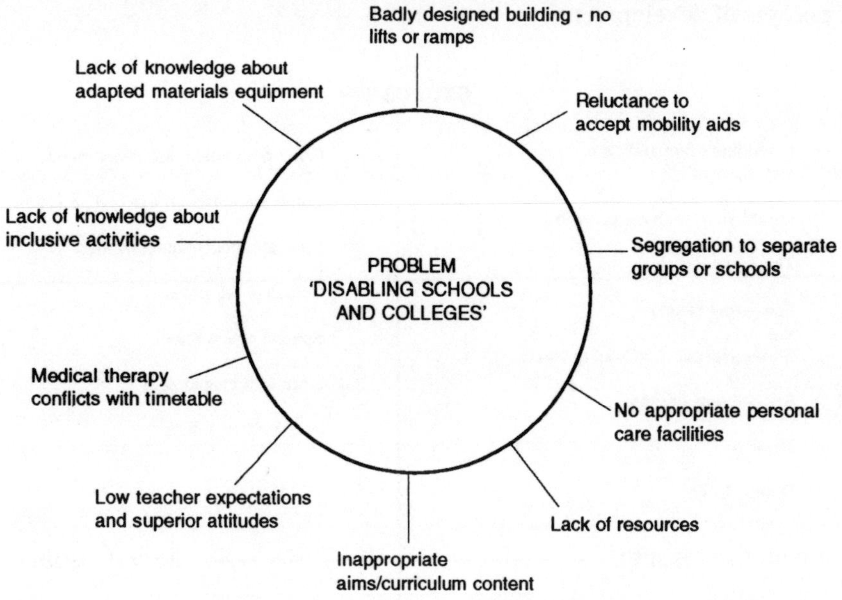

Figure 3.2 The Social Model

Possible solutions to the problems described in this figure are no longer the province of the medical profession. They do not depend on a cure, neither are they an attempt to change an individual disabled person. People are unique; it is the responsibility of all those concerned with education to ensure that provision is appropriate.

Reliance on the individual model of disability has encouraged the development of segregated education provision for many children who are physically disabled, either in a special school or in a special unit/group in a mainstream school or college. Hadley, Wilkinson and Rodwell (1993) compared some aspects of education for children with movement disabilities of primary age, in a rural and a metropolitan LEA. They found that, even when disregarding multiple disabilities, many of those with movement disabilities were still educated in special schools and colleges. Although only a small study, the figures suggest that moves towards integration are still slow. There are also many instances where, although in a mainstream school, integration is only either social or locational. Even the use of the term 'integration' implies that the benefits are mainly for those who are being integrated. The notion of 'inclusion' with benefits for the whole community is still limited to a few isolated pockets of development.

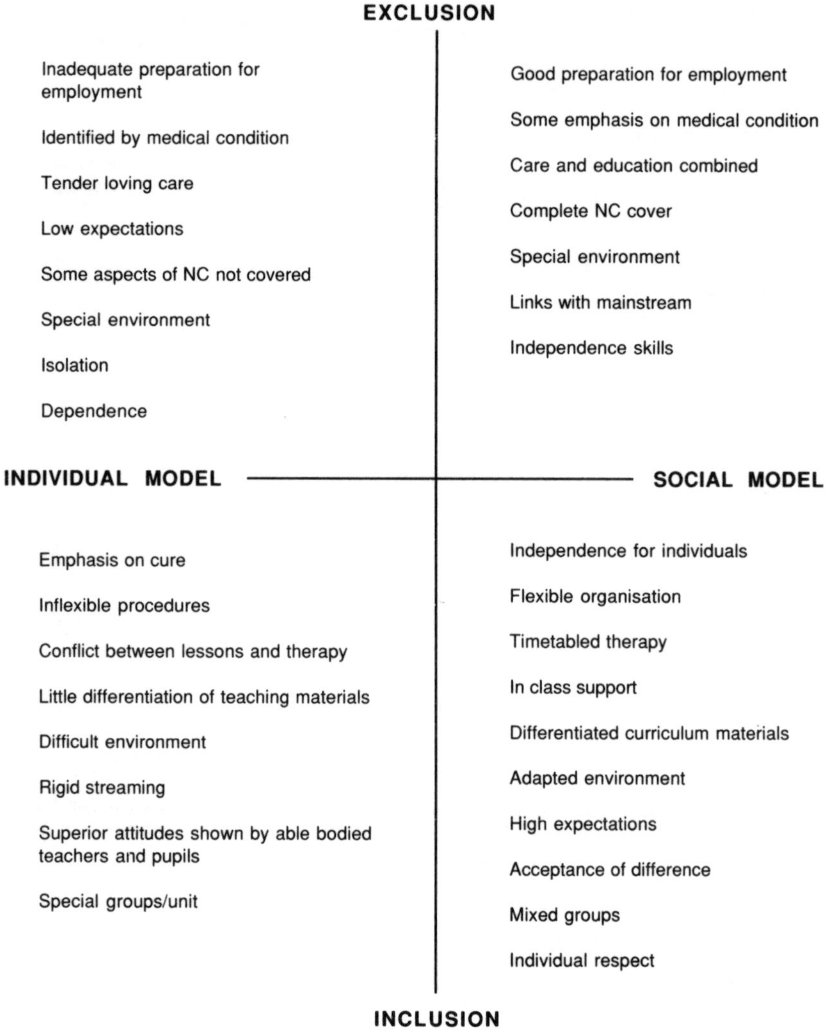

Figure 3.3 Characteristics of Schools using Differing Models of Provision

Figure 3.3 illustrates how the use of different models of disability, combined with different organisational procedures based on either exclusion or inclusion, can create school situations with enabling or disabling characteristics. Little educational research has been focused on the benefit to society of reducing disabling characteristics of the school. Instead the emphasis is on how to more quickly identify and effectively respond to special needs.

Recognising the barriers

Many of the structures established by schools and colleges and central and local government in response to special needs, reduce the possibility of enhancing equality of opportunity. Instead, these structures help to build bigger and even more insurmountable barriers for children who are physically disabled which prevent them from achieving their potential. These barriers are not unique to schools and colleges or to disability and have been recognised and described by those investigating discrimination in many other situations. Figure 3.4 illustrates three main types of barrier which acknowledge the inextricable links between them and the eventual cumulative effect on any individual.

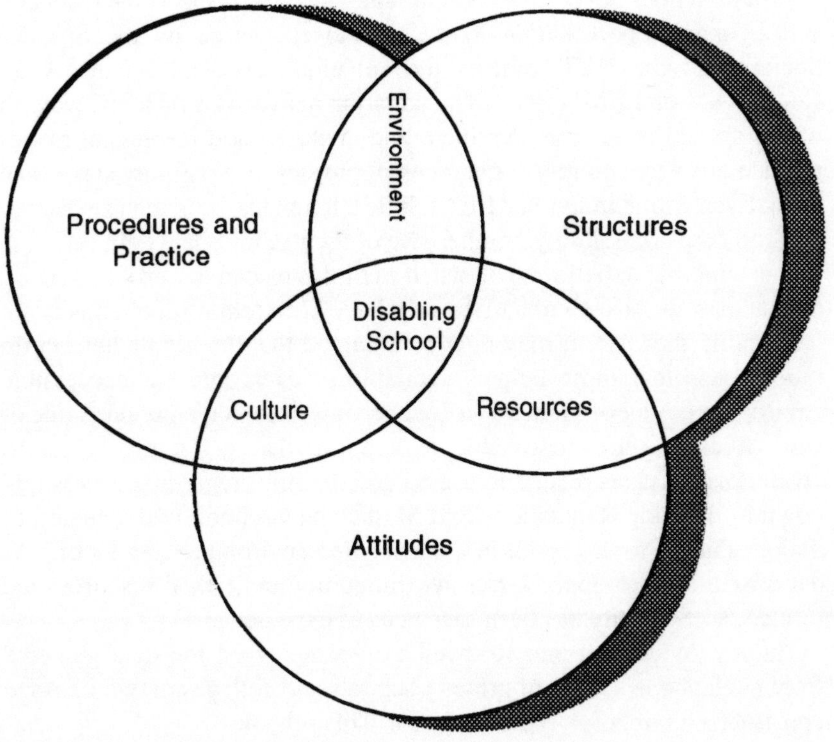

Figure 3.4 Barriers to Inclusive Education

There is no reason why children who are physically disabled should be seen as necessarily having any learning difficulty. However, the definition in the Code of Practice could be said to make this assumption from the outset. A child is described as having special educational needs if he or she has a learning difficulty which calls for special provision to be made. It then goes on:

> .... has a disability which either prevents or hinders the child from making use of educational facilities of a kind provided for children of the same age in schools and colleges within the area of the LEA.
>
> (Code of Practice, 1994)

Using this definition, it is the individual's disability which makes the physical environment inaccessible. In fact, many school buildings are inappropriate for all children and particularly disabling for some.

Because the emphasis is usually on altering the child not the school or college, little attempt has been made to identify or measure the disabling factors in the school or college environment. Indeed, even very basic information does not seem to be available. In some respects the Cooper's and Lybrand report *Within Reach* (1992) sponsored by the Spastics Society and the NUT, mirrors the situation described by the Audit Commission and HMI (1992). The variation between LEAs in the ways in which special needs are identified, and analysed and resourced, makes problematic a meaningful comparison of physical accessibility at national level. Even within individual LEAs, little attempt has been made to survey and audit the accessibility or otherwise of their schools and colleges.

It is tempting to believe that, when a child is placed in a special school, then at least the structural barriers will have been removed, but this is not necessarily the case. It may now be assumed that the high adult : child ratio means that more help is available to overcome an inaccessible environment. Independence as a goal becomes submerged under a tide of care. It also seems reasonable to suppose that given the increased awareness of issues related to access and the rules regarding access laid down in Building Regulations Part M, then new schools and colleges, or major rebuilds would result in a barrier free environment. In fact LEAs have been able to apply for crown immunity and, when resources are limited, accessibility has been sacrificed to expedience.

Hadley, Wilkinson and Rodwell (1993) analysed the data gathered from a telephone survey of primary schools and colleges in two LEAs to construct a model of a 'typical' school. This school:

> .... has steps, does not have either a level site or toilets adapted for wheelchairs and has distances between teaching areas of 20-100 yards.
>
> (Hadley, Wilkinson and Rodwell, 1993)

They went on to measure the effect of the environment on children who were physically disabled. Not surprisingly they found that an adapted, or enabling environment, reduced, and in some cases eliminated, the 'disablement' scores which were calculated for the study children.

Removing physical barriers has far reaching financial implications (Coopers and Lybrand, 1992), but too often the argument that this reduced the limited resources for all children fails to take account of the following important factors:

1. *A considerable proportion of the money available for education as a whole is spent on special schools and colleges.* It has already been suggested that some of these schools and colleges have an environment which is disabling and much evidence is available that the social consequences of segregation increase discrimination and levels of dependence (Barnes, 1991; Rieser and Mason, 1990). Special schools and colleges cater for a very small number of students, and the money spent on them has no benefit for any other pupil.

   Initially the cost of adaptation for a mainstream school may be high, particularly if it is seen as being for a very small number of students, but from a wider perspective, a much greater range of people can benefit. These issues are discussed in detail by Coopers and Lybrand (1992) who recognise the cost of opening up access for students into neighbourhood schools and colleges, but who go on to say:

   > However, we would argue that the conversion of public education premises to permit effective access for adults with disabilities (parents, Governors, staff and the general public) should itself be a priority irrespective of how many pupils with disabilities subsequently go there. It is not unreasonable to regard some of the premises conversion cost talked about here as reflecting this more general purpose.
   >
   > (Coopers & Lybrand, 1992)

2. *Many school buildings are in a deplorable condition and create a physical environment which is inappropriate for all members of the school community.* The additional cost of providing effective access is small when considered against the overall costs of maintenance of poor, dilapidated buildings or premises conversion costs. Improvements for effective access will also be improvements for everyone using the building.

3. *With very few exceptions, school managers, LEA officers, school governors, teachers and architects are not disabled.* Although access officers are increasingly being employed by local councils, the majority of decisions about access are made by able bodied people who have made little or no attempt to consult with people who are

disabled. Such adaptations as are made can end up by being an expensive waste of time and resources.

In terms of the physical environment, achieving equality of opportunity is dependent upon an accurate survey of the disabling factors in school buildings and a realistic building programme which ensures the provision of access for all. The additional resources required should be both a national and local responsibility.

Procedures and practice

> 'You can be as angry as you like, Esther, but that does not alter the fact that you are not doing the best you can. If you want to be treated as an equal by everyone else you had better start behaving like one. And you had best not forget, my dear, that since you are handicapped you are going to have to work harder than ordinary people just to be considered their equal'. (p.148)

So says Margaret to her granddaughter Esther who has cerebral palsy. Esther is failing to make academic progress at her special school, in the story, *Skallagrig*, told by William Horwood (1987). However, Margaret focuses only on Esther's responsibilities in her fight for equality, not on those which rest with society. All school and college students are encouraged to do the best they can, but, for some, no matter how hard they work, the barriers erected by the procedures and practices of the organisation ensure that equality of opportunity remains out of reach.

The traditional patterns of organisation adopted by most schools and colleges often appear to have much more to do with serving the interests of teachers than they do with meeting the needs of individual learners. This creates particular problems for students who are physically disabled. Features of the disabling school or college which discriminate against these students include:

- *the design and structure of a timetable* which dictates where and when learning will take place, and the distances to be covered when one lesson finishes and another begins;
- *the layout of furniture* in classrooms and the positioning of teaching resources;
- *the journey to and from school* which can be a miserable and exhausting experience for many who have to travel long distances and are subject to interminable delays;
- *the lack of appropriate training* for members of the school or college community;
- *bureaucratic procedures* which fragment a child into unconnected parts.

Organisational discrimination may not be intentional, nevertheless the resulting oppression of disabled students contributes to the failure of integration policies described by Fulcher (1989). Lack of awareness cannot be an acceptable excuse for failing to address the needs of any individual. Some disabling factors in schools and colleges and classrooms can be reduced or removed without cost, through giving more consideration to the way that learning is organised. Who will suffer if year 5 are housed on the top floor in a building with no lift because that is where they have always been? Is it the teacher, the other students, the parents, or is it only the child who is unable to climb the stairs and must either be carried or, even in some cases, moved to a different school? Will anyone suffer if the class is moved to an accessible ground floor room? Can maths only be learned if it is taught in the room at the top of the tower block, while English, the lesson before, takes place in a mobile classroom at least 50 metres from the base of the tower block? The opportunity to learn should not be dependent on physical ability. The physical resources of a school may not be ideal, but effective grouping of students combined with careful location of teaching spaces can greatly increase equality of opportunity while maintaining an inclusive approach to education.

Even in schools or colleges where functional integration is the norm, and pride is taken in the inclusion of disabled students, discrimination results from lack of awareness. Too often the layout of classroom furniture restricts the occupant of a wheelchair to a small space close to the door. In a particular instance, in a resourced school, the classroom teacher was not even aware of this situation until an Adviser, who used a wheelchair, wanted access to all the students. The teacher was embarrassed, but only concerned for the adult; for the student it was considered acceptable.

Freedom of movement is prevented not by a physical condition, but by thoughtless procedures which needlessly limit and separate disabled students from their peers. The deployment of a support assistant might also serve to emphasise physical and emotional separation. To employ a non-teaching classroom assistant may reduce expenditure, but, without careful staff training and planning, can be educationally unsound and wasteful of scarce resources.

The whole issue of disability equality training is one which has yet to be addressed. Students who are labelled as having special needs are seen to require special policies and to be the responsibility of special staff. The training which is available is frequently limited to these 'special' staff and even then may only be offered to teachers. Support workers are often poorly paid, receive no training and have no opportunity to consider their role as facilitators of equality of opportunity. Where support is provided by teachers, they are usually selected on the basis of having space on their timetables and are given no time to plan with the class teacher, or to consider how to maximise their effectiveness.

Even when the need for training is highlighted, its provision is often limited to the medical factors related to specific conditions. The opportunity for exploration of personal values and attitudes towards disability has yet to be considered important.

The Code of Practice

It would be difficult to leave this section on the barriers created by organisational procedures and practice without making reference to the Code of Practice on the Identification and Assessment of Special Educational Needs. At the time of writing, schools and colleges struggle to make sense of this lengthy document, but will it make any real difference to the factors which discriminate against disabled students? Positive features in the Code include clearer definitions of when action needs to be taken and detailed descriptions of structures which should be in place in schools, colleges and LEAs. Legislation should now prevent the long delays which denied some students the resources they needed and attempts have been made to ensure that parents have real choices and an effective voice in the decision making process. Descriptions of who is supposed to do what and when, make clear who is accountable and the necessity to link outcomes to resources is spelled out.

However, the statements which allow segregation remain, as does the reliance on an individual or medical model of disability. The structures proposed emphasise difference and do little to reduce the fragmentation of a student into a series of unconnected problems. Co-operation between agencies is encouraged, but how it should be achieved is then left to individual interpretation. Assessment of a student is based on national curriculum testing, but this has yet to gain acceptance with the majority of teachers.

Much is said about the provision of resources to meet needs, either by schools, colleges or LEAs, but, when they are already struggling to stretch inadequate budgets, sufficient funding is a very real constraint. There is a danger that over-specification of practice can produce a level of bureaucracy which drains the available, already limited resources. It remains to be seen whether the right balance has been struck between prescription and flexibility. The term 'equality of opportunity' does not appear and its relationship to special needs provision is not made clear. It could be argued that it is implicit in the whole document, but if the relationship is left to interpretation, it could also be argued that little has changed and an important opportunity has been lost.

Attitudes

> .... disabled people are poor, pathetic, helpless victims of subnormal intellect and substandard education who need to be treated in 'special' ways and given charity handouts.
>
> (Mildrette Hill, 1991)

Is this just an extreme, exaggerated view of the popular image of disability or does it contain elements reflecting widely held attitudes which serve to maintain the barriers faced by disabled people? The recent failure of the proposed 'Civil Rights' bill to become law, suggests that, while no longer 'politically correct', such a statement might indeed be used to describe the beliefs held by many non-disabled people.

Structures and procedures which create the barriers have been designed by society. They could be dismantled. Inclusive education could replace segregation. The disabling school could become the enabling school. This cannot happen until the widespread oppression of disabled people by society as a whole is recognised and overcome. It cannot happen while campaigning by disabled people is described as 'tyranny' and when, from the same article, the view is held that:

> It is surely obvious, however much one sympathises, that disabled people .... cannot enjoy the same freedom of movement and opportunity as the rest of us – unless, that is, billions of pounds are to be spent on altering the environment.
>
> (Richard Ingrams, *The Observer*, 1993)

Schools and colleges rarely initiate change; they reflect and perpetuate the predominant values and beliefs of society. Inequality in education mirrors that which exists for people who are physically disabled in every other aspect of their lives.

Negative attitudes towards disability have been prevalent throughout history and have been further entrenched through the process of industrialisation and the development of the 'welfare state'. Such attitudes encourage and reinforce the building of barriers. Only when they are changed will all members of society work towards creating a physical and emotional environment in which difference is celebrated and individual worth guaranteed.

Society's attitudes towards disability are reflected in the expectations of schools, colleges and teachers. The majority of disabled students are not expected to be high academic achievers. They are more often to be found in lower sets in comprehensive schools, colleges or special units where the education they are offered reflects the popular image of disability. They may have to choose between lessons which develop the intellect and opportunities for medical therapy. There is little chance for the physically dependent to exercise choice or demonstrate control in their lives. Disabled people are cared for or done to, the expectation is not to work with. When, despite expectations, a disabled student succeeds, his or her image now conflicts with that which is generally accepted. Jenny Morris (1987), a college lecturer with a PhD who is paralysed below the waist, described one way this conflict is addressed by non-disabled people:

> It is difficult, if not impossible, for people to reconcile the two images. To some extent, they only manage to deal with the fact that I have this contradictory position by ignoring my disability. I thus become an honorary able-bodied person, in the way that many women holding high-status positions become honorary men.
>
> (Morris, 1987)

Disability cannot and should not be disregarded. Equality of opportunity results not from attempts to minimise differences, but from recognition and provision for individual need without prejudice or discrimination.

Summary

What is the difference between meeting special needs and providing equality of opportunity?

- Where does 'special needs' end and the concept of 'normal' children begin? Current educational structures and procedures indicate that there is a difference, although clarity of definition is lacking.
- There should be no distinction; all students are special and catering for individual difference should be a matter of usual practice.
- Everyday experience in education suggests that the change in perception necessary to create such a learning environment is still a long way off.

Education should provide equality of opportunity.

- The culture surrounding special needs suggests that individuals who are identified in this way cannot be equal.
- While difference remains, the respect and value which people who are seen as being different are accorded by society is less.
- The classification of people into groups denies the fundamental differences of people within the group and reinforces inaccurate stereotypic images.

'Special' has largely come to mean 'inferior'.

- It suggests that there is a better way to be, a way that everyone can reach, a way that everyone wants to be.
- The label of 'special' can be acquired at any time from birth onwards and it inevitably results in prejudice and discrimination.
- 'Special' children are no longer equal. They are to be feared, pitied, made whole again – almost anything but to be valued as they are.

Concentration on disability as personal weakness, that belongs to an individual student, focuses attention away from the disabling factors that exist within schools and colleges.

- Recognition of the social causes of disability encourages the identification of the barriers constructed in education by negative attitudes, inappropriate procedures and practice and inaccessible physical environments.
- We can accept these barriers and argue that the availability of resources must dictate which needs can be met.
- We then fail to uphold the right of every individual to equality of opportunity. Prejudice and discrimination will continue and inclusive education remain a dream.

CHAPTER 4

The Challenge of Inclusion

This chapter explores and reflects upon the nature of support, the process of setting up support services and the issues surrounding schools and colleges in meeting the challenge of inclusion. It considers in some practical detail how choice and opportunity might be supported through recognising diverse abilities in assessment, creating opportunity through programmes of study and in the day-to-day organisation of schools and colleges. The inclusiveness of a school or college is still dependent on the wider cultural, social and political factors that have been reiterated in the previous chapters. It is also the will and commitment of those involved at the point of delivery of educational experience that will enable schools and colleges to become inclusive settings.

Stumbling blocks or ramps?

Inclusion, like beauty, is in the eye of the beholder. There have been many stumbling blocks, even when teachers are, in general, well disposed towards including pupils with physical and sensory disabilities compared with other sub-groups in the special needs spectrum. They also found that many teachers have experience of teaching pupils who are physically or sensory disabled. Sheila Howarth, in 1987, pointed out that good levels of service and resources to support inclusion could help staff to view a disabled pupil or student as an asset, rather than a liability. This view must be tempered in 1995, with the reservation that financial (or resource) gain without preparation, training and commitment could be a recipe for short-termism and a disaster for disabled pupils and students.

According to Moses, Hegarty and Jowett in 1988, the most common type of help provided when a physically disabled pupil attended a school or college was a support assistant. This type of help was also provided, particularly at primary level, for a wide range of pupil needs. There was seldom a coherent strategy about the employment and role of such support assistants. There was considerable variation in practice and it was much more usual for the assistant to be attached directly to an individual child at a particular school or college. This was often on a temporary basis and did not form part of a considered policy, plan or support service.

In 1992, Terry Clayton reported on the general support for special educational needs in 67 schools. This followed much work he has done over the years in looking at welfare and learning support assistance in schools (1989a, 1989b, 1990a, 1990b, 1991 and 1992). He found (in 1992) that only one-third of the schools had access to specialist equipment, materials and facilities. These consisted almost entirely of equipment and facilities for pupils with physical and sensory disabilities. They included such things as adaptations to the building such as ramps and special steps, special toileting facilities, equipment such as standing frames and wheelchairs to assist balance and mobility, fine motor aids, specialist equipment for physical education, hearing aids and radio microphones for hearing impaired pupils and desk top hardware such as a computer and a Lecta activity switch for use with cassette recorders.

He found that out of 67 schools:

- only 5 used equipment, materials and facilities provided by the District Health Authority (DHA);
- 34 (50 per cent) received therapy or medical services from DHA;
- all schools received advice and assessments from DHA colleagues.

There was support for 12 schools (just under 20 per cent) by teachers of hearing impaired (ten schools) and visually impaired (two schools). Apart from the obvious discrepancy between the hearing impaired support and visually impaired support, it was clear that support for pupils and students who are physically disabled or experience medical conditions was non-existent, there being no designated support services or specialist teachers. Since 1988-90 many local education authorities have either allowed the development of 'grass roots' initiatives or have actively set up services. One of the most effective and enduring services seem to be those set up through a 'resourced school' model. Usually, it is the special school (or schools) in an authority that become the 'network base', overtaking the concept of 'resource centre'. A network centre implies much more of the activity surrounding effective support than a static 'store' of resources. Clayton (1992) divides the kind of support available into four main categories:

- equipment, materials and facilities
- teaching and therapy
- advice and assessment
- training

An example of an integrating support initiative

We could do worse than look at a well-established (since 1985) County Education Service for Physical Disability (CESPD, Humberside. Paul Donkersloot, 1991). My own experience has given me the opportunity to work with over forty different local authorities; a significant number have developed, or are developing, such services. CESPD is one of those and is an example of the change from a specialist (physically disabled) school into a support network. It aims to maximise the opportunity of disabled pupils and students to go to their own local schools, whenever possible. Any resourced school initiative such as this is a visionary act on the part of those who undergo the radical changes involved. They (the resourced schools becoming network support centres) will also recognise the inevitable and desirable conclusion that they may, at some time in the future, cease to exist as 'special schools' when all children are eventually, and successfully, catered for in their local schools.

This is not a negative issue, nor is it a battle of wills between the integrationists and the specialists. It is an inevitable journey we are already on, the road to inclusion, despite the mountains, valleys and potholes of fear, ignorance, the need for power and just plain apathy. In this chapter we look at the three dragons (fear, control and change) that act as barriers to inclusion (Forest and Pearpoint, 1991). The use of a special school as a network resource, enabling disabled pupils and students to attend mainstream school or college, is a current example of the inevitable and welcome growth towards more inclusive education. The closure of special schools in this country has been seen as an enormous threat to the choice of services available, to the livelihoods of staff involved, to the 'expertise' of specialists and as a reduction in resourcing. It must not be a reduction of resources and support. If anything, it is an increase in both commitment and resources. As an ex-Head of a residential special school, it was clear to me that the change was coming, back in 1985. This is an altogether positive development as long as all parties concerned, with their skills and commitment, are involved.

So what kinds of support are offered by CESPD and other similar services? In Donkersloot (1991), there were some clues about the intentions and organisation of CESPD:

(1) **Building**: Concerned with early identification of major or minor building alterations following approval by the LEA statementing panel. These would follow the carefully reported and identified needs of the young person concerned and involve the support of a County Access Officer.

(2) **Equipment**: Loan and maintenance of appropriate equipment (from pencil grip to full computer rig). In association with a child's occupational therapist and physiotherapist, equipment and activities are discussed that will assist with mobility and functional independence.

(3) **Teacher's Aides**: Subject to fulfilling the child's needs, the support services will assist in making clear and consistent recommendations. These must be jointly developed and have a clear rationale before presentation to the statementing panel. The service will continue to work alongside the teacher's aide and provide in-service training. The resourced school allows new teacher's aides to gain valuable skills and experience before moving out into local school placements.

(4) **Curriculum Support**: Working alongside learning support services, hearing and visually impaired support services, it concentrates on information relating to physical management and independence, exam regulations and a vital link with the careers service, giving specialist advice and continuity.

(5) **Integration**: Attempting to ensure quality integration for all students and pupils in the classroom, around the school, at break times and in extra curricular activities.

(6) **Consultation advisory support**: In relation to annual reviews for statemented children by providing annexes to education forms and statements. Liaison with other agencies through a 'key' person. Clarifying and interpreting medical advice (say, in the case of a heart condition). Health and safety issues. Help the formation of parent support groups. Database information service.

The above framework is a general model for delivery of support to mainstream schools and colleges that has been tried and tested. There are many other models of support and they generally fit into two categories:

- *special schools* with (multi-disciplinary/specialist expertise) are additional resources (by LEA or by schools as purchasers) as providers of in-school and regional support;
- *an additional support service* that is set up as an external provider resourced by the LEA or by school purchase for a child.

Support that is not carefully planned tends to lapse into a medical or individual model and is predominantly seen as support for the individual pupil or student and as an additional burden on the school. It places the burden of change back on to the individual and continues to marginalise that individual, educationally and socially. The CESPD example (above) clearly shows an ecological and effective approach. Pupils and students who are physically disabled or have medical conditions quite rightly point out that, like all of us, they cannot change their physical attributes. You can't get rid of cerebral palsy, muscular dystrophy is not curable, psoriasis comes and goes, asthma can be managed. Chapter 2 argues that the individual support approach is not productive and will not allow the school or college to grow and develop, as a whole.

'Visions' of inclusion

The 1992 Further Education Act and the 1993 Education Act (including the Code of Practice that has emerged from it) herald significant developments for colleges and schools. Some of the ramifications have been explored earlier in this book. Despite the fact that, in 1995, no new money is being made available to schools generally, the 1993 Education Act in particular makes significant demands and requirements for change. Schools will have to draw up a policy that addresses all the issues laid down in the regulations and report to parents from academic year 1994–95 onwards. SEN policies will reveal:

- Who is the school's special needs coordinator?
- Any specialist SEN provision.
- Information about access for disabled pupils.
- How resources are allocated 'to and between' SEN pupils.
- How much SEN pupils join in the general life of the school.
- Relevant staff qualifications.
- The governing body's policy on training.
- Links with special schools, voluntary organisations, social services and the LEA.
- The number of pupils with special needs and the number with statements.

The fear is, with some justification, that without appropriate training provision, what is a very positive development will be doomed to failure. Every school or college is required to have a Special Educational Needs Coordinator (SENCO) or a 'key' member of staff and this will eventually have a positive impact on disabled pupils. However, the previously patchy appointing of SENCOs and the relative level of GEST 12 funding means a slow process of 'skilling' such personnel.

> The documents now spell out in greater detail than ever before, the support which should be available to pupils with SENs both in ordinary and in special schools. But the documents say little or nothing about how teachers are to be trained to provide this support.

> The Code of Practice goes into detail on how all classroom teachers in ordinary schools should identify pupils' SENs and take initial steps to meet them. How are beginning teachers, and those in post, to be trained for this responsibility?
>
> (Klaus Wedell, 1994)

The 1992 Further and Higher Education Act adopts a slightly different approach. Current commentaries in general have welcomed both Acts and the Code of Practice as a very positive step forward in fuelling change for inclusion and given access or entitlement to all. However, as seems to be typical with legislation in education, since 1986, the laudable and progressive intentions of entitlement for all and integration of all pupils and students has to be tempered with some acknowledgement of reality. The movement to Local Management of Schools (LMS), the additional accounting requirements of the national curriculum, the current exigencies of budgeting and central resourcing of local budgets have meant a growth in class sizes, an increase in teacher stress, an eruption of paperwork and low morale in schools and colleges. These factors all militate against inclusion in the face of positive statements and overall guidance (Clayton, 1992).

Headteachers, Heads of Department, governors and staff in schools and colleges will need to make development plans and use budgets to resource smaller classes and release teachers, particularly the Special Needs Coordinator, from teacher duties (Rieser, 1994). There will be a greater amount of time required for preparation and planning in direct relation to the diversity of needs and abilities of the class or course group or subject group. It is not for nothing that special schools have more generous staffing levels recognised in Local Management of Special Schools (LMSS) and DES Circular 11/90.

Ideological statements in legislation that are distanced from the real practical issues will cause many problems in managing the finances and resources. However, given the will and intention to change and grow, even these are not insurmountable in time. We can, through strong partnerships at different levels (politicians, LEAs, governors and schools), make an impact, particularly in the area of training, and there are many groups currently taking up the gauntlet. Individual monitoring groups are making representations to the DFE and to Ministers. In 1993, their growing concern led them to come together to form the Special Educational Needs Training Consortium (SENTC), and to link themselves to the special needs Voluntary and Professional Bodies, through the auspices of the Council for Disabled Children. The SENTC has been joined by observers from the Associations of Metropolitan Authorities and County Councils, OFSTED, the DFE, SCAA, and the

Further Education Funding Council. After lobbying about the special needs aspects of teacher training in the 1994 Education Bill, the SENTC is now engaged in discussions with the DFE.

Unfortunately, the demands of legislation in 1988 and in 1993 have generated considerable fear and concern amongst teachers and educators generally. The 'fear' aspect has dwindled in 1994 when the impossibility of 'policing' demands has become apparent and is being gradually superseded by a more co-operative 'What is best for learners or students?' approach. Nevertheless, there are deeper and more insidious fears that still lurk (and have done for many, many years) under the surface, ready to sabotage growth and development. These fears are intertwined with the resourcing issues and often used as an excuse for inaction. Only a part of it has to do with resources. Much has to do with existing attitudes, lack of awareness and the need for challenging training. Any initiatives and school or college support needs to address these barriers at the same time as supporting any individual pupil or student. See figure 4.1.

Preventing physical segregation and encouraging social integration are two very important first steps towards inclusion. But we need to go much further than this if we are to take up the challenge. Including disabled pupils and students means:

- *overcoming the fears or barriers* to growth and change;
- *sharing control*, developing open management by appointing a SENCO or 'key' person to school or departmental/faculty management teams;
- *developing learning environments* that can sustain diversity, not always conformity and 'averageness';
- *energising growth and change through partnerships*, enabling technologies, in school or college support systems and using the curriculum in a positive way;
- pushing forward boundaries, being clear about what can be done, what is effective and what is desirable through *whole school approaches and policies.*

Policies and strategies for inclusion

The 1993 Education Act sets out regulations and stipulates which issues must be addressed by school or college special educational needs (SEN) policies (Schedule 1 to the Education (SEN) (Information) Regulations 1994). These were well summarised in *New Learning Together Magazine* (April 1994) and bear repeating here:

- The name of the teacher (or lecturer) who is responsible for overseeing the provision of education for pupils with special educational needs at the school, and the arrangements that have been made for overseeing the provision of education for pupils with special educational needs at the school.
- The admission arrangements for pupils with special educational needs who do not have a statement in so far as they differ from the arrangements for other pupils.
- The kinds of provision for special educational needs in which the school specialises.
- Access to the school buildings by disabled persons. *Access to learning through planning and differentiation.*
- Facilities for pupils with special educational needs at the school.
- How pupils with special educational needs are identified and their needs determined and reviewed.
- How pupils with special educational needs engage in the activities of the school together with pupils who do not have special educational needs.
- The qualifications and experience that staff have in relation to special educational needs.
- The governing body's policy on in-service training for staff in relation to special educational needs.
- The use made of teachers and facilities from outside the school.
- The role played by the parents of pupils *or students* with special educational needs.
- The links with outside support, *such as* special schools or *specialist facilities in the area/region*;
- The links with local authority child health, social security and educational welfare services and any voluntary organisations which work on behalf of children with special educational needs.
- How the governing body evaluates the success of the education which is provided at the school to pupils with special educational needs.

(Rieser, 1994)

(*Author's additions in italics*)

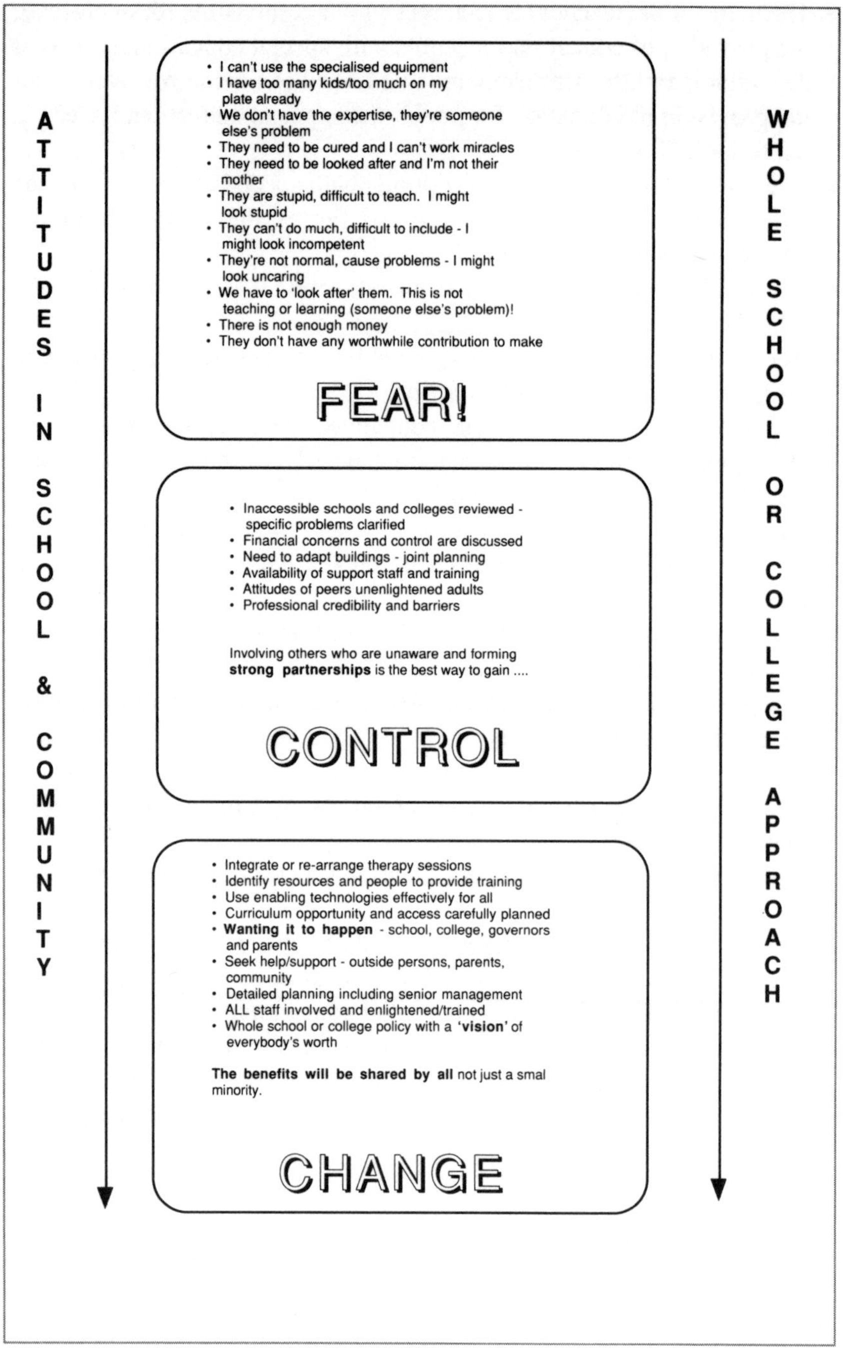

Figure 4.1 DEVELOPING CHOICE AND OPPORTUNITY (Expanded by groups of teachers from a model by Forest and Pearpoint, 1991)

It will be a number of years before the full practical outcomes of this guidance are plainly visible in schools and colleges. If we add to this the requirements on policy laid out in the 1992 Further and Higher Education Acts, there is plainly a stage set for positive action. Below are listed the requirements on Further Education Funding Council (FEFC) Local Education Authorities (LEAs) and Colleges:

- Sufficient facilities to be secured for full-time education suitable for disabled students (16–18 years).
- Adequate facilities for part-time education over 16 years and full-time for those over 19 years:
  - leading to academic and vocational qualifications;
  - entry into higher education;
  - preparation for the above courses;
  - teaching basic skills (including independent living and communication skills).
- LEA retains responsibility for disabled students and to ensure:
  - part-time provision for students between 16 and 19 years;
  - provision for young people with statements who remain in school
  - (including independent school);
  - availability of discretionary grants, transport and fair treatment on full-time courses for those over 16.
- Proper consideration for the needs of individual students (over 19).
- Ensure that funding for students at 19 years is not automatically withdrawn.
- Consider independent institutions where maintained provision is not available for disabled students between 16 and 25 years.
- Attract additional funding by assessing clearly the additional cost of providing for disabled students.

In many ways the practical activities that ensue from taking these policy matters seriously could be guided, in detail, by an 'Equal Opportunities Policy'. All schools and colleges are now required to have such a policy by the OFSTED Framework (1992). The detail of these policies provides the key to day to day opportunity in learning and taking part in the whole process of becoming educated.

Policy Making as a commitment to pratical opportunity

- Access to the environment.
- Access to the curriculum (*ability, motivation and self-esteem*).
- Including disability issues *and awareness* within the curriculum at all phases.

- Assessments and Statements of special needs (*validating environmental change*).
- Curriculum *differentiation and meaningful learning experiences.*
- Support staff (*their status and training*).
- Co-ordination of peripatetic services, e.g. occupational, speech and physiotherapy.
- Communication (*an environmental approach not just specialist*).
- BSL (British Sign Language) as a 'mother tongue'.
- Language (*use of terms, jargon and labelling*).
- Images and culture (*social perspectives and stereotypes*).
- Abuse, name-calling and harassment.
- Transport.
- Trips.
- Medication and nursery assistance.
- Liaise *and co-ordinate complex partnerships.*
- Obtaining and maintaining 'special' equipment.
- Consultation with parents/*carers/enablers.*
- Self-representation of disabled pupils/*students.*
- Employment and support for disabled teachers and other staff.
- Disabled parents, *governors and other role models.*
- Physical education and physical disability.
- Sports and 'able-ism'.
- Clubs and extra-curricular activities and services, e.g. play centres.
- Medical emergencies. *Generate confidence and awareness.*
- Health and safety.
- Involvement of Trade Unions and staff representatives.
- Representation of disability and learning difficulties on Governing Bodies.
- INSET for teachers, support staff and governors by Disabled Trainers.

(Adapted from Richard Rieser and Micheline Mason, 1991, from *Disability Equality in the Classroom*). (*Author's additions in italics*)

The above exhaustive list provides many opportunities and challenges for schools and colleges, *not just to meet the needs of physically disabled pupils and students in isolation but to begin to set up an inclusive learning environment* for education and socialisation.

Making the vision a reality – first steps

The process of identifying the 'vision' for school, college or service development begins with the first stage of development work, that is, to gain a clear idea 'where we are now . . .' through a process of audit or review. School or college management has to make the opportunity to look at the school or college 'as a system' and to build up a picture of its current position (i.e. policies, curriculum strategies, the number of pupils or students who are disabled, where they are, who they are, what resources (including human) are available, the appropriateness of current provision/services, their location and ethos).

The next stage of development requires an opportunity to evaluate the range of general school or college provision (in the light of discussion), curricular approaches, methods, quality of life and overviews provided by the Code of Practice and by considering equal opportunities as a whole. Examining whole school or college issues, in relation to pupils/students who are disabled, enables further consideration and sharing views about observations and possibilities through in-service training or planning workshops. Many schools and colleges have very effectively involved their disabled pupils and students in this evaluation. Some have based their action plans on the reports of disabled pupils and students.

Systematic problem solving involves:

- Reviewing the current situation with appropriate data and information.
- Identifying overall areas of need for growth and development.
- Selecting and prioritising specific area(s) for school/college teams or departments to consider;
- Applying systematic or problem solving strategies to the situation.
- Analysing carefully what is involved in the process and management of 'change' and who is involved as the 'agents of change'.
- Detailing clearly strategies and plans based on including pupils who are disabled, their quality of life and the wider needs of all concerned (e.g. staff training, welfare support, physical environment).
- Evidence of what has been done to instigate or bring about positive steps towards including pupils (e.g. policy and strategy documents, curriculum differentiation, facilities and technology).
- Evaluation and further analyse of what impact the change(s) have had, or you hope will have, on the quality of life and learning for all pupils.

Including individuals – recognising diversity

The basic principles of the Code of Practice (1993 Education Act) mark an important recognition of the movement towards including disabled pupils or those with diverse abilities into mainstream education. It also tries to re-affirm the importance of parents' choice of school but then proceeds to virtually negate these with three 'weasel' clauses:

1. The school (chosen) is unsuitable to the child's age, ability, aptitude or

special educational needs.

2. The placement is incompatible with the efficient education of other children.
3. An inefficient use of resources.

(1993 Education Act – Schedule 10 Regulations)

The marshalling of these (particularly number 3) would, in effect, be able to destroy almost any arguments, no matter how powerful or persuasive, by a parent. There is a right of appeal to a Tribunal, independent of the LEA, but the effect of such Tribunals is yet to be ascertained. These regulations make it even more important to have genuine partnerships (see Chapter 6) with parents at all stages of assessment and provision.

The Code of Practise – Content

I – Introduction: Principles and procedures.
II – Stages 1–3: School-based stages of assessment and provision.
III – Stage 4: Statutory assessments.
IV – Stage 5: Statements
V – Children under 5 with SEN
VI – Annual Review of statements

(1993 Education Act)

The Code of Practice clearly outlines a model for assessment of needs in five stages of increasing complexity and detail. It still continues to promote the tendency for the individual pupil or student to be seen as the source of any problems generated. This is often an intolerable burden for pupils/students with special needs and for their parents, learning support assistants or other advocates/enablers. It can be ecological and environmental if interpreted widely, but often it is not, and the problem remains with the individual with little real change in their learning and social environment. The third problem is that it leaves all the work to teachers, schools and colleges, whilst stipulating a lengthy shopping list of requirements. This could be acceptable if it went hand in hand with an acknowledgement of the need for more planning time, smaller classes, more (and more effective) initial and in-service training or education, more training for learning support staff, effective co-operation (or even presence at times) of outside support personnel and broader changes in society (e.g. Civil Rights – Disabled Persons Bill in Parliament).

The Code of Practice requires many things but gives little clue, in practice, about positive interventions or where the additional resources are to come from. Again, this would not be so bad (we seem to have got used to this) if there weren't other factors actively militating against inclusion. For instance, there is the current growth in class sizes – the author resides in a county with the highest pupil : teacher ratios in the UK (DFE statistics, 1993). The way that budgets have been delegated makes a child's special educational needs (and the stages and triggers) seem like a race for more cash or resources, rather than a planned process of intervention to make educational opportunity available. Other factors such as school 'league tables', open enrolment and purchaser-provider networks all make the inclusion of SEN pupils at best, a complex process, and at worst, make for an exclusive school and an undesirable one.

Children and young people who are physically disabled are blessed and cursed at the same time. Many physical disabilities (though not all) are visible. There has always been a greater degree of sympathy, if you like, for their difficulties and often a greater acceptance into mainstream schools. This has also been a curse because sympathy and charity sometimes fade when the consequences of the unaltered learning environment become clear. Either they involve a much greater degree of physical/environmental change or the consequences for learning and development have not been fully realised. Deprivation of access to experience and learning does not disappear overnight and many pupils/students who are disabled still have to complete their studies in difficult, if not hostile, physical and social environments. In addition, there will be the academic consequences of having missed 'chunks' of learning or curriculum in earlier educational provision.

The Code of Practice – internal stages

Stages 1–3: These stages are internal to the school but require informal partnership with parents and other agencies. It is the overall responsibility of the Governors to ensure that identification, assessment, monitoring, provision and partnership with parents and outside agencies is effective in support of pupils with special education needs.

- Definition of SEN
- Governor's responsibilities
- School SEN policy
- Role of SENCO
- Identification and record-keeping
- Partnership with parents
- Information available
- Child health and protection services – liaison

The five stage model suggested in Part II to IV raises some further issues. Stage I, for example, is seen as internal to the school/college and essentially informal. Nevertheless, this informal stage can lead to an enormous amount of collected information and teachers will need to be supported in efficient ways to do this, by in-school recording systems that are not excessive or burdensome with overly bureaucratic requirements. Also, by sharing and developing these on a local and national basis.

Stage 1 – Information collected

School

- class records (including previous class/school and their particular arrangements);
- national curriculum attainments and ways in which it is made accessible;
- standardised tests or profiles, with reservations about their reliability or validity;
- records of achievement in their broadest sense (e.g. creative ways that achievement has been fostered and recorded);
- reports on pupils in school settings (this must include comment about the accessibility of learning and social environments);
- known health or social problems (see Child Health Services).

Parent

- views on pupil's or student's health and development generally;
- perceptions on performance, progress and behaviour including their view of the appropriateness of the educational facilities;
- factors contributing to any difficulty (e.g. particular ways of communicating, bullying, low self-esteem);
- other agencies parents would like to involve.

Child

- personal perceptions of any difficulty (e.g. time taken to allow for communication);
- how the pupil or student could address them and what they need from the teacher/school/college;
- any other adults the child would like to involve.

Doctor or GP

- a child health surveillance report (see Child Health Services).

It is important, at Stage I, that the parents are included and that the onus is not entirely on the pupil/student to make changes or adapt to circumstances.

Liason with child health services

SENCO (Special Education Needs Co-ordinator) ensures effectiveness of services/systems for:

- keeping individual records;
- drawing together information (GP, school health services, health visitor, paediatrician, consultant);
- transfer of relevant medical information and sharing appropriately;
- ensuring the elimination of underlying medical causes for learning or behavioural difficulties whenever possible (e.g. pain, discomfort).

By definition, there is likely to be medical information that needs to be interpreted, clarified and shared in an appropriate format. It is important that this information is carefully ‘sifted’ with the involvement of parents and the student. Many negative assumptions can be made about the consequences for learning and development when information is only partially communicated or partially understood.

Individual(ised) Education Plans (IEPs) – a social model?

There is an inherent paradox, in practice, in defining a national curriculum for all and then suggesting that ‘Individual Education Plans’ must be drawn up for ‘special’ pupils or students. It is tempting to say ‘Either it is a curriculum for all, or it isn’t’. In reality, educators are expected to take the national curriculum framework and find creative ways to deliver this, or make it accessible to a particular group. A large comprehensive may have more than 80 pupils for whom time will be spent in drawing up and implementing *individual* education plans. The Special Needs Coordinator (SENCO), the class or subject teacher, departmental heads or headteachers, learning support staff and sometimes external personnel or agencies may be involved. This is a substantial logistical task. In fact, the national curriculum has to be interpreted for *all* pupils, in programmes of study, courses, lessons and in recording achievement or progress. What is a normal process of planning for teachers has become additionally complex and specialised by this *individual* approach.

Stage 2: Individual Education Plans (IEP)

The introduction of this concept also has arguments about 'individual' versus 'individualised'. In short, an IEP should contain:

1 – Curricular needs
2 – Teaching requirements
3 – Non-curricular needs
4 – Review arrangements.

Stage 3:

This stage involves more extensive intervention, internal consultation (Headteacher, SENCO, parents) and varying degrees of external support and involvement. In brief this involves:

1 – SENCO recording advice and arrangements
2 – SENCO convenes review meetings
3 – Referral for statement – information and evidence.

TRIGGERS: These are events which can set in motion the next stage of the 5 stage model outlined in the Code of Practice (e.g. SENCO, teacher and parents consult with Headteacher to trigger Stage 3) involving more intensive intervention and external support.

There is a danger here of seeing all the responses to making education accessible by an individual approach and centring all efforts around an individual. The greater the number of individual education plans, the greater the drain on scant resources (financial, time, human effort and teaching materials). A balance needs to be achieved between:

- the needs and abilities of the individual;
- classroom or subject planning and facilities to support it;
- the curriculum support available in school (human resources);
- the whole school and environmental factors;
- external support available and its organisation.

Individual(ised) Education Plans – what is involved?

1. **Curriculum needs**	– precise curricular priorities; – learning objectives and criteria for success; – monitoring and recording arrangements.
2. **Teaching requirements**	– teaching strategies and – techniques;

	– staff involved; – size of teaching groups; – equipment and materials; – frequency and timing of support.
3. **Non-curricular needs**	– pastoral care arrangements; medical requirements.
4. **Review arrangements**	– review date; – people to be involved in review.

In truth, the education plans should not be truly individual. This is separating the individual pupil or student onto a divisive curriculum. The overall aims and objectives should be the same for all. The modes of delivery, specific teaching materials, equipment or resources used and the changes in the learning environment as a whole will enable the experience of learning to be individualised. In Chapter 5, the issues of learning support in proximal zones of development, differentiation, access and the way in which a learner can be supported are explored. Meeting the challenge of inclusion involves further development of the whole school or college learning environment (as discussed in Chapter 3) and the quality of partnerships in Stage 3 planning (Chapter 6).

SENCO should record:
- what further advice is being sought;
- arrangements pending receipt of this advice;
- review arrangements.

SENCO convenes review meetings to discuss:
- progress made by child;
- effectiveness of Education plans;
- likelihood of referral for statutory assessment;
- update of informants and advice;
- future action.

The diagram (figure 4.2) regarding 'an assessment process' still has its limitations. These are the limitations imposed by a view of the assessment of a pupil or student as a relationship with teacher, assessor and other professionals. Of course, a physically disabled child or young person exists in a much wider context and with a great deal more to offer than the limited response to assessment exercises. *Thorough participation of the individual* (and, for younger pupils, his or her parents) in the process will reduce this narrowing but the choices and opportunities will be dependent on bringing forward a much wider view. Any assessment must recognise certain key issues, some of which are discussed in Chapter 2. Table 4.1 (Humphreys, 1992) is a deliberate polarisation of the issues to illustrate the possibility of moving towards a more inclusive assessment model.

Central Notions	Traditional?	Progressive?
Individual uniqueness	group referenced and standardised	individual and self-referenced
Different people's views	single judgment by teacher	multiple perspectives valued including the pupils'
Truth	based on a assessor's bias	based on consensus by all end users
Ownership	evidence owned by testers	evidence owned by pupils
Negotiation	assessment unchallenged by the pupils	assessment open to negotiation or dialogue
Motivation	competitiveness allows only a few to succeed	shared involvement allows a wide range of 'success'
Context	based on formal tests (often paper and pencil)	based on natural responses in daily context
Integration of curriculum and assessment	assessment led curriculum	curriculum led with integrated assessment
A whole view	narrow reference based on academic achievement	broad with reference to the whole person
Outcome	supports selection process within the system	supports the process of personal development

Table 4.1 Pupil and student assessment – some contrasting issues

The Code of Practice (1994) goes some way to achieving participation and consensus in the process of assessment. Stage 4 concerns referral for statement with written information and evidence including:

- actively sought and recorded views of parents and pupil or student;
- information from educational and other assessments (including medical and health);

- clear statements about the school's intervention in Stages 1 to 3;
- properly organised and implemented educational plans;
- a record of regular reviews, their progress and outcomes;
- a coordinated approach also involving external agencies and professionals.

Perhaps the obsession with advice, assessment, diagnosis and labelling has some of its roots in the insecurity that teachers generally feel about pupils with 'special needs'. There is an enormous need to classify and it is true to say that recognition of different or diverse abilities is a 'key' factor in including pupils who are disabled. Our current assessment practices for pupils and students who are physically disabled still leave a lot to be desired in:

- the amount of participation by the pupil or student in the whole process;
- acknowledgement of spatial or perceptual consequences in early learning;
- attention to basic (and often subtle) vision and hearing effects;
- the focus or basic 'access' to learning (position, seating, comfort);
- establishing an effective means of communication for the pupil or student, *no matter what* ability levels are inferred;
- creating proper partnerships, protocols and quality assurance for multi-disciplinary assessments;
- ensuring that resources and arrangements identified through *proper assessment* (whether a legal 'statement of educational need' or not) *are actually being made or allocated.*

Taking into consideration these factors (i.e. those that support or militate against a proper assessment) leads to a model of assessment that fits well with the 5-stage Code of Practice model. However, the diagram (figure 4.1) illustrates quite clearly that the Code of Practice on its own is no more than a piece (or many pieces!) of paper. A full understanding and commitment from those involved (Chapter 6 on 'partnerships') will make it live and affect positive change. The role of ongoing 'assessment through teaching' (ATT) has been marginalised by the imposition of standard attainment targets (SATs) and standardised tests. These are entirely inappropriate, as a sole measure of ability for pupils who are disabled. They can, however, contribute to *ongoing assessment through teaching activity.*

The more detailed model for assessment (based on Davies, 1995) must carry with it the assumption that the pupil or student and parents (for younger children) are thoroughly involved throughout. This involves establishing some form of effective communication, right from the start.

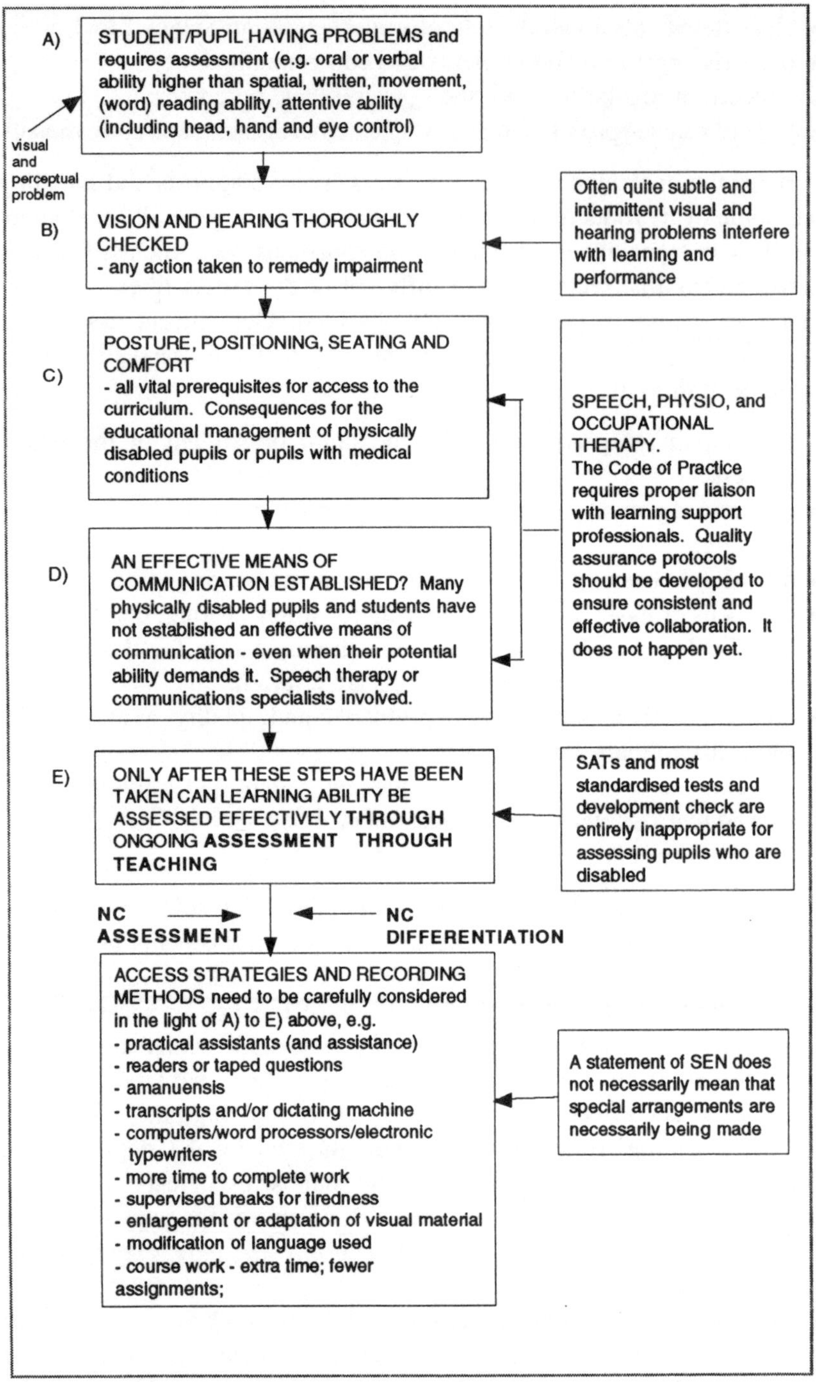

A)
STUDENT/PUPIL HAVING PROBLEMS and requires assessment (e.g. oral or verbal ability higher than spatial, written, movement, (word) reading ability, attentive ability (including head, hand and eye control)
visual and perceptual problem
B)
VISION AND HEARING THOROUGHLY CHECKED - any action taken to remedy impairment
Often quite subtle and intermittent visual and hearing problems interfere with learning and performance
C)
POSTURE, POSITIONING, SEATING AND COMFORT - all vital prerequisites for access to the curriculum. Consequences for the educational management of physically disabled pupils or pupils with medical conditions
SPEECH, PHYSIO, and OCCUPATIONAL THERAPY. The Code of Practice requires proper liaison with learning support professionals. Quality assurance protocols should be developed to ensure consistent and effective collaboration. It does not happen yet.
D)
AN EFFECTIVE MEANS OF COMMUNICATION ESTABLISHED? Many physically disabled pupils and students have not established an effective means of communication - even when their potential ability demands it. Speech therapy or communications specialists involved.
E)
ONLY AFTER THESE STEPS HAVE BEEN TAKEN CAN LEARNING ABILITY BE ASSESSED EFFECTIVELY THROUGH ONGOING ASSESSMENT THROUGH TEACHING
SATs and most standardised tests and development check are entirely inappropriate for assessing pupils who are disabled
NC ASSESSMENT
NC DIFFERENTIATION
ACCESS STRATEGIES AND RECORDING METHODS need to be carefully considered in the light of A) to E) above, e.g.
- practical assistants (and assistance)
- readers or taped questions
- amanuensis
- transcripts and/or dictating machine
- computers/word processors/electronic typewriters
- more time to complete work
- supervised breaks for tiredness
- enlargement or adaptation of visual material
- modification of language used
- course work - extra time; fewer assignments;
A statement of SEN does not necessarily mean that special arrangements are necessarily being made

Figure 4.2 An assessment process for pupil or student who may be disabled (adapted and expanded from Davies, 1995)

Support for learning within the school or college

Pupils or students will need to receive support within a school or college in different areas:

- in the classroom, subject department or general learning facilities;
- around the school or college generally;
- through whole school strategies and guidance:
  - in-service education and training;
  - (senior) management team(s);
  - access to 'community'.

In the *classroom, subject department or learning facility* there will need to be an awareness of the individual background factors that affect choice and opportunity in the learning environment. Physical disability is a very broadly defined group and therefore will include pupils or students with no mobility (or physical access) problems through to epileptic students who may have few mobility problems but require other facilities.

The following points should be borne in mind in considering physical, mechanical or technical changes for an inclusive classroom:

- *Is the pupil able to communicate their personal needs and feelings adequately?* (this is a right, not a privilege).
- I*s there sufficient space in the classroom*, department and surrounding facilities for a wheelchair to move about or park? Are structural alterations required?
- Has there been consideration of changes that might require structural alterations, extra equipment or resources? *Are these going to provide general benefits*, not exclusive to one pupil or student (e.g. more space, less space)?
- What work will pupils or students be doing until these alterations or enhanced resources arrive? Will the work fairly reflect the pupils' abilities? Will there be an *interim phase to full inclusion?* Is the classroom isolated in terms of access to other facilities in the school or college?
- What strategies can be used to minimise the effects of *absence from the classroom because of therapy or movement round the school or college?* Are all rooms accessible? Not all disabled pupils will have special requirements for physical access. Friends can help move about between lessons but fire routines and using lifts should be considered separately.
- What *drawbacks could there be in the course* for pupils with, for example, special communication needs, a movement disability or a

potentially painful medical condition?

- What changes could be made *to enable the pupils or students to meet the assessment targets* or exam requirements of the courses or programmes of study offered?
- *What strategies can be used to minimise the written workload* for pupils or students who find writing tiring or painful? Can work be recorded on computer, audio or video tape, photographs or by an amanuensis/facilitator/support assistant?
- *Is the furniture suitable?* Can the height be adjusted, for example, in science laboratories? Is there room to sit comfortably at a desk? Will the pupil or student have to remain in a wheelchair all day?

In addition to the physical, mechanical or technical changes to the learning environment, there are requirements for learning support assistants (or facilitators) or classroom assistants and their effective deployment. Classroom assistants or learning support facilitators need:

- job descriptions to be clearly specified and *their role to be discussed and clarified;*
- to achieve consistency across subjects, school areas, learning environments and between different staff or departments. This can only be properly achieved by *their participation in development meetings, and whole school training*;
- to help children gain access to curriculum and help, when necessary, with medical and personal needs. They will also need to *listen carefully to the pupil or student and, often, use advocacy skills in this support*;
- to be skilled at identifying the needs of pupils by *listening to them* and balancing their feelings and views against school or college demands;
- *to be well informed* through involvement in school/college or curricular planning whenever possible or through pre-class discussion and briefing or by daily/weekly planning meetings with teachers and therapists;
- to allow pupils to become as independent as possible. To know *when to adopt a 'hands-off' approach* is as vital as knowing when to help;
- to work with other children or do resource materials/preparation; so becoming *less clearly identified with one child and reducing the stigma* attached to that child by their presence.

In the classroom or learning facility, consideration will need to be given to good seating and posture. To achieve a basic level of functioning in the classroom, a younger pupil will need to achieve *an upright, stable, symmetrical and comfortable sitting position.* As the pupil or student matures through primary school he or she will need to learn to take increasing responsibility for achieving this, with guidance and help. This mainly applies to pupils or students who have a significant physical or movement disability but it also applies to others who may have less obvious disabilities. It can help a child who has any form of perceptual or motor disability to achieve access to educational experiences.

Why is position and correct seating so important?

- It helps to achieve better trunk and head control, enhancing sitting balance and the possibility of *more independent posture*.
- It leaves the *hands free to engage in productive desktop* activity rather than waving around trying to maintain sitting balance.
- *Symmetrical* sitting is necessary to enhance *eye-hand co-ordination skills* as far as possible.
- It helps a child or young person *use scanning techniques by moving their head independently from whole body movement*. It enables a person to pay attention and focus on what is going on around them.
- The acquisition of *useful visual perceptual skills* is also dependent upon scanning and eye-hand co-ordination (above).
- It provides *greater opportunities for socialising* and interacting with peer groups, taking part in group work or communicate with the teacher. (The position of the chair in relation to the teacher or the focus of group work is vitally important).
- A child or young person needs to be released from having to pay too much attention to their physical needs and use *every opportunity to access learning activities and generalise skills*.

The aim is to enable access and choice through correct seating and position. Above all it must be comfortable!

By the time a student reaches secondary education, these particular physical management issues should have been properly sorted out. Whatever type of seating is used, this should be done in conjunction with occupational or physiotherapy support. Clear and simple guidance can be found in Tingle (1990) and in North Yorkshire County Council Education Committee (Guidelines for Schools – Physically Disabled Pupils, 1992). It should not totally remove any responsibility for posture and position from the child or young person themselves. Unless a young person has developed their own sense of a comfortable and useful sitting posture (aided or unaided by physical support), they will not achieve independent responsibility for themselves. In turn, this will hamper personal and social development. This means that adults do not 'take over' the physical management aspects but use them productively as a learning experience, whenever possible. The comments from Year 11 students in the next section clearly illustrate a developing sense of choice and control. This is vital for personal, academic and social development.

By the time a student has reached Year 11 in secondary education, they are usually expressing the wish to exercise CHOICE. This relates to other people's assumptions about what kind of help is needed and what kind of help should be given. It is all too often assumed that a non-disabled person (particularly with a student-teacher relationship) knows what a disabled pupil/student can and can't do, particularly in what is called 'independence skills'. The key feature of independence is having a realistic appreciation of *your own skills and limitations*. When we realise our own limitations, we can then take steps to overcome them, by learning our way out of them. If this is not possible, as is often the case, then we take the next step which is either to get some form of *personal assistance* from someone else or use *some form of aid, tool, extension or adaptation* (e.g. car, directory, telephone, bicycle, bus). If you find yourself lost in a strange city, you resort to using a map (if you can get one!) and, even with this, you may need to resort to asking someone where you are. This requires recognition of your own abilities and limitations and then the skills to acquire the resources or the help you need from others. If the local population are fearful, uncaring, antagonistic or assume *they* know where you want to go, then you've got problems!

Around school or college (personal and social requirements)

The school or college management team devolves responsibility for pupils with physical disabilities; key staff will probably have responsibility for ensuring that everyone in the school or college is sensitive to the needs of people who are disabled, through the medium of the school's personal and social education programme. Further to this, there should be positive and varied role models for disabled pupils and students evident in all teaching materials; some awareness of the difficulties faced by disabled people in the community through traditional and cultural oppression (see Introduction and Chapter 1); personal, social and health education (see Chapter 2) initiatives and science material covering, for example, movement studies looking at the body and its mechanics. This may seem a little contrived but until disabling and many less obvious medical conditions are accepted as a natural part of the human condition, we need to compensate for past oppression and segregation.

The personal and social development of all pupils, including those with physical disabilities, will also be the responsibility of key members of staff. In the case of FE and HE colleges, responsibility for guidance and support will be from a Learning Support Centre, whose presence is common knowledge and is available for use by students. Many schools and colleges have produced pupil or student booklets and from these booklets a student could check that their particular needs are met in the school or college's programme of pastoral care. Also that learning support is organised or available for pupils or students if there is to be prolonged absence because of illness or medical treatment.

In more detail, what form should this personal and social support take? We could do far worse than look at comments of disabled students themselves (figures 4.3 and 4.4), taken from Aileen Webber's *Integration and Independence* series (Webber, 1991).

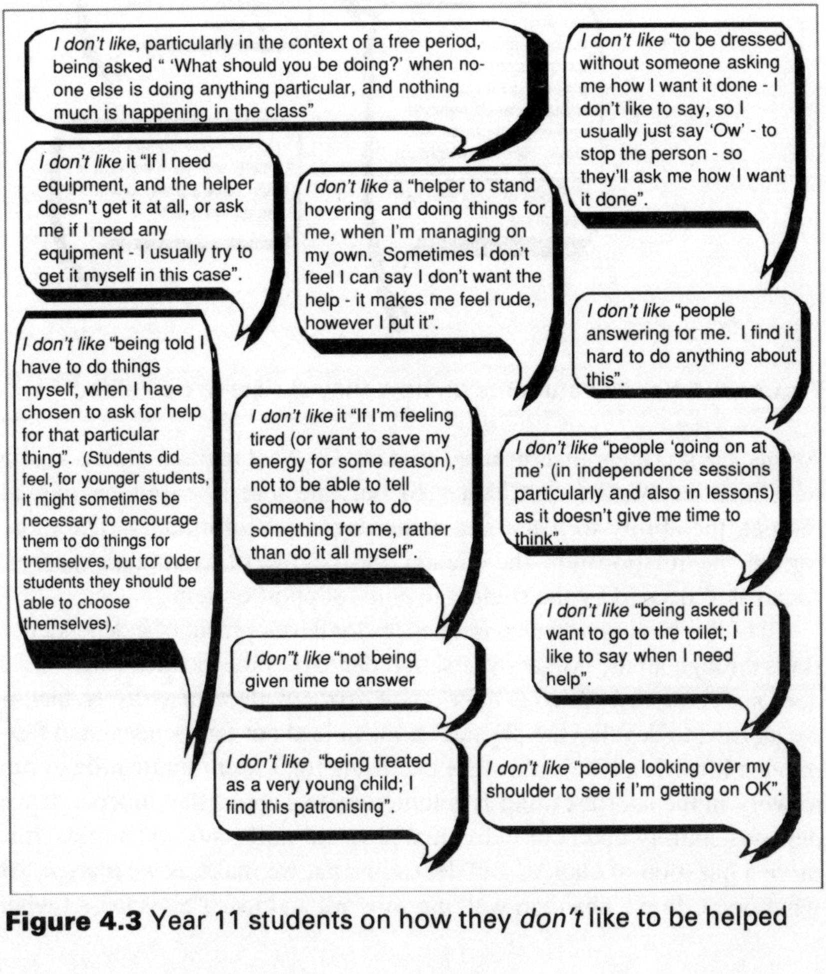

Figure 4.3 Year 11 students on how they *don't* like to be helped

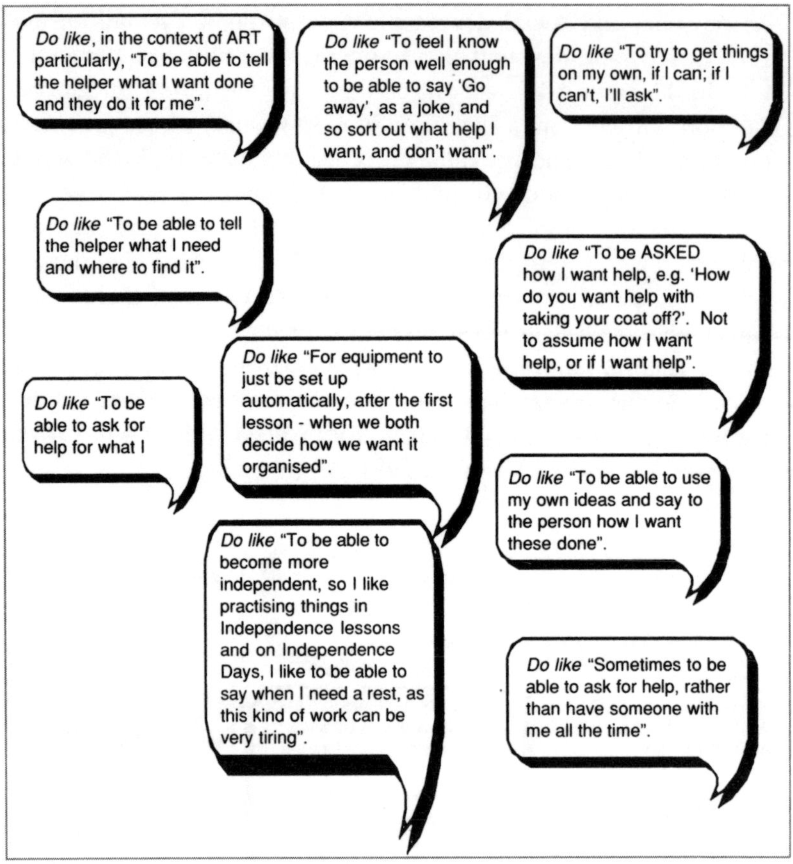

Figure 4.4 Year 11 students on how they *do* like to be helped

At this age it is clear that disabled students do want to have a relationship with their enablers (see Chapter 6) but one that is based on mutual respect, the ability to listen and some degree of informality. The more formal the relationship, the greater the degree of communication or social skill needed by the student to enlist support or help.

All of this has important consequences for development of independence skills throughout the primary years. In order to become independent, a child does *not necessarily have to develop an array of physical skills*. In fact, if we all tried to develop the physical skills to lead our independent and fast-moving lifestyles, we would all be practising for a four minute mile to run to work in the shortest time! It is ludicrous to suggest that independence depends entirely upon our individual physical skills and capabilities. It is more a question of choices and decisions that we make as we mature. At what point do we abandon walking to work and use a bicycle? At what point do we put aside the bicycle and take up a car? How do we compensate, through planning, leisure and recreation, for the fact that the speed and demands of modern work mean a physically unhealthy lifestyle? A child or young person needs to develop awareness of his or her own abilities and limitations through positive experience, alongside non-disabled peers. He or she does not necessarily need to be pushed through years of punishing physical routines in order to achieve a somewhat insecure standing position or a limited capacity to walk. This is likely to be abandoned in the teenage years (in favour of a wheelchair) to keep up with friends moving around.

Catering for the personal and social requirements begins at preschool where an attitude of independence can first be fostered. An independent attitude (for example, ability to make choices, solve problems, recognise abilities and limitations) is fundamental to further (independence) learning. It will provide the motivation to develop skills, become a social being and communicate effectively in order to achieve personal goals. This is in stark contrast to the attitude of passivity that is often fostered in disabled children from a very early age by adults who 'know better what is good for you . . . .', who demand rigorous physical performance whose outcome or prognosis is dubious and who are unable to listen to the choices that the child is trying to make. It is, of course, a matter for further debate within preschool, primary, secondary and tertiary institutions how much they can tolerate an attitude of independence in the face of the requirements for conformity and acquiescence that some of our current educational institutions seem to require from all pupils.

The (senior) management team and key personnel

There is little doubt these days that an inclusive approach requires affirmative support and action on the part of Principal or Headteacher and (senior) management teams. For the reasons examined by Dr. Christine Barton in Chapter 3, anything other than a concerted approach (whole school or whole college) will be doomed to failure or minimal success. Any actions will just be chipping away at the surface and placing disabled children and young people in potentially hostile environments. Of course, not everybody in a school or college will suddenly become a convert to disability equality. Many teachers have no interest in these endeavours, even when there are disabled pupils attending their lessons. Systems must be set up that will encourage collective responsibility and enable choice, opportunity and entitlement for all pupils, including those with diverse abilities, (see figure 4.5).

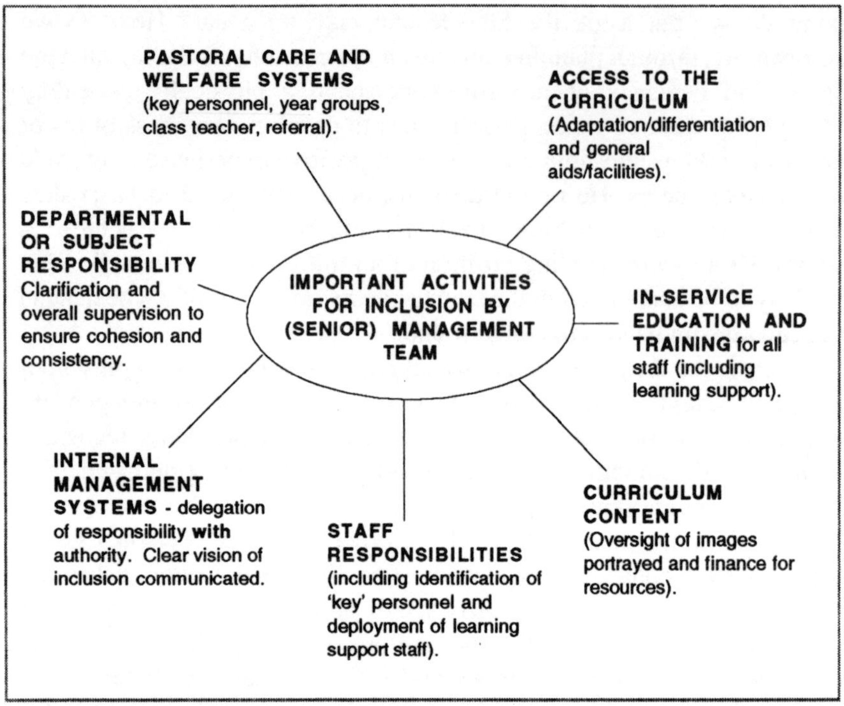

Figure 4.5 Systems for inclusion

The quality of partnership between school or college management, teachers, learning *support staff and pupils or students* is vital (see Chapter 6).

Departmental or subject responsibility does not end at planning the content of courses (e.g. topics and programmes of study). *Inclusion, like learning, is a process, not an outcome*. Differentiation and adaptation are also processes not outcomes. The result of all of these may well be a change in thinking or behaviour or a change of content, mode of delivery or other change (see Chapter 5 on differentiation). By understanding the process, teachers and learning support staff can work more effectively with pupils or students who have diverse abilities. This means that planning and initial discussion of curriculum access, programmes of study and modes of delivery should involve 'key' designated staff in the secondary school or college. Or, in the primary sector, class teachers should involve the SENCO or specialist support teacher in this planning. The role of a 'key' or contact teacher, the SENCO and any additional learning support is to help class, subject teachers or departments review and make changes necessary to make the (national) curriculum subjects accessible to pupils who are physically disabled.

Access to the formal curriculum should not be left to one individual teacher in a school or college. Responsibility for entitlement, access and differentiation should not be left for just a 'key' person. The following list is intended as a check that a disabled pupil is being enabled in his or her access to the formal curriculum, appropriate learning environments and equivalent (to non-disabled peers) choices in school life.

- *Adapted equipment or specific aids* may benefit a disabled pupil or student. What sources of advice and support are available? What facility is there for ongoing training of staff in their use?
- *Access to equipment*, for example, typewriter, word processor or laptop computer. How can this be arranged? What rooms/space is available? What arrangements are made for maintenance and breakdown?
- *Notice board and pupil/student information.* Are the sources of information equally accessible to disabled students?
- *Classrooms and specialist subject rooms/areas.* Are these accessible and is the (specialist) equipment, say, for science accessible to disabled pupils or students?
- *Courses, programmes of study, special lessons and broader curricular activities.* What sources of advice and support are available in (a) planning, and (b) delivering these?
- *Learning support staff, facilitators, classroom assistants.* What is their availability? How can access be arranged in the absence of support staff? What are the systems to feed back to (senior) management regarding their deployment?
- *Timetabling.* Schools and colleges are currently under pressure to fill and account for every moment. How does the timetable tie in with the movements around school or college?
- *Activities off school site or campus.* Do arrangements allow pupils or students to participate fully in off-site educational activities (for example, educational visits, work experience, swimming . . .)

Management responsibility for pastoral care, personal and social development is as important, in learning terms, as the management of delivery of curriculum content: not just for disabled pupils or students, but for all. An unhappy or lost student will not learn and reach their capacity. Pupils and students, as a group, who do not feel part of the community of the school or college will tend towards disaffection and will not participate fully, even when they can. It is no good having the most comprehensive and visionary formal curriculum plans and policies if the human resources are not managed effectively to achieve them. Of course, pupils are the most important human resource, aren't they? This area has been called the informal or 'hidden' curriculum; it is pastoral care or just the totality of school life. The management of a school or college can widen access to personal and social development by considering the following points:

- *Loss of valuable social and personal contact.* Due to a number of factors:
  - school/college outside local neighbourhood
  - pupils/students having special transport
  - special arrangements for fire drill, play . . . . there is a need to compensate for artificially induced social deprivation.
- *Allocation to teaching or course groups.* Are they the most appropriate ones or are they allocated because of lack of expertise, facilities, using wheelchair or special equipment (not satisfactory)?
- *Unstructured times (break, play, lunch) and extra-curricular (social activity).* Are disabled pupils or students able to access the same activities, experiences and facilities as the non-disabled?
- *Role models and attitudes.* Does the school or college have positive (and visible) role models for disabled pupils? Have all the staff and pupils (or students) where appropriate been properly prepared for developing an 'inclusive' social atmosphere in the institution?

In summary, this chapter has sought to outline the various levels of activity in response to the challenge of inclusion. Using examples of good practice in existence, such as CESPD, Humberside, is one way to learn about the various elements that contribute to success. It is apparent that, for successful inclusion there needs to be planning, activity and ongoing review at various levels, from individualised teaching through to whole school management. Preparation, training and open discussion are key elements in generating and maintaining commitment to inclusive or affirmative practices in schools and colleges. Choice and opportunity for disabled pupils and students can be achieved in such a way that it is part of the general evolution of our education system. Quality education for the minority of diverse learners will mean sharpening and improving the skills of teachers and organisation of schools or colleges, to the benefit of all.

CHAPTER 5

Entitlement, Access and Differentiation

Entitlement to what?

The introduction of the national curriculum following the Education Reform Act (ERA), 1988 has placed obligations on schools and educational services to acknowledge that all pupils are entitled to a broad and balanced curriculum. The definition of that curriculum was to be found in the national curriculum standing orders and papers that accompanied the legislation. At the time, it was generally observed, no reciprocal acknowledgement was made of the special, diverse or individual needs of a substantial proportion of pupils in both mainstream and special education provision. This was an implicit contradiction to the Warnock Report and 1981 Education Act which recognised the level and extent of special educational needs that existed within the education system as a whole. The 1993 Education Act incorporating the Code of Practice gives more detailed guidelines about the practicalities of this broad concept of entitlement through access to the school curriculum and recognition, once again, of categories of special need.

In this chapter, the concept of 'breadth and balance' is explored in relation to choice, opportunity and inclusion for pupils who are physically or movement disabled. In broad terms we have the welcome movement towards collective responsibility in the education system to ensure entitlement and access for all. This is set in the context of the Code of Practice that now defines special needs in terms of broad, but compact, categories. At one time there were 10 'categories of handicap' and even then, as we now recognise, many children slipped through the net and their educational needs and abilities were not recognised within those categories. More fundamentally, practical concerns in trying to implement and deliver this very detailed and prescriptive curriculum have emerged. It was as if the 'detail' of the new national curriculum orders actually militated against its own principles, reducing entitlement for all and even breadth and balance in many instances.

Learning and promoting positive experiences

Medical terminology such as 'dyspraxia', 'Down's syndrome' and 'dyslexia' is part of a system whose aim is to clearly define 'symptoms' (visible signs) or other characteristic signs of disorder. This is useful for medical professionals who wish to treat the disorder and make it go away, get better or to restore the patient to 'normality'. This is not an appropriate ethic or approach for teaching. Remedial teaching has been based on the identification of these specific 'deficits' and is called a 'Deficit Model' of teaching. However, this alone is not enough because children do not learn in neat compartments and remedying (or attempting to remedy) one specific aspect in isolation will never work totally. A contrasting model is the 'Enrichment Model' which emphasises the use of the whole learning context (including the teacher) and the *whole abilities of the student to provide alternative ways towards achievement and success.* The learner who is given the choice, opportunity, support and guidance, will take responsibility for solving learning or access problems, usually in his or her own way.

(Micheline Mason, 1992)

In this chapter, the relationship between the needs of pupils and students who are disabled, and the breadth and the depth of the national curriculum, is discussed. The view of experienced teachers who have also listened, and actively noted, the views of their pupils (Cornwall, 1992) is that the range and extent of these needs go well beyond that which is catered for by the national curriculum. The work done by Aileen Webber (1991) in her four volume *Independence and Integration* series illustrates comprehensively the extent of personal, social and mobility requirements that should be taken into account in working alongside students with disabilities. The construction of a suitable learning environment to access and supplement the national curriculum should be guided by two main things:

(1) An understanding and acknowledgement of the cultural and legislative history that continues to impact on the education and lives of disabled students.

(2) The increasing information and advice from groups which actively promote the civil rights and the views of disabled people, young and old.

The problem with labelling, identifying syndromes or working on a deficit model is that:

(1) It implies that there is some specific 'cure' or remedy which is rarely true with learning or behaviour difficulties.

(2) It can 'blind' you to a whole variety of other relevant factors involved with any particular child or 'bind' you to irrelevant factors.

(3) It doesn't help to plan 'the way forward' in learning or curricular terms. In other words, it is only a *starting point for positive intervention, not an end in itself.*

It is important for teachers to use their powers of accurate description and all of the relevant information provided by careful observation and discussion with the pupil or student, in order to make their own informed judgments and decisions. There may be a need to incorporate or combine parts of the methods outlined in Chapter 8 and synthesise new approaches. *This is where time spent on creative joint discussion/review is rarely wasted.* Schools or colleges that are including pupils and students who are disabled must be able to set aside this 'creative review' time. The teacher and other adults working alongside disabled pupils and students play a vital role as mediators in assessment of needs and abilities as well as in accessing the learning material and environment.

The idea of mediated learning is particularly relevant to pupils or students with a physical or movement disability. It applies to all learning situations where either a human (teacher, learning support professional or assistant) or a computer, teaching machine or adapted aid is involved. People who are disabled in general have far more people mediating in their lives (Prosser, 1992) with possible consequences for the amount of choice and control they can exert. (See figure 5.1).

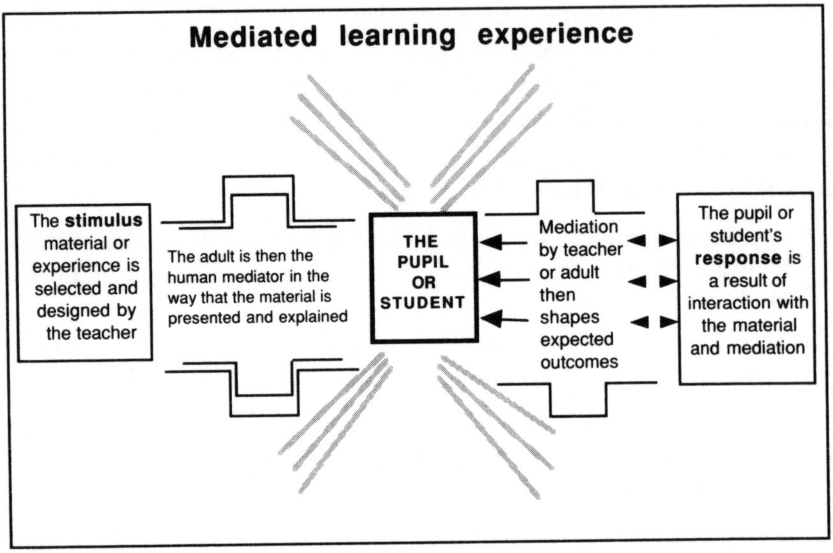

Figure 5.1 Mediation must not reduce the student's choice and control

As we will see in Chapter 6, the quality and nature of partnerships have a vital impact on the quality of life and learning for children and young people in schools and colleges. From the learner's point of view, it is important that choice and control are retained. The experience of mediation can be either empowering and facilitative or it can become confusing, distracting and dissociated from the task in hand.

A positive and holistic assessment of needs

Nowhere is potential fragmentation more apparent than in the assessment of needs or of curricular attainment.

In 1992, Klaus Wedell expressed widely held general concerns over NC assessment (in Bovair and Upton, 1992). There was, in practice and despite the rhetoric, a clear separation of assessment from day-to-day teaching. According to Wedell, there were three main questions that needed addressing in considering assessment and the NC:

1. *Planning the next step* for the individual child's learning.
2. Answering teacher's and pupil's questions about '*levels of achievement*'.
3. Answering teacher's, parent's, governor's, LEA's and finally the government's questions about the '*quality of education*' *that is being offered*.

What is national curriculum assessment for?

In addition to this, the OFSTED Framework (1992), clearly defines and discriminates between 'standards of achievement' firstly as measured against 'national norms' which are calculated via demographic information about the type of school and national statistics, and 'standards of achievement' which have to do with the pupil or student's own progress in relation to his or her own potential. It is this second aspect of 'standards of achievement' which provide the key to giving all children confidence, raising their self-esteem and boosting their overall performance. Comparison against national or competitive 'norms' for many children (and not just those who are disabled) can easily have the effect of destroying confidence, self-esteem and increasing anxiety levels with consequent and clearly observed effects on educational or academic performance.

Planning the next step

The list below is extracted from Wedell (1992). It points to ways of thinking beyond the national curriculm.

- Concentration on the 4 'key stages' vs. the need for continual assessment and evaluation based on day-to-day teaching.
- The aims of education cannot be realised within the confines of a subject-based curriculum (NCC, 1990).
- Records of achievement, a broader view, are not part of the current statutory requirements.
- In practice, in mainstream schools, statutory and effective assessment is still going on within the limits of the subject model NC.
- Attainment targets and standards of achievement represent *only two dimensions* of the curriculum map:
  - content
  - progression
- *NC is at best an approximation*, it is still in the process of evolution. A fact not made clear in statutory and other publications on the implementation of 1988 Act and subsequently the 1993 Act.
- Programmes of study contain ideas for . . .

- range of experiences offered
- good teaching method (e.g. project work)
- teacher based assessment
- development of curriculum 'framework'

Effectively including pupils who are disabled and enabling their curriculum entitlement depends largely upon having *whole school policies* (see Chapter 3). Effective assessment and monitoring requires a shared ethos, with positive expectations, inclusive intentions and confidence in problem-solving. The fact that all attainment targets and are on 'orders' (NCC, 1989) is not providing a structure within which teachers, pupils and students can develop meaningful programmes of study by discussing and selecting objectives. This is more motivating and more manageable for both the youngster and the teacher or lecturer.

> Current administration of SATs in their present form meets neither the requirements of individual assessment, nor of the general monitoring of standards. The answer lies in increased investment in moderation, both within and between school staffs, for the development of a curriculum based assessment.
>
> (after Wedell, 1992)

The key factor for pupils and students who are disabled is often the output mode or judgment of understanding and skills from limited responses. Time, listening skills and encouragement are vital commodities and all too often in short supply, squeezed out by the pressures and requirements on the adults, not necessarily related to an individual student.

Differentiating within the limits

Differentiation is seen as the key to including pupils who are disabled and providing access to the (national) curriculum. 'In real terms', to use a common phrase these days, teachers have been differentiating for years. It is not something new to teaching at all. The best practice in teaching has always sought to include *all* the pupils in a group, one way or another. The problem is the narrowness of our current definition of differentiation. Teachers have felt that they now have to learn 'what to do' and this has narrowed the view down to easily trained and quantified, mechanistic strategies. What does the terminology of differentiation *really* mean and can we make better use of broader and more creative interpretation?

Teachers talking about differentiation (1995) stress:

- The process of identifying, planning and providing according to need.
- Individualised expectations and work. To enable each individual to achieve success and progress.

- For each child to realise their full potential, the curriculum must be wide, *flexible and all encompassing*.
- Identifying each child's needs and setting a task that will provide successful learning.
- A process of enabling children of all abilities to work to their full potential. 'Differentiation is synonymous with good classroom teaching' (Moore, Owen et al, 1994).
- Is what we have been doing for years – but it didn't have a name – well, a posh one!
- Differentiation is: a means of every child being given access to the national curriculum at a level to suit their individual needs.

Teaching and learning objectives are now required to be stated within the pupil's Statement of Educational Need ('objectives the child is expected to achieve . . .' p.4 DFE 1992 – Circular 22/89). The key to providing access and entitlement to pupils with SEN is through differentiation. This is far more creative than merely stating additional different objectives. Differentiation is achieved by:

- good curricular planning
- experienced and creative staff.

Differentiation

- is synonymous with good teaching (Moore, 1992).
- enables pupils and students to demonstrate what they know, understand and are able to do.

It is allowing the learner, or assisting the learner to *make their own construction* of the knowledge or task in hand. The institutionalisation of learning in schools and colleges, during the late twentieth century has made it necessary to re-visit the whole concept of individualised learning and education for diversity. The concept of differentiation challenges expectations and relationships in the classroom. It assumes a high degree of skill and training on the part of the teacher, a suitable environment in which to teach and, above all, knowledge of each pupil or student. It is debatable, in the current state of our education system, whether these conditions are being met. For reasons discussed elsewhere in the book, the school environment, the level and content of training for teachers and the size of schools/classes often militate against efforts to differentiate and discriminate between pupils in large or changing groups. The practice of targeting the teacher's presentation, the organisation of learning activity and the response from pupils for smaller groups, or even individuals within the class, is vital if all students in a larger group are to make progress. But, differentiation also depends upon wider factors (whole school approach and local or national government support).

The national curriculum both limits and extends the teacher's efforts at individualising or 'grouping' her teaching activities. (See figure 5.2).

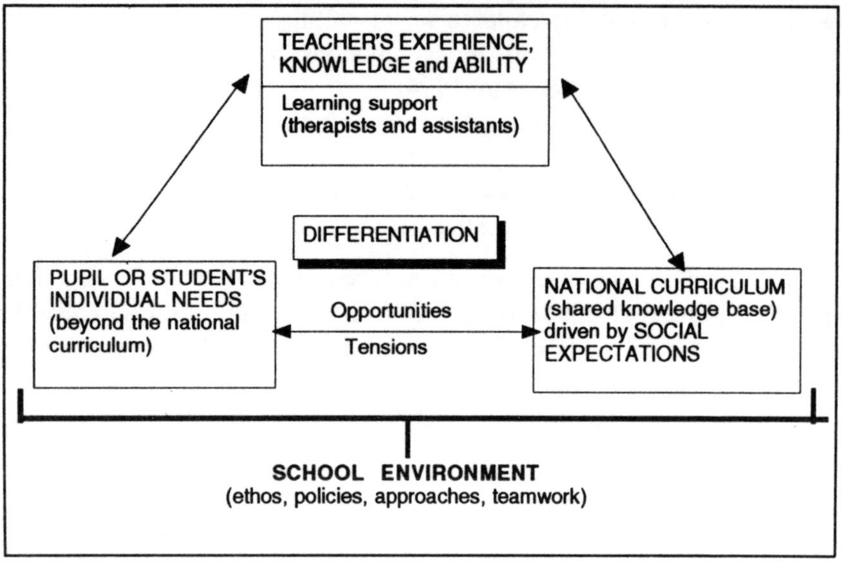

Figure 5.2 The vital mediating role in differentiation

The national curriculum or course requirements may constrain the teacher or lecturer in the pressure to achieve a measurable amount of subject based learning within time limits. It also gives opportunities to use the subjects of the curriculum creatively to attend to the disabled youngster's individual needs (see later).

Access

> .... imaginative and innovative learning routes to make pupils and students active participants within the curriculum, the school and the wider community.

In the context of children and young people who are physically disabled, the concept of 'access' has to be separated from 'entitlement' and 'differentiation'. It is also far broader than when it is applied to other areas of special educational need (SEN). Differentiation is one way to enable participation in learning activities but it is of limited use if the student cannot get into many of the learning areas (e.g. the science laboratory) of the school or college. Access takes on additional dimensions when a physical element becomes involved but there is also more to it than the purely physical. The student needs access to (for example):

- Physical spaces
  - for comfortable working in class/lectures
  - for subject specialist activities and areas
  - for recreation and social activities (not marginalised)
  - for personal and hygiene (with dignity) needs
- Curriculum/materials
  - library or reading materials and areas available
  - speed and mode of presentation (+ catch up time)
  - pre-copied materials/take away (good planning)
  - tape recorded lessons or video material (other media)
  - alternative ways of representing outcomes/ work production
  - aids for communication and work production
- Enrichment activities
  - spaces around school to work/enquire
  - IT materials and equipment to replace movement
  - facilities to join rest of group on trips
  - extra time to 'catch up' basic work
- Learning support
  - assistants not 'whisked away' arbitrarily (planned support)
  - assistants with some training/empathy
  - (therapies) integrated with educational activity
  - planned process of getting equipment/aids
- Personal support
  - inclusive attitude all round (friendships, etc.)
  - additional social spaces and activities
  - disability awareness (civil rights recognised)
  - not treated differently as a human being
  - referral to counsellor or 'key' person on request

ACCESS IS A BIG WORD

It is impossible to think of access to the curriculum without thinking of a whole range of physical and social factors that impact upon learning. Choice and opportunity do not exist where the physical, social and learning environments are not planned to include pupils and students who are disabled. This is because schools, colleges and educative processes have marginalised and segregated such pupils and students for the past 120 years. It is not surprising that we now have to work hard to convert our institutions into more user-friendly places for all. The physical conversions of buildings and learning/working spaces have to be preceded by a change of heart and vision, by somebody at some level. This is the start. The rest of the process may take time but it will eventually get there.

Balance

> ...between the demands of the national curriculum and the teacher's interpretation of individual or personal need.
>
> ... between subject demands, the 'core' curriculum and core competencies to maintain access to the curriculum and school life.

Mechanistic teaching of self-help or independence skills is not much good if the environment then denies choice and the opportunity to practise them in real situations. Aileen Webber's (1991) *Independence and Integration* series provides much useful practical material aimed at encouraging disabled youngsters to communicate their needs confidently and clearly. This is complemented by activities that encourage helpers and enablers to become more sensitised to an individual's needs and abilities. To achieve the kind of balance necessary, between national curriculum subjects, core skills for independence and the individual's needs beyond the curriculum requires:

- well developed PSE (Personal and Social Education) and pastoral programmes;
- creative use of subjects (literature, drama, science);
- acknowledgement of needs beyond curriculum;
- full inclusion but with 'catch-up' time;
- a properly planned physical environment.

Responsibility for learning is often seen as the sole responsibility of the class teacher. Indeed, teachers are often afraid to include pupils and students who are disabled, simply because of the perceived weight of this unrealistic expectation. Physical disability or medical conditions carry with them more obvious physical and outward consequences and will often cause concern, worry and even rejection, before a pupil or student arrives. It becomes 'someone else's problem' (Moore and Morrison, 1989). John Moore (1992) clearly divides the responsibility for differentiation between:

- the classroom;
- the key stage or department;

– the whole school.

Differentiation for diverse abilities with reference to physical disability and medical conditions has clear practical and daily implications not only for teachers and learning support personnel but for the whole school.

Teachers and support staff need to be confident in their knowledge of both the subject matter they are working with *and* the needs of an individual pupil/student who is disabled. This involves:

- aids and adaptations (making teaching accessible);
- conducive and user-friendly environment (physical access);
- same topic or subject but different input and product;
- all needs (e.g. physical/therapy/emotional) seen as part of the learning process and 'integrated' (communication/teamwork vital).

Planning coherent and progressive programmes of study (which is effective practice anyway) allows the teacher or lecturer to:

- anticipate physical/mobility/access problems;
- develop or adapt input materials;
- allow for different outcomes or responses;
- plan for extra time needed to complete tasks;
- plan for and use enabling technology.

This is best facilitated within a departmental or school framework that also has a coherent overall expectation or work programme.

The teacher/lecturer chooses from a range of *topics and materials* and identifies priorities through his/her knowledge of the individual, group and broader social needs.

Relevance

. . . . age appropriate, motivating, purposeful, interesting and useful learning experiences.

Adapting the materials, choosing the topics/subjects/areas of knowledge with due consideration for the individual (as opposed to the 'national') requirements is almost bound to make it more relevant. Making it more purposeful related to the long term aims of both the student and the adult involved.

The quality of relationships and group processes at different levels will have a facilitative or inhibitive effect on the teacher's ability to differentiate successfully. These factors will allow the teacher/lecturer to use groupings more flexibly, to 'share' teaching and learning environments, to make use of each other's ideas and adaptations. This will also reflect sensitivity and response to individual needs. A group whose individual members are also respected and have individual expectations is more likely to unite around the task (Adair, 1986).

Making it happen in real life

Progression

> . . . . skills and understanding generalised or used in a variety of contexts thus achieving mastery or fluency.

Ensuring progression involves monitoring progress through responses in a wide variety of situations and circumstances. It involves checking the following factors:

- **Content** – the same subject or topic can be covered by different content for individuals.
- **Interest** – the same content/subject will have different interest value or parts may have more interest value than others (how do they relate to the learner's experience?)
- **Pace** – pupils and students who are physically disabled will often require different expectations and arrangements regarding the pace of:
  - learning and assimilation;
  - reproduction of ideas/work;
  - planned extension or supplementary activities to learner's view point;
  - clear criteria for measuring progress (not just written!);
  - attention to conditions and materials used;
  - involvement of pupil/student in monitoring progress.
- **Preparation for learning**
  - what groupings does the individual prefer?
  - pupil's/student's confidence and frustration levels
  - what activities/subjects are motivating and rewarding?

There is no point in subjecting any physically disabled pupil or student to a 'balanced' diet of curriculum subjects if some of these become inaccessible because their needs 'beyond curriculum' (e.g. access to science laboratory, time to complete notes, 'catch-up time' for missed lessons, tests or notes) are not properly considered. On the other hand, there has to be very good reason to lower academic expectations. There is a need to adapt situations, materials and output expectations to allow the pupil or student to show what they understand, know and can do (Moore,

1992). Where academic expectations are lowered, this should only be seen as a slowing of a normal process of learning and in the face of clear evidence that the pupil or student is not coping. In our education system that relies largely on paper and pencil work, it is the narrowness of the way that curriculum is delivered and responses are measured that cause problems for a disabled pupil or student.

Breadth

> . . . to ensure that all pupils are given the opportunity to experience as many, varied and interesting educational experiences as other children . . . to make sure they do not get stuck in a 'remedial rut'.
>
> **Cross-curricular**
> Skills . . . e.g. communication, numeracy, problem-solving, information technology, studying . . .
>
> Approaches . . . e.g. topic work, themes.

Overall, then, the activities associated with 'differentiation' are no more or less than those that teachers who are effective with diverse abilities have always undertaken. The danger is that by defining a set of jargon associated with teaching groups with diverse needs and abilities, we then limit the activity to a more bureaucratic or mechanistic process. How to combine the 'checks' to make sure we are covering important aspects and including everyone but at the same time maintain the spontaneity of good learning experience is an ongoing discussion point for teachers.

The national curriculum is not the whole curriculum

There are often tensions between the demands of an academic (including national) curriculum and the broader individual needs of pupils who are disabled or have medical conditions. Specifically the tensions can be between:

- personal care, health education and social skills;
- motor development, physical therapy or movement activity;
- emotional development through positive relationships;
- personal autonomy through choice and opportunity;
- support (e.g. medical and therapy) services being consistent and integrated;
- gaps in perceptual-motor development and experience.

These tensions occur because the broader needs of pupils and students who are physically disabled are seen as separate or even opposing (e.g. therapy programmes not connected to child's actual daily movement or

PSE (Personal and Social Education) studies unconnected to disability or equal opportunities/civil rights issues). Teachers and lecturers who work with pupils and students who are physically disabled, and particularly those in mainstream schools or colleges, often talk about the problems of physical management and the demands of the curriculum as being two conflicting forces. They describe problems with:

- **Time** – away from curricular or subject-based work. This includes timetabling problems and additional therapy programmes.
- **Staffing** – often inconsistent and general lack of staff trained to work alongside pupils and students who are disabled. Skills, expertise and whole school awareness.
- **Access and choice** – almost inevitably limited by physical layout, furniture, particular aids or other resources (over and above basic facilities – e.g. ramps and toilets).
- **Fatigue** – the 'cost index' (Gage, 1987) has both intellectual and emotional components, in addition to the physical component which contributes to tiredness.
- **Space** – for special equipment and adaptations as well as for their storage and maintenance. Classrooms overcrowded already leave little space for wheelchairs and equipment.
- **Aims and targets** – many of these are not necessarily related to the needs of individual children and therefore require considerable adaptation and development.
- **Dignity and privacy** – the facilities and layout but mostly attitudes in schools and colleges sometimes compromise these.
- **Testing and assessment difficulties** – most obviously apparent when physical skills are needed to produce a 'testable' response (ranging from written to spoken or movement and dexterity).

Implementing the national curriculum, since 1990, has given many headaches and heartaches associated with the considerable tensions between unreal and unnecessary curriculum requirements and physical or individual needs. At the same time, teachers have also talked about the opportunities that investment in a 'broad and balanced' curriculum for all can bring.

- **Entitlement** as a concept has given pupils who are physically disabled the same educational rights and opportunities as their non-disabled peers.
- **The whole child** is involved, not specifically identified parts. This gives opportunity to enjoy activity rather than 'slog away' at limited skills all the time.

- **Positive expectation** is necessary if pupils who are disabled are going to be included in school life and curricular experience. This comes from training, knowledge, experience and confidence.
- **Openness and collaboration** is needed in planning both purposeful and meaningful activities for pupils who are disabled. Often across professional boundaries.
- The **starting point for planning**, within the curriculum entitlement, is the individual ability of the pupil or student (expressed in an Individual Education Plan).
- **Spontaneity and flexibility** within a structured approach allows for diverse needs and abilities to be included.

This positive view must be qualified by pointing to the many factors already outlined that currently militate against pupils and students who are disabled or have medical conditions. 'Access' and 'entitlement' are the 'book-ends' that push together the ethical and policy statements with the practical activities in a school or college. (See figure 5.3).

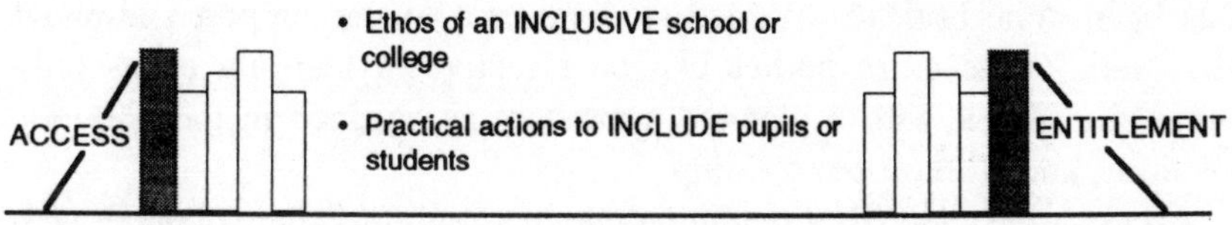

Figure 5.3

In an inclusive school, that generates inclusive policies for all pupils and students with special educational needs (SEN), affirmative and appropriate practical activities will ensue. However, a considerable part of the problem, and one that impacts on disabled youngsters, is limited and uncreative interpretation of national curriculum requirements. In short, sticking to the 'letter of the law' and ignoring the 'spirit of the law'.

> Teachers point out that, for all pupils with special educational needs and pupils who are exceptionally able, the national curriculum provides only part of the curriculum. Access to developmental work across the curriculum, personal and social education and enrichment activities in particular, should be given equal status with access to national curriculum subjects and religious education. It is a question of getting the balance or the context right.
>
> NCC, 1993

Teachers must be allowed and encouraged to interpret the national curriculum more creatively and more liberally. This means a reduction in the 'hard-nose' percentages approach (allocating all time to subject-based work, teaching to SATs, enlarging cross-curricular and topical themes, attending to more fundamental areas such as motivation and communication). It also means reducing the bureaucracy of accountability that seems to hang over schools and colleges like a 'sword of Damocles'.

The proper way to improve the quality of education *for all* is through professional development programmes, professional autonomy and a much less detailed and mechanistic 'accounting' system. I use the word 'accounting' because the mechanical or technically detailed system of testing could well have been drawn up by a group of overworked accountants who thought they were assessing the quantity and quality of sausages produced from a sausage factory. Much of the subtlety, the nuances, the human element, the creativity and the spontaneity of learning has been lost over the past ten years. Most important though, is the effect this has had on enabling teachers to provide for flexibility in the classroom to include disabled pupils and students. One way this problem has been attended to is to throw more bodies at it in the shape of welfare or learning assistance. This is not a solution in itself and a great injustice has been done both to disabled students and to the support personnel involved. These extra bodies can be effective in learning terms only when they work with a planned approach, as outlined in the previous sections, and with proper training.

Access to the national curriculum is part of a total curriculum of pupils with special educational needs but other elements across the curriculum remain essential. Pupils demonstrate achievement inside and beyond the national curriculum: all these achievements should be recognised (NCC, 1993).

General

- complete physical access to social and educational facilities
- time management – length of day, movement time, therapy and timetabling issues
- personal physical needs (e.g. seating, posture, positioning and comfort)
- therapy and medical needs (including diagnosis) translated into learning approaches
- change management – attitudes, training and organisational changes

Perceptual

- identification and staff awareness of range of difficulties encountered in 'modes of presentation'
- organised school environment that does not cause additional confusion
- appropriately presented work – planned with colleagues and specialist knowledge
- additional adult support where necessary and small group work

- additional help with specific difficulties (e.g. epilepsy, visual or hearing impairments)

Emotional and behavioural

- atmosphere and facilities preserve dignity, responsibility and self-help
- awareness of emotional needs through relationships with – peers
  – staff
- 'named person' the student can go to for advice or feedback
- consistency in approaches to immature behaviour (e.g. attention seeking)
- sensitivity to family and supportive relationships (natural support systems)

Personal and social

- enhancing self-esteem (choices, responsibility, positive feedback)
- creating social interaction and friendships within school or college
- social skills to engage help, express needs and fulfil wants
- communication of affirmative attitudes and to make relationships
- adult relationships with helpers not dependent or child-like

Learning

- whole staff awareness of student's possible learning needs/abilities (e.g. attention, gaps in experience, need for sensory experience)
- a realistic, usable and effective 'Individualised Education Plan'
- involvement and responsibility for self-assessment or evaluation of learning

Curricular

- due care and attention to access (transport, safety, field trips, technology and communication needs)
- differentiation through careful planning by creative experienced staff
- continuity, progression and relevance to the individual
- broad and balanced experiences creating opportunity
- practicalities of some subject areas (e.g. technology)

Parents and community

- ongoing support – recognition of the importance of the natural support networks
- general level of awareness of disability – parents as experts informing professionals
- attitudes to disabled people and equal opportunities or civil rights
- particular (extra) burden on parents generated by society's or professionals' negative attitudes

Some of the above factors will be in common with other special needs and some in common with all pupils and effective educational planning. Nevertheless, they could act as an initial checklist from which teachers, special needs coordinators and others might select particular priorities for any given individual. Let us, as an example, consider one area in greater detail, that of 'personal physical needs' (above). Michael Davies (Senior Educational Psychologist, 1992) has this to say about the importance of personal physical needs in relation to teaching and learning:

> A child concentrating on maintaining balance is not a child that is attending fully to the lesson in hand. The child whose head is forever on the move is not a child who can visually fixate on important features in the teaching. A child who cannot maintain a symmetrical position and keep their head in alignment will not be able to adequately attend to the teaching and furthermore an asymmetric sitting position needs to be corrected and correct posture encouraged and maintained. A child who finds it difficult to reach and grasp target objects is not a child who will continue to try unless their efforts are facilitated and they are helped to succeed. If the child is having to expend a great deal of energy maintaining physical control and not achieving much success then the capacity left for learning and the motivation to achieve are somewhat reduced.
>
> Correct posture is crucial to a child's development . . . Bad posture means poor learning opportunity.
>
> (Davies, 1992)

Thus individualised planning would also specify the conditions necessary to attain maximum comfort and enable the child to attend to and become responsible for his/her learning. It is to be hoped that, by the time secondary education has been reached, suitable seating and adaptations have been found. However, conditions change as a person grows and it is necessary to be ever vigilant regarding posture, comfort and the position that a child adopts. As the pupil grows, he/she may well be able to take more and more responsibility for ensuring that they maximise their own learning opportunities. This could also be part of an individualised plan.

Individualised education programmes – a balancing act?

- Ensure that statemented pupils receive their entitlement to a broad, balanced and differentiated curriculum.
- To demonstrate that a school is meeting its statutory obligations to a statemented child.
- The above principle can be extended to all pupils with SEN, including those termed 'talented and gifted'.

(Adapted from Butt and Scott, 1994)

First of all they should be called 'Individualised' . . . not 'Individual . . .'.

Individualisation is not the same thing as an 'Individual Curriculum or Programme'. Although this may seem semantic it is important to understand and clarify the difference between individualised curricular activities and an individual curriculum that separates and marginalises. Therefore the IEP is definitely not a completely separate programme from that which other pupils will follow. It needs to show specific information and guidance about how the normal set of learning experiences, curricular activities and teaching methods are differentiated or adapted to allow the pupil access to the curriculum generally. For example, a pupil may have a difficulty where writing is a particular but substantial problem. Rather than lengthy assessments of so called 'writing skills', and a special programme of writing activities, the IEP should simply indicate that the pupil uses a word processor or alternative means of producing written work. He or she may need more time for creative writing and for producing response to homework, worksheets or other tasks.

Each school or college will develop its own particular framework for individualised or small group educational planning. It is not the intention of the book to hand out specimen pro forma, a tendency all too common these days as those outside schools, colleges and classroom attempt to prescribe what form this planning should take, (and hence limit the creative process).

Planning for learning in upper secondary and college environments

Much, if not all, of the previous sections on assessment, differentiation and additional needs of students who are disabled is applicable to post-compulsory education. There are certain considerations, mostly to do with *transitions* (from school to college, adolescence to adulthood – see Chapter 4). Programmes for all students need to be planned with long term outcomes and aims in mind. This is also true of students who are physically disabled. Their aims for adulthood will have similar characteristics (e.g. responsibility, financial independence, family, accountability, employment). Individual pupils who are physically disabled, whilst having similar aspirations in principle to anyone else, will have particular requirements with respect to certain aspects of, say, skill development, communication, the environment and the transition to adulthood. This transition provides the theme for some of Aileen Webber's set of course materials (Webber, 1991) in which aspects of the preparation and transition from adolescence to adulthood are well dealt with in practical and teaching terms.

Being in control and exercising choice will include:

- **Personal care**: to develop his/her potential for independence in personal care and domestic needs.
- **Mobility**: to develop the student's capacity for independent mobility.
- **Education**: in addition to basic numeracy and literacy to cope with the demands of living in modern society. To extend his/her knowledge and interests through providing genuine curricular and subject choices.
- **Recreation**: to develop social and leisure interests already established and to find new ones. Friendships and partnerships.
- **Personal development**: to enhance self-esteem and a sense of personal achievement in order to enjoy a significant and rewarding lifestyle.
- **Work**: to develop the student's potential for employment and productivity.

Planning for learning and including students who are physically disabled in upper secondary and college environments involves some broad areas for consideration:

- What are the benefits and problems associated with (multi-disciplinary?) partnership between your college and associated local services ?
- What professionals and services are involved locally ?
- How are the students involved in the process of education and learning ?

Many colleges now have a policy relating to the concerns of pupils with special educational/training needs. The extent to which these policies are implemented and the familiarity of staff with their contents varies considerably. Consider the following areas for possible attention:

- What is the college's specific policy relating to provision for students who are disabled or have special education/training needs?
- Does the college have a policy on 'Equal Opportunities'?
- Is there a specific/named person who has responsibility for ensuring that the special needs and/or equal opportunities policies are implemented?
  - What is their position/status?
  - How would you contact or communicate with them?
- What are the key *procedures* which f*acilitate full participation* by students who are physically disabled (for example, access, admission procedures, enrolment, teaching methods)?
- Are there any procedures or aspects of life in the college which you feel *inhibit full participation* by students who are physically disabled?
- What kind of learning support services or multi-agency co-operation exist alongside your teaching/lecturing role? How does this work?

Choice, opportunity and learning into the millennium

> The view we take of the future and of our ability and willingness to shape and change it is inevitably private and personal as well as professional and political in its widest sense. Nor is it easy to think about the future when the pressures of today and the demands of tomorrow seem overwhelming.
>
> (Mittler, 1992)

The way in which the national curriculum was hurriedly imposed was an act of intellectual, academic and social piracy which has sought to define, in a narrow way, what education is about. The educational agenda has been hijacked by politicians. It has occupied educationists, teachers, schools and local authorities to the extent that the underlying issues of the long term (and historic) perspective of including pupils who are physically disabled has been put on the back burner. Indeed, the issue of including all pupils with special educational needs or disabilities has been set back on many fronts (Mittler, 1992; Vaughan, 1992; Barnes, 1991; Rieser and Mason, 1992; Swann, 1992). Physically disabled pupils have been the first group of pupils to be significantly integrated into mainstream education (Moses, Hegarty and Jowett, 1988). This was partly on the misconception that all that was needed was welfare assistance and some physical or building changes.

Summary of the points in this chapter

'Proximal zones and scaffolding' – support into the curriculum:

- A 'broad, balanced and differentiated curriculum' (Mittler, 1992) is desirable, as is 'entitlement for all'. It is teachers' skills, training and professionalism that will make this possible, not a system of bureaucratic accountability.
- Home-school or college link for all pupils that makes the school or college part of its local community is important. The school as a community, not a separated or academic institution heralds a more cohesive society of the future.
- Real and active partnership with parents, making changes together and planning to maximise learning, particularly at an early age. Parents have expertise.
- The particular need for pupils and students (and their families) to deal with statutory agencies as a whole and not as individual services (LEA, SD and Health or Paramedic Services) which fragment people into professional chunks.
- Inclusion (not integration) of all pupils and students with physical disability or medical conditions into the mainstream of education in practice, rather than ideology.

- Developing the concept of 'individual abilities' to supersede the Code of Practice categories and even the concept of 'special educational needs'.
- Repairing the damage done by the imposition of the national curriculum without any regard for pupils with disabilities whose access to curriculum, school life and learning experience (rather than ATs) is vital.
- Take up the torch of integrated learning (through cross-curricular work) and of personal and social developments through which the inclusion of pupils who are physically disabled can be made a reality.
- Examine in greater detail the personal and social effects of LMS, LMSS and the new funding councils on allocation of resources for pupils who are disabled. The effect that identification of resource needs (through the statement of educational needs) and evaluation of school performance and popularity has on attitudes and provision for disabled pupils.
- Turn around the obsession with 'standardising' attainment (including the worrying trend back to paper and pencil tests) and move the agenda back onto evidence of a range of achievements and programmes of study that will reflect more diverse abilities.
- Restore the professional integrity of teachers (who have been deskilled by prescriptive attainment targets and SATs) and allow them to exercise judgment, develop their skills and understanding of the individual needs of their pupils with disabilities through restoring teacher assessment to its proper place. Don't drag FE and HE into this prescriptive 'stew'.
- Build on the positive aspects of the 'Code of Practice' which focus observation on the broad and additional needs of pupils who are physically disabled, through 'Individual Education Plans'.
- Remove the threat that open competition between mainstream schools and local colleges or national universities places on pupils and students who are differently able and will not necessarily be perceived as academically successful.
- Build on the positive work that has been done on developing whole school or college approaches (to cater for pupils with disabilities) and their effect in fostering a more co-operative, communicative and encouraging learning environment for all pupils.
- Our schools' and colleges' ethos today plays an important part in shaping the communities of the future. The preoccupation with narrow academic attainment will further marginalise pupils who are disabled. Education is not about passing tests but about becoming a rounded, participating and thinking member of the community.

The terms 'zone of proximal development' and 'scaffolding' (after Vygotsky, 1962) broadly describe the process of enabling access to the curriculum through differentiation and appropriate support. The Code of Practice (1993 Education Act) provides an opportunity to broaden the 'zones' in which educationists work and may heighten the chances of including pupils who are disabled. It could also improve the learning environment for all pupils. The choice is ours. Is it to be an exclusive and competitive system, promoted by selectivity and limited prescription of priorities leading to marginalisation and segregation? Or can we develop an education system that includes and supports diversity, creating a more cohesive society where everyone's abilities are valued?

Learning opportunity and empowerment through the curriculum

Body Language
by Simon Brisenden

my gesturing for words
becomes a stutter

my touching at the sky of faces
is but a whisper

my moving through the halls of eyes
has no grammar

my writing on the streets of motion
has no reader

my dancing on the mirror of colours
is so deliberate

my body has a language with no alphabet

Tackling issues of disability, equality and opportunity does not have to be restricted to the usual personal and social education (PSE) domain. Creative use of all parts of the curriculum in schools and colleges can provide the opportunity to look at within-school, community and national issues, without marginalising disabled students or placing them in an uncomfortable spotlight. Once disability is seen as an integral part of all aspects of life and living, a whole range of possibilities and opportunities become available to the teacher or lecturer.

Primary topic work

This can include many aspects of life:

- **Personal, Social and Health Education**
  Sport – variety of sporting events, including alternative Olympics, and

sport that allows diversity of physical ability. Schooling – learning support, integrated schooling, special schools.

- **Religious Studies** if discussing equal rights/opportunities, respect for each person, healing. People who are disabled are a contributing part of the community.
- **English** for speaking and listening work, e.g. taking part in discussions, for written work, e.g. writing letters, articles, poems, speeches for a discussion. Communication (as part of language), for example: lip speaking, sign language, finger spelling, braille, moon alphabets, large print books, speech impairments (does not mean unintelligent – need time), telephone adaptations, minicoms etc., sub-titling on TV, signed meetings, theatre performances, audio description of films and theatre performances, signs and public address systems, information leaflets needed in large print, braille, etc.
- **Science** particularly when the body is being discussed.
  My body – when studying movement, hearing, sight, etc., then consider disability as well.
  Transport – wheelchair users and buses, trains, tubes. Visually impaired people and the transport system. Disabled people and flying.
- **Technology** particularly when using activities related to problems of access as a stimulus for design. The environment, including the home – adapted homes, ramps/lifts not stairs, wide doors and parking spaces, bleeping crossing and different pavement surfaces, braille or raised letters on notices/instructions, items that may help people with disabilities.

Secondary and further education curricular activities

Again, these is plenty of scope for curricular activity and content. These could be a normal part of learning and discussion. An opportunity to raise awareness and change attitudes. Any subject can include reference to the work and contribution of disabled people. This would include mention of individuals in a variety of areas to ensure that the school is able to select instances which match the curriculum offered.

- **Home Economics**
  GCSE in Child Development – topic areas on 'mental handicap' and 'physical handicap'.
- **General Studies**
  Vocational Care courses, e.g. GNVQ in Health and Social Care and A Level Home Economics – sections on community care and disability. Youth and Community wings/departments – where used to prepare

young people for community service work and to help integration.

- **Personal and Social Education**
  Prejudice leading to discrimination, e.g. for jobs. Disability equality in the curriculum – secondary programme: definitions of disability – the social and individual models compared, images of disability – the role of the media and charity, disability in the framework of equality of opportunity and oppression, the language of disability, recognising barriers – structures, procedures and practice, attitudes, independence and choice for people who are disabled. Opportunity to reach potential. Everyone has different talents and abilities, we just need to find them. Education best suited to needs, whether integrated or segregated. Learning support. Work/employment – the right to work, contribute to society, pay taxes so not need allowances. Law about employment of per cent of disabled people, grants available to adapt equipment etc. at work place. Rights – the right to allowances that allow independence in work, travel, etc. Charity – are disabled people viewed as objects of charity? Do disabled people have a say in the affairs of disability charities? Is the Government relying on charities to find money for help, care, etc. Access – to places and to information. Transport – on trains, buses, tubes, plane. Communication – lip reading, sign language. Speech difficulty does not mean lack of ability. Marriage – should disabled people marry? Having children – should disabled people have children? Housing – adapted, sheltered housing.
- **Home Economics and Science**
  Child Development courses – physical and mental disability. Cooker – adapted kitchens. Vocational caring courses, e.g. GNVQ Health and Social Care – topic of disability. More detailed work on body mechanics, health, fitness, the human condition. Emphasis on diversity and variety (natural biological variety) in nature.
- **Technology and Design**
  Designing items and equipment that help people with disabilities. The disabling school, access surveys, design briefs related to access or adaptations, the role of technology in improving access, environmental controls, etc.
- **PE**
  Inclusive activities.
- **Cross-curricular Themes**
  Civil rights, models of education, environmental design.
- **English**
  The importance of the media in determining the image of disability, the relationship between concepts and language.

The body musical
by Simon Brisenden

I've got a piano in my head
and an orchestra in my heart
I've got a singer in my feet
and a guitar in my private parts

I've got a piano and a violin
in the cabaret behind my ears
and a pair of sequined lovers dance
in the ballroom of my thighs
when I die
I'm going to donate my body
to music

Colleges of Further Education

- Health and Community Studies departments
  e.g. in GNVQ levels 2 and 3 Health and Social care, NNEB courses, Family and Community Care courses (City and Guilds), Nursing courses, Learning Support Certificate (City and Guilds).

Colleges of Higher Education

- Medical Colleges, Nursing courses, Therapy courses, Social Studies
  For disability awareness issues, changing attitudes.
- Education departments
  Postgraduate Certificate of Education, BEd courses (City and Guilds), Certificate in Continuing Professional Development (Special Needs).

The challenge for schools and colleges

A great deal of this book so far has been committed to the theme of provision for disabled children and young people to be seen as 'holistic', environmental or ecological. The consequence of this is that it is not solely concerned with schools and colleges as lone 'institutions' or teachers and lecturers as having sole responsibility. They key to effective development lies in community, in partnership and in recognising everybody's worth.

The school curriculum can be used to deal with what are currently difficult issues but, in doing so, develop a recognition of the importance of the richness of *natural variety*. The opportunity for learning about our own beliefs and about our fellow citizens is never ending.

Cruelty without beauty
by Simon Brisenden

you can have your body re-designed
to suit the ghetto in your mind
and the menu is obscene
it's devoid of all protein
in the spoons catch a reflection
of your magnificent malnutrition
it's the only place for dinner
where you end up getting thinner

the service is by men
with a camera and a pen
they give everyone a label
as they lead them to their table

Everybody that is alive grows and learns, without exception. This fact alone should be enough to give some momentum to teachers at all levels, and cause schools and colleges to take seriously the matter of including pupils and students who are physically or more severely disabled. We have looked at some brief examples of a rich, diverse and stimulating approach to the curriculum and to making this curriculum accessible to pupils and students who are disabled.

CHAPTER 6

Making Partnership a Reality

What partnerships?

It is a bit of a truism to say that partnerships are involved in the education of children and young people who are disabled. It is also true that the more people involved, the more difficult they are to manage and the more unwieldy the process can become.

It is sometimes surprising how many professionals and agencies can become involved with children who are physically or movement disabled or who have specific medical conditions. It is a complex and often fragmented process. A child whose profound and complex difficulties may require advice and intervention from as many as ten professionals at any one time, will be subjected to diverse training backgrounds and to differing management and professional structures. It is no surprise that, from the child's point of view, the delivery of education and therapy programmes, even within the national curriculum, are fragmented and sometimes deliberately divided. One constantly recurring issue is the competing demands of physical programmes as against academic or cognitive work. This will never be reconciled whilst teaching exists within a structure which inherently divides the child up into service or subject areas, each competing for the child's time. The quality of life and learning for children with physical disabilities or medical conditions, therefore, is directly related to the quality of teamwork and partnership that surrounds them. This chapter considers the processes of partnership, their reality in relation to children and young people who are physically disabled and the ways that positive examples can overcome some of the barriers to collaboration and growth.

There is no doubt that there are great problems facing professionals in this country who need, and more often than not, want to work together in a positive, collaborative manner. There is still a lack of understanding of, and ability to realise, effective teamwork and partnerships. Where there are positive intentions, the mechanisms, structures and management systems are still lagging behind. There are three main problem areas:

- attitudes and professional encampments or roles and lack of attention to client's/patient's own perceptions;

- organisational factors and managerial practices that have become established, even entrenched;
- lack of interpersonal skills required to enable the positive development of relationships.

The fact that the requisite skills are very under-developed is not surprising. Previous (and following) discussion outlined the mechanistic and extensive demands on teachers as 'curriculum deliverers'. Within the current education framework it is squeezing out the all important relationships between teacher and pupil. In addition, the medical ethic applied to both social and education services (even used as definitions of disability in the Children Act – Chapter 1) has reduced the importance of an equal partnership between professional and client or patient and hence the chances of successful partnership.

The formation of proper and efficacious partnerships requires ongoing and consistent hard work to maintain. The complexity of our systems for delivery

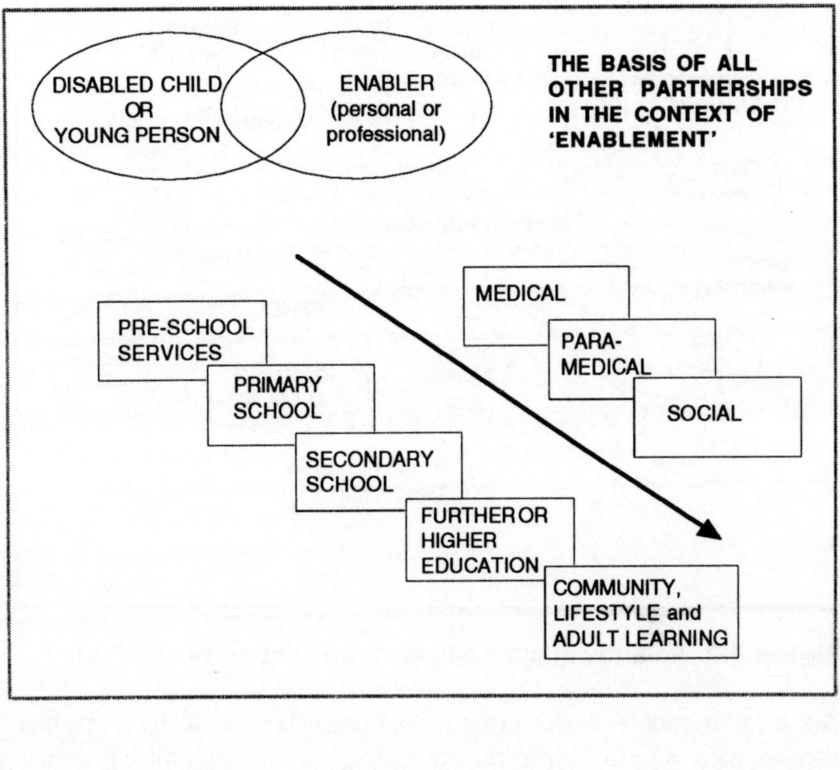

Figure 6.1 Progress through the Education system into Adulthood

of services to children and young people who are physically disabled is such that some fairly radical change of procedure, practice and attitude is necessary. New concepts of 'networking' and advances in technology (e.g. TV conferencing or virtual reality) may provide opportunities to make partnerships more real and meaningful to the one person for whom they exist. Just like everyone else, disabled children and young adults have a right to social, personal and friendship partnerships and these relate directly to the whole process of educational and social enablement.

It is a sad indictment of our education and culture that many disabled children go through our education system having more partnerships with paid professionals or volunteers than with friends or even family. The disabling effects of our culture still militate against young disabled people having a range of opportunities to socialise and make friends.

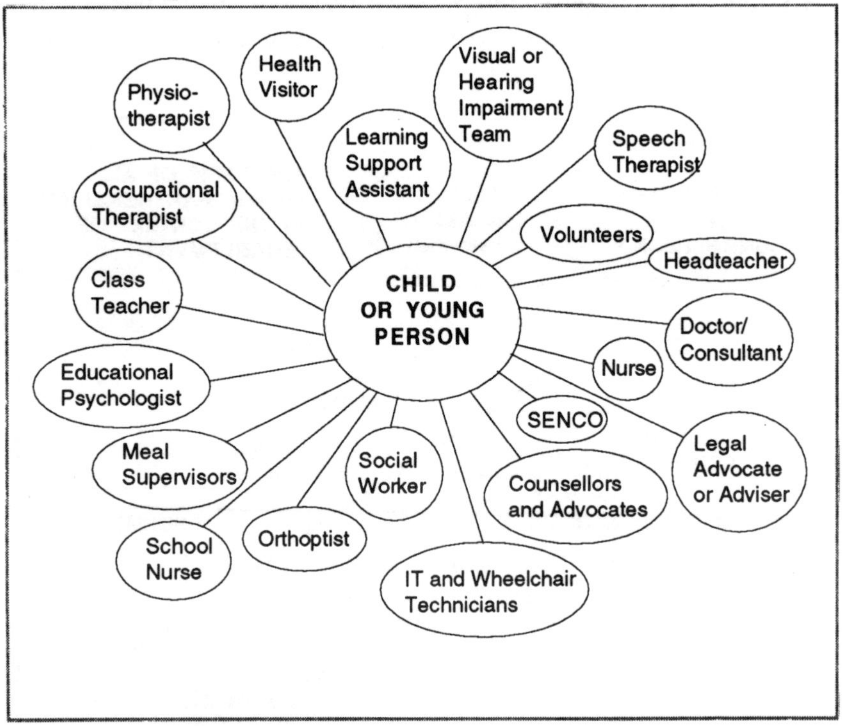

Figure 6.2 An array of people paid to provides services or help

An array of people shown in figure 6.2 consists specifically of people who are paid to be in the presence of a disabled youngster in an enabling capacity. They will each have differing perceptions of the person at the centre, of his or her abilities or needs and of the ways in which that person could be helped. Above all, each of the professionals will have their own training, jargon and agenda that they will bring to the child or young person. This can be a very confusing soup. If, as often happens, each professional or helper wants to 'prescribe' or insists on imposing their own solutions to the problem, we have a recipe for conflict, chaos and, ultimately, a fragmented and frustrating set of experiences for the child or young person. Contrary to a popular, or perhaps, naive view, that all these professionals are working together, the reality is that images of a unified process are highly contrived and superficial. Each of the professionals has their own views and is constrained by the limits and definitions of the services to which they belong. The child (and parents) or young person at the centre must be able to maintain or develop control of this complex set up for it to have any meaning.

There is, of course, another group of people who form partnerships at various levels, (figure 6.3).

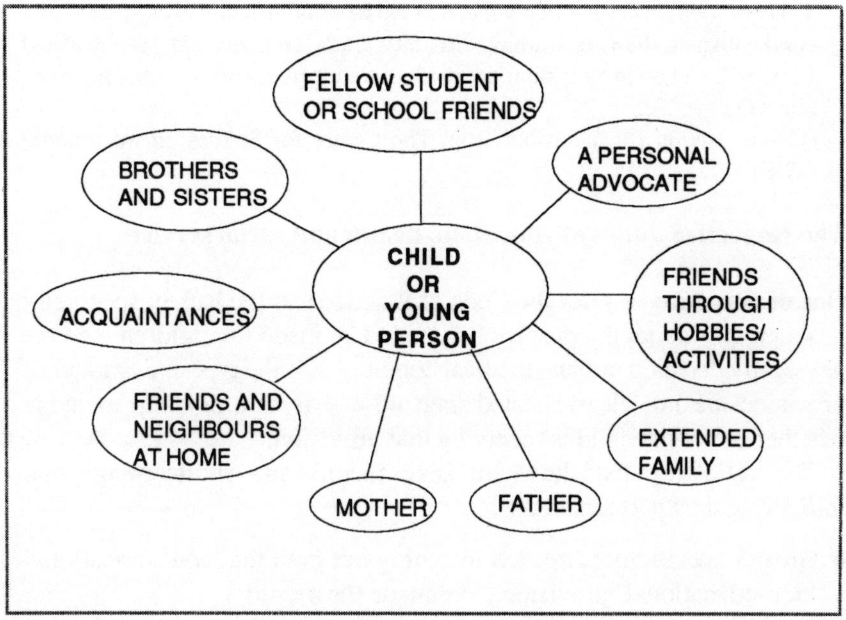

Figure 6.3 The Natural Partnership System

This natural partnership and support system is not seen as such a potent force in the education and development of the young person. In most cases a child can spend around 15,000 hours (Rutter et al, 1982) in their school career. This leaves around 28,800 hours that he or she could spend with carers, family and friends before attending school. It also leaves 96,360 hours that a person spends with family, friends and carers during their school career. This points to the natural support systems having a very substantial effect in shaping the life and learning of a young person.

> **What is your dream for Carla?**
>
> Parents of children with disabilities often have not had the opportunity to think about what they want most for their children. This question restores their ability to have a vision based on what they really want for their child, rather than what they think they can get. Sometimes this is the first time professionals have had the opportunity to hear what parents hold in their hearts and minds for their children's future. Carla's parents said they dreamed Carla would be able to go to high school with her brothers, to get a job, and one day to live with some friends in the community.
>
> **What is your nightmare?**
>
> This question makes explicit what is in the heart of virtually every parent of a child with a disability or learning difficulty. Carla's parents said, 'We're afraid Carla will end up in an institution, work in a sheltered workshop and have no-one when we die.'
> (From: 'Action for inclusion' from The Centre for Studies on Integration, CSIE).

The respective duties of education, health and social services

One of the concerns prior the Code of Practice was the lack of specificity in statements about the provision that is to be made for children who are physically disabled or have medical conditions. If the type and amount of provision are not clearly stated then no-one is in a position to judge whether or not the child is receiving that provision.

The following list shows divisive factors and shortcomings that militate against partnership:

- Greater specificity is needed in setting out both the 'educational' and 'non-educational' provision to be made for a child.
- A clear basis for deciding what constitutes educational and what constitutes non-educational needs and provision is needed. There are currently many children awaiting speech therapy provision because health and education are each hoping that the other will provide. It remains to be seen whether the new Code of Practice will have an impact on this situation.

- There should be a duty on health and social services to assist education in making the provision specified in the statement. This duty is equivalent to the duty on health and education to assist social services in meeting their duties under the Children Act, and would help considerably in promoting a more co-ordinated approach to meeting children's needs. The Code of Practice makes this clear but there is no statutory obligation. The reality of the situation is that the three statutory services are still required (by market forces) to look inward first and resource themselves on a competitive, rather than a co-operative basis. There are some notable exceptions to this situation.

Levels of partnership

Level 1: A disabled child or young person and their immediate enabler(s) – shown in the arrays of people paid to enable and the natural support partnerships.

Level 2: In-school or college partnerships between governors, professionals and between professionals and parents.

Level 3: Partnerships between the school or college and other statutory and community services (e.g. in the transition into adulthood towards less specialised generally available services).

The **level 1 partnerships** have been illustrated by the previous arrays of people paid to enable and by the natural partnership system. These involve the growth and sustenance of immediate relationships, both personal and professional. Ideally, in the nature of growth into adulthood, there is a progression from degrees of dependence in childhood to increasing autonomy and choice in adulthood.

> The disabled individual's mobility is mediated by others. This affects the learning process, a large component of which is exploratory or active.
>
> The desire for independence is constantly frustrated, and there are inevitable strains . . .
>
> (Prosser, 1992)

It is these partnerships that will provide continuity and progression for a child to the young adult. Herein lies the problem for a young person who may have grown up experiencing a predominance of professionally oriented relationships and whose natural support systems may have become subservient to professional intervention or negative social attitudes to their disability.

Stereotyping makes it difficult to form equal partnerships:

- Disabled people can't interact socially ('Does he take sugar?').
- We have to be cheerful.
- Negative aversive attitudes (Noonan et al, 1970), related to personality of non-disabled person (e.g. authoritarianism, ego, strength and body concern).

(Adapted from Prosser, 1992)

The greater the impairment, the greater the level of paid intervention and the greater is the potential fragmentation of personal development. Taking on this paradox requires an appropriate level of personal enablement without the direct intervention of an array of paid or professional enablers.

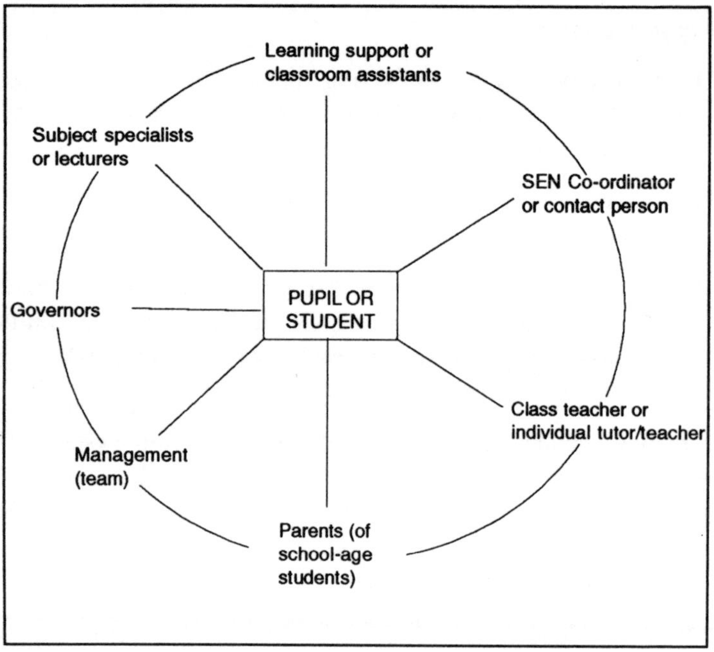

Figure 6.4 In-School or College Educational Partnerships

At level 2, on entering full-time education, the young disabled person will experience a whole range of new relationships. These often involve tensions between the individual needs of the pupil or student (more likely to be recognised by those on the right of the diagram, figure 6.4) and the overall school, college and subject requirements (more likely to be promoted by those on the left of the diagram). The quality (continuity, accessibility, entitlement, expectation) of education experienced by a young person is directly related to the quality of the in-school partnerships that are formed and sustained.

It is at level 3 where the inherent complexity of the support systems and their relationships can lead to a reduction of choice and opportunity for the individual.

At this point the child or young person becomes more dependent upon the quality of the partnerships between his or her school and the wider community (including external services). Decisions can be taken for the individual that relate to the availability of the community services and the school's ability to access them. A disabled young person may be attending a school away from his or her own local community (a 'designated' secondary or special school/unit). Again, many of the natural support systems that would provide alternative links to community services, or even alternative possibilities, may have been compromised. In a sense, a young person who is disabled can be channelled towards a lifestyle dictated more by the needs and objectives of the services than his or her own aspirations and needs. There are specific consequences to this. For example, the lack of provision and take up in adult physiotherapy services. The increasingly negative view of physiotherapy (Jones, 1992) amongst disabled teenagers is explained by lack of understanding and full participation by the individual at a younger age, followed by the interference with schooling and social life during the teenage years.

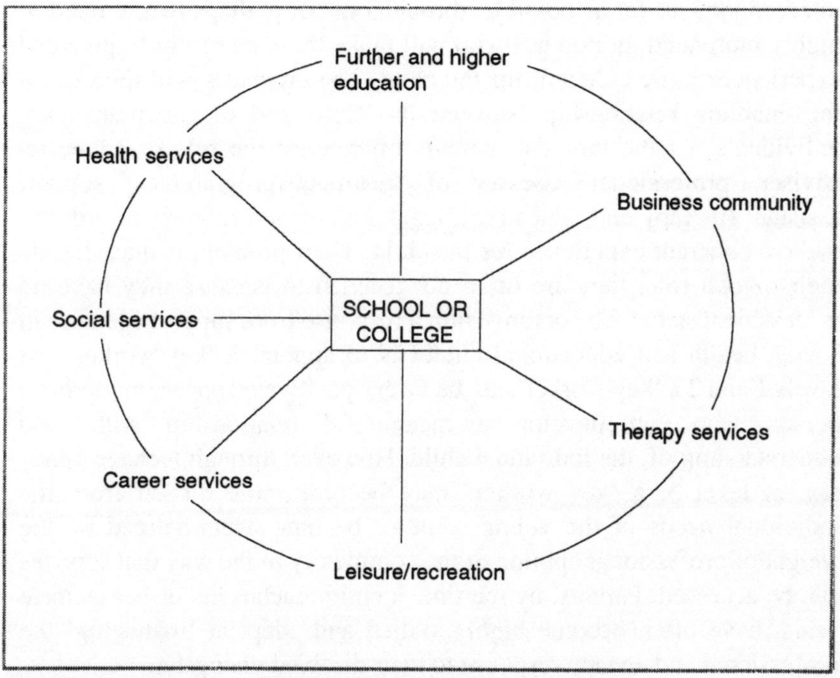

Figure 6.5 Partnerships between School/College/Learning support and wider community

During time in school and college there has been an increasing trend to deliver health, teaching and therapy programmes, particularly in the primary years, as a single, integrated process, through the auspices of either the classroom (or learning support assistant) or class teacher. The unification of these approaches acknowledges the importance of the whole person and makes it more of a *learning experience*. It is extremely important that choice, control and relevance to daily life and immediate needs is preserved. Otherwise the system continues to do things *to* the disabled pupil with little personal involvement and reduced long-term gains. Even very young children face continual direct interventions from a battery of medical, health, psychological, social, and finally educational professionals. Often, the greater the impairment the more daunting is this battery. This can be detrimental to the personal and social development of the disabled youngster, decreasing choice, control and opportunity and hampering growth into autonomous adulthood. Disabled children are often plunged into a world of adult and professional relationships, with all their 'baggage' of social and professional expectations. Children who are not disabled are protected from this kind of hurly-burly, being allowed more space to grow as individuals.

One way of dealing with this problem would be to channel all interventions, as far as possible, through one, or perhaps two, trained or highly motivated individuals who will make these currently fragmented experiences more coherent for the child. The emphasis will then be on the enabling relationship between the child and one, perhaps two, individuals. At the moment, parents often fulfil the role of advocate, adviser, professional assessor of treatments/programmes, support assistant (therapy and education), legal adviser and teacher, in order to make a coherent experience for the child. Their problem is that, despite their pivotal role, they are often not listened to because they have no professional status. The organisational response from support agencies in social, health and educational circles is to appoint a 'key worker'. At levels 1 and 2 a 'key worker' can be a very positive response, involving a person who can develop a meaningful relationship with, and understanding of, the individual child. However, through teenage years, say, at level 3, a 'key worker' may become more distant from the individual needs of the young adult or become overwhelmed by the weight of professional opinion or the complexity of the way that services can be accessed. Parents, by the time a child reaches his or her teenage years, have often become highly skilled and adept at 'managing' the professional and agency response to their disabled youngster.

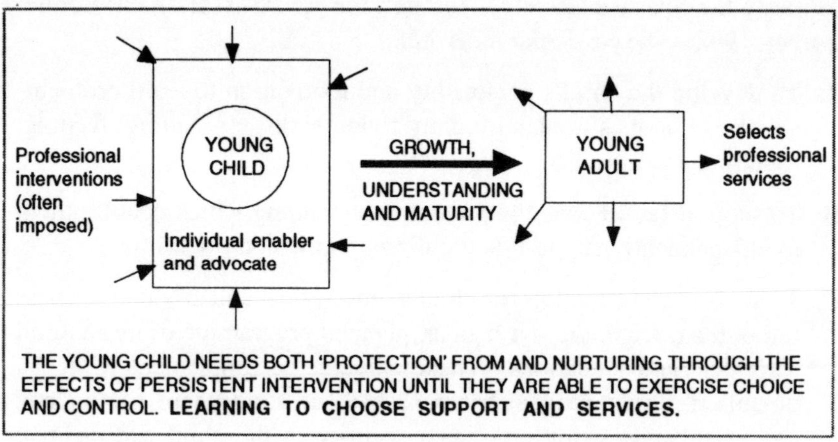
Professional
interventions
(often
imposed)
YOUNG
CHILD
Individual enabler
and advocate
GROWTH,
UNDERSTANDING
AND MATURITY
YOUNG
ADULT
Selects
professional
services
THE YOUNG CHILD NEEDS BOTH 'PROTECTION' FROM AND NURTURING THROUGH THE EFFECTS OF PERSISTENT INTERVENTION UNTIL THEY ARE ABLE TO EXERCISE CHOICE AND CONTROL. LEARNING TO CHOOSE SUPPORT AND SERVICES.

Figure 6.6 Learning to choose support and services

One way of dealing with this problem would be to channel all interventions, as far as possible, through one, or perhaps two, trained or highly motivated individuals who will make these currently fragmented experiences more coherent for the child. The emphasis will then be on the enabling relationship between the child and one, perhaps two, individuals. At the moment, parents often fulfil the role of advocate, adviser, professional assessor of treatments/ programmes, support assistant (therapy and education), legal adviser and teacher, in order to make a coherent experience for the child. Their problem is that, despite their pivotal role, they are often not listened to because they have no professional status. The organisational response from support agencies in social, health and educational circles is to appoint a 'key worker'. At levels 1 and 2 a 'key worker' can be a very positive response, involving a person who can develop a meaningful relationship with, and understanding of, the individual child. However, through teenage years, say, at level 3, a 'key worker' may become more distant from the individual needs of the young adult or become overwhelmed by the weight of professional opinion or the complexity of the way that services can be accessed. Parents, by the time a child reaches his or her teenage years, have often become highly skilled and adept at 'managing' the professional and agency response to their disabled youngster.

An example of the interaction of personal, physical and emotional factors in gaining access to the curriculum and learning experiences is found in the *'Curricular Aims for 'Schools for Parents'*, (SCOPE –

formerly the Spastics Society – through the Acorn Assessment Centre, Barnet, 1992). The curricular aims are:

A. To develop the child's personality and motivation to learn problem-solving strategies to acquire daily living skills, e.g. sitting, feeding, toiletting and mobility.

B. To support families by the provision of training which enables them to independently support their children in the home setting.

C. To awaken and stimulate the child's senses, self- and group-awareness through participation in a regular, planned programme of meaningful activities and situations. These should be implemented in an organised, structured environment and an atmosphere of fun and enjoyment, promoting emotional security in the child and positive expectations from the parents.

D. To implement an holistic approach which 'develops the whole personality of the child, encompassing the physical, cognitive, emotional, social and 'spiritual' aspects through active learning', and thus realises the child's full potential.

E. To give each child the time and space needed to achieve its goals.

F. To provide the child and family access to a broad and balanced pre-school education leading to a future school placement which will ideally be within the local community.

The nature of partnership and growth

Children and young people who are physically disabled are not the only people whose lives can become an enjoyable adventure through the quality of partnerships. Life can become a nightmare through callous lack of consideration of this human principle. People whose choices and opportunities are reduced by the environment or community in which they live will have additional difficulty in forming productive partnerships. Many liaisons (not partnerships) will be imposed on them. There will often be a struggle to be recognised as an equal or positive force within that partnership. This is true of personal, organisational, community or educational endeavours.

> Successful schools recognise the value of a partnership which places the child at the centre and extends beyond the school itself to the Local Educational Authority, the community and central government.
>
> (National Association of Governors and Managers, NAGM, et al, 1991)

This is a dynamic, complex, interactive process that is hard to quantify but that needs full consideration at the various levels outlined by the previous section. We have seen that partnerships are key processes from the individual (one-to-one) level, through small groups or teams, up to whole organisations or schools and their communities (both within and around). Partnerships are often described at a formal level, using formal tasks and responsibilities to define their existence and meaning. To rely on these formal descriptions alone is a futile and meaningless pursuit. Formal parameters and descriptions may be necessary but the quality of outcomes and success of the process depends on the quality of personal interaction between the contributors to that partnership.

Partnership is a term that also includes the overall emotional and social growth and development of a group of two or more people. A description of the life of a group will reflect a combination of the feelings, hidden agendas and unconscious needs of individuals, and how these interact to influence the development and 'feel' of the partnership. Understanding and making sense of the quality of partnership is often enormously difficult. Yet the term 'partnership' is bandied around in educational policies (national, local and in schools or colleges). It is hard enough to understand what motivates just one individual to behave in the way she/he does. When a number of individuals are interacting the difficulty is greatly amplified. At any one moment in a group it is likely that, if a number of individuals were asked to describe what they thought was happening, each would have a different interpretation. Attempting to assess the life of a group accurately is important, because of the large influence unconscious and irrational forces have on the extent to which group tasks are successfully achieved and enabling partnerships maintained.

Perhaps the first step should be to consider some overall factors that contribute to success or can make a partnership less than an enabling experience for those involved:

- *The number of people in the partnership*. An enabling partnership may be a disabled student and his/her helper or a team of people working on making learning experiences accessible.
- *Whether members work together, know each other*. Good teamwork also depends on trust, anticipation, flexibility and commitment. These can be as important as specific skills or professional qualifications.
- *Whether members chose to join the partnership or whether they were sent*. Of course, 'choices' in reality are always relative but they do have consequences for personal agendas and an impact on the other members.

- *How long the partnership will be together.* Membership may be long-term or short-term or mixed. Acknowledgement of this will affect attitudes, roles and the contribution that each member can make.
- *The style of leadership or conditions of membership.* These will affect the balance of the partnership and the quality of participation by its members. Leadership is a dynamic, shared process.
- *Whether the environment is comfortable.* Individual members or groups within a partnership can be disabled, hampered or undermined by being placed in a 'hostile' environment (physically, socially or intellectually).
- *The personal agendas which individuals bring to the partnership.* Ideally, these should not be hidden. Successful partnership means understanding the motives, at different levels, of other members.
- *What the membership is in regard to ability, talent, gender, race, class and age.* Perceived or invented 'imbalances' in these areas will cause great tensions (e.g. 'I am more able generally than you, therefore I should control the partnership. . .').
- *What the partnership task is.* When the task in hand is defined by only one person in a partnership, the other member (or members) have to 'accept' the task. Joint success is more likely when all members of a partnership have some control of the definition of the task.

Learning about, and understanding, group life, group processes and how to form partnerships, is one of the all-important keys to changing the attitudes that marginalise, exclude and segregate disabled youngsters. My own experience and much research (recent example Maras and Brown, 1991) shows that there is much work to be done in preparing groups to accept and include children and young people who are disabled, beyond the superficial integration that can make life even more uncomfortable for a disabled youngster. This can often lead to parents and young people choosing segregated provision in living, education and leisure.

Children and adults who are disabled cannot help but become painfully aware of the potential conflicts and sometimes polarised attitudes that their very presence may herald, though not *cause*. The causes of these conflicts (for example, arguments about resources, hiding deeper problems) often stem from lack of affirmative intentions, leadership or vision and fear of outside educational and social pressures. All of these can lead to either complete physical exclusion, or locational integration but social and educational exclusion or, at minimum, marginalisation.

The importance of understanding group processes lies in their effect upon the lives of young children and young adults. Decisions are often made by groups of professionals who are not working together as a team and whose relationships could hardly be called partnership. Superficially, parents and disabled youngsters may be brought into the decision making process. In effect, they are often marginalised by group processes and professional agendas, including polarisation of opinion and conflicts between the sub-groups involved. Chapter 7 provides far more real, graphic and painful illustrations of this phenomenon from parents' viewpoints.

Much of what goes on between health, education and social services professionals, either planning or delivering programmes of intervention for children and young people who are disabled, could not be called 'teamwork'. Even co-operation is difficult when the personal agendas of the professionals are concerned. The planning and implementation of multi-disciplinary approaches, strategies and programmes are rarely undertaken by a cohesive group and guided by any form of trained or competent leadership. Many professionals, including consultants, doctors and psychologists, have had little training in managing working teams or managing groups. The assumption is that they will naturally be able to lead because of their professional expertise or area of knowledge. This is often not the case and is one factor that contributes to the ineffectiveness and inefficiency of multi-disciplinary team and multi-agency support.

In education and social services, this model is heavily weighted towards 'the task', with a heavy reliance on 'the individual' as the key. As long as 'the task' is the overwhelming element, a wealth of opportunity and creative potential to improve the quality of the service will be lost. Where whole school or college approaches, departmental teamwork and the relationship between a disabled youngster and their enabler (say, classroom assistant) have been carefully considered, there have been many and varied benefits with far reaching and long-term positive consequences.

Barriers to change, partnerships and growth

Children and young people who are disabled or have medical conditions demand an appropriate confident, open, cohesive and honest response from the various services who purport to be available to them. With the exception of pockets of effective practice up and down the country, this is simply not happening. Where collaboration, co-operation and genuine teamwork exists, and when a disabled individual is an equal part of that team, there is a noticeable, if not measurable, change in the quality of experience for all involved.

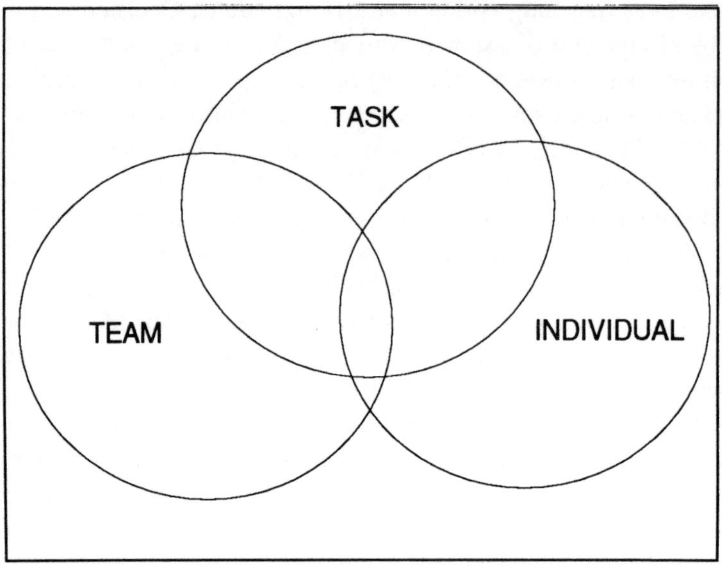

Figure 6.7 Balance between the elements is essential (from John Adair, 1986)

These barriers to change, partnerships and growth have been described earlier under three headings or levels. Let me now add more:

1. Problems associated mainly with individuals.
2. 'In-school' or 'college' problems.
3. Local and localised 'team management' problems.
4. Problems associated with 'professionalism'.
5. Management at Government, or Authority (county, district) level.

Some of the factors involved are described in the following pages and all of them can be remedied by processes involving encounter, discussion, team development, skill training and awareness raising exercises. They are not insurmountable, although to practitioners in the field they may often seem so with attendant frustrations and time wasting consequences. Many of the problems at management levels ((4) and (5)) work downwards to disrupt and destroy relationships between practitioner (e.g. teacher, physiotherapist, social worker, learning support worker) and their clients, pupils or students (the service users). Inappropriate ethics of the overall service can lead to 'hardening of the categories' (Kelly, 1955) and increased cynicism all round. Similarly, at levels (3) and (2), managerial practices and professional demands, that are not client or 'person-centred', will damage partnerships or require additional energy in maintaining them.

There are specific barriers that can be identified. These stem from my own work with multi-disciplinary training groups, Lacey and Lomas (1993), Moses, Hegarty and Jowett (1988), and others. Level 5 barriers to change and partnership are:

(5) At Government or Authority Level

- Lack of management training (or resourcing for).
- Unplanned service growth.
- Imposed changes need enablement, resources and means of evaluation.
- No ownership of common objectives.
- Confused pay and allowance structures or differentials.
- Confused or widely variable terms and conditions across disciplines.
- The inconsistencies and tensions of local management and competitive climate/financing.

Government ministers have recently sought to divorce policy making from operational matters. This removes or substantially reduces the means to alter policy according to feedback when it becomes operational. Responsibility for policy and the subsequent enactment of policy lies with those involved at all levels. The problems outlined below only exist because of deeper organisational flaws such as lack of information flow, genuine vision, long-term planning or listening to the needs of service users. Analysis of the organisational structures involved in service delivery should, at the very least, indicate some productive movement towards choice and opportunity for those who use the service.

Most of the changes in education, health and social services that have taken place over the last ten years have been imposed by legislation and then 'sold' by narrow inductive training programmes. In all this change and development, it is no wonder that disabled children and young people have to contend with the inconsistencies and frustrations of the professionals around them as well as their own communication, mobility or co-ordination difficulties. The quality of the services provided depends partly on professional endeavour, partly on the individual (or through advocates, associates) and partly on wider social attitudes that reflect themselves in government and local authority politics and policies. Level 4 barriers to change and partnership include:

(4) Problems associated with 'professionalism'

- Inability to change or challenge their specific knowledge base in relation to other disciplines.
- Professional boundaries or demarcation – job insecurity.
- Hierarchies – drones, creators and bosses.
- Professional mystique and vested interest – status across the different disciplines.

- Issues of credibility across the professions – often preserved by establishing a private knowledge base.

It is assumed that at the centre of all professionals' efforts is the pupil, student, patient or client. Unfortunately, this is not the case. When we examine 'barriers' like this, it becomes clear that in most professional endeavour much time is spent dealing with the requirements of bureaucratic accountability, (other) professional expectations, maintaining credibility amongst peers, coping with lack of resources, balancing budgets, trying to arrange communication and meetings, trying to reduce the caseload or class size, trying to understand the ramifications of the latest politico-legal impositions, and so on. For most professionals, the time and energy that they can actually expend developing personal and professional partnerships with disabled children and young people is shrinking. There needs to be enough time for proper peer consultation, co-operation and collaborative planning. If these kinds of human resource problems are not attended to, in the education system particularly, disabled youngsters will become increasingly marginalised and offered more and more fragmented and inadequate learning experiences and environments. There are a number of initiatives that put the student/client at the centre. There are also many parents up and down the country battling both in support of, and against, professional efforts in order to co-ordinate a coherent approach to their son or daughter (see Chapter 7).

There are also Level 3 barriers to change and partnership:

(3) Local or localised team management problems

- Too much in-fighting (very subtly!) – proper relationships not established.
- Does not really include the disabled person (or parent) as an equal or integral part of the effective team.
- Lack of management or leadership training.
- Status inequalities across the disciplines (e.g. doctors have tended to hog the limelight although this is changing).
- Lack of consistency and clarity in 'team membership'; the team never progress to 'getting organised' or 'mature closeness' (Francis, 1987).
- An appropriate base to work from (both physical and knowledge bases).
- Time allowed for planning and discussion.
- Inability to use individual (or creative) skills of the team effectively.
- Lack of vision or skilled, dynamic leadership (or agreed leadership) within the group.

When we get to this level of 'barriers', it becomes clear that the previous barriers (at political/social levels) are having an overall impact plus some new considerations. Creative planning that includes disabled youngsters and parents at anything other than a superficial level is not common at the moment. Level 2 barriers to be sumounted are:

(2) In-school or college problems

- Inadequate job descriptions or clarity of roles – particularly concerning learning support or classroom assistants.
- Pay/rates/allowances vary but are not always consistent with responsibility (or effort!)
- Increasing size of classes or groups militates against adequate provision for special needs.
- Physical access and facilities militate against coherent whole school approaches.
- Individual school or college teams are unaware, lack information about services, and are isolated.
- Lack of clear vision and leadership leading to confusion and fragmentation.
- Lack of whole school approach or positive affirmative policies towards physically disabled pupils and students.
- In-school hierarchies and management problems (e.g. clear organisational communication).
- Lack of *joint* training initiatives with members of other services (e.g. speech and physiotherapists).

Achieving a quality service in schools and colleges requires collective responsibility by all concerned. Or, if the institution actively decides to segregate or exclude without concern for further provision, then collective social irresponsibility. Selectivity and exclusivity in schools and colleges may last long enough to satisfy the current doyens of so called excellence but their days are numbered. The changing social climates and the enormous impact of enabling technology (see Chapter 9) will have a far greater effect on education, socialisation and learning than the invention of printing. This may become more apparent in the next decade. Modes of learning will change; schools and colleges will come to accept, and be able to provide for, a much wider diversity of ability than is currently the case. Children and young people will have the choice to remain within their own community.

Finally we come to the Level 1 barriers to change and development:

(1) Problems associated mainly with individuals

- Personal characteristics (e.g. under stress or lack of empathy).
- Living a 'nomadic existence' (Lacey and Lomas, 1993) – having no satisfactory personal, physical or ideological base.

- Insecurity – concentrating on maintaining own credibility (sometimes at the expense of others).
- Lack of training in working collaboratively.
- Lack of advisory, support or enablement skills (see later).
- Lack of assertive skills and commitment to influence change or growth.

These individual or personal barriers mostly speak for themselves. It is clear that without the hearts and minds of individuals no change or growth will stick. It is the worst nightmare of parents that their children will be taught by teachers who regard their work as 'just a job'. True professionalism involves a high degree of personal commitment and empathy. Once this is apparent and visible, the rest is a matter of education and training. It is useful and expedient, for the purpose of discussion and analysis, to separate out levels of partnership. Nevertheless, they are not as separate as this. The individual barriers to change and growth (level 1) will exist within senior management or, as we see recently, central government. Individual problems and understanding will impact on national directives and vice-versa. The stresses and strains on teachers currently is evidence of the reducing control they have had over their professional lives. This has had a major effect on the quality of partnership both adult to adult and adult to pupil or student generally.

In-school or college partnerships

Talking to and working alongside disabled youngsters, and the professionals who work alongside them, leads to the conclusion that a school or college must be able to *meet their needs as people first*. Children and young people who are disabled are not different in this respect from their non-disabled peers. However, they will have their own particular needs in gaining access to curriculum and school life generally, in addition to the regular educational requirements. The quality of in-school or college partnerships are the cornerstone to developing positive and affirmative whole school approaches.

> It is essential that these professionals collaborate in order to provide a service for the whole person. Such an holistic approach to meeting the needs of young people with disabilities is necessary to ensure that their impairments do not become handicapping. Educationalists more than any other professionals are aware of the interdependence of all aspects of human development. They use sensory and emotional aspects to build up readiness for learning and teaching methods which incorporate cognitive, physical and sensory aspects to ensure and reinforce this learning. This use of any appropriate mode to create active learning and to capture attention and point the way is the hallmark of a good teacher. This very characteristic of the expert educationalist may be the thing

> which clouds judgement when that same educationalist is 'confronted' by someone with a physical disability. If I use active methods to enable young people to learn, then I may feel inadequate when I see someone who I presume cannot take advantage of such methods. This presumption is misplaced. Physical disability may lead to passivity but it need not. Active methods are possible for all pupils.
>
> (P. Halliday, 1989)

For a disabled pupil or student, access to curriculum and school life generally is more dependent upon collaboration and partnership than it is for non-disabled peers. Paula Halliday's hopeful comment at the end, should now, six years on, be taken further. With enabling technologies (Chapter 9), appropriate curriculum planning (Chapter 5), movement studies, activating methods (Chapter 8) and high quality partnerships, active learning is indeed possible.

As we have seen earlier in this chapter, in-school or college partnerships exist at various levels and are also likely to be unique in their interactions and quality. Individual and personal characteristics like creativity, commitment and communicating skills will all have an overall impact on partnerships. Physically disabled pupils and students will need a range of partnerships involving paramedical and therapy staff. These are made very difficult by the way that the services are currently managed, (see figure 6.8).

This *systemic problem* requires some radical changes. The question is one of allocation of resources, training, awareness of need and quality of professional partnerships.

> It was proposed that this would be done in consultation with occupational therapy, teachers and a medical physics technician where appropriate. There was, however, no extra funding allocated to create supporting posts for the above professionals. Current liaison between the speech and language therapist, occupational therapist and teacher is inadequate and depends upon the 'goodwill' of the professionals concerned.
>
> (ICAC, 1994)

There are some examples of health and education managers agreeing to work to a different model. SCOPE (formerly Spastics Society) special (residential and day) schools operate a model that enables them to work as a team and, often despite the distances involved, include parents in the team's work and planning, (figure 6.9).

In addition to the working conditions and managerial frameworks of teachers and therapists, there is a question about the nature of the partnership. Proper respect for the disabled child, their parents or the young person means that professionals will not expect them to 'hand

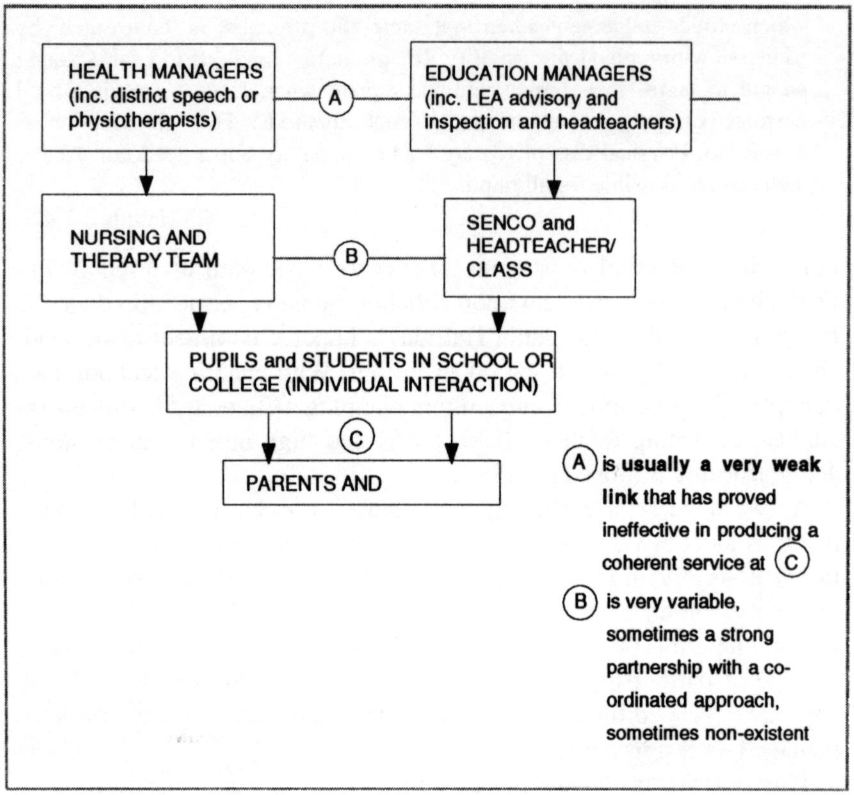

Figure 6.8 The current fragmentary model of service delivery

over' their responsibility. No professional 'owns' a disabled child or young person. They are part of a team that works with the whole child or young person, not detaching parts or attempting to 'take over' any particular aspect. This is important because there is still too much 'fear' involved in working with disabled pupils and students, although this is gradually decreasing.

> This means that the educationalists are not alone, nor do they have to become tame paramedics. Teachers may need to learn to be a part of a wider team. They need not become 'disability experts'. Expertise and advice are available. Parents, other professionals and young people with disabilities all have expertise. Teachers add to this pool of expertise but to be effective they also need to withdraw the help of others from it. To do this they need to know the remit of other professionals and how and when to access their skills best to meet the needs of young people.
>
> (P. Halliday, 1989)

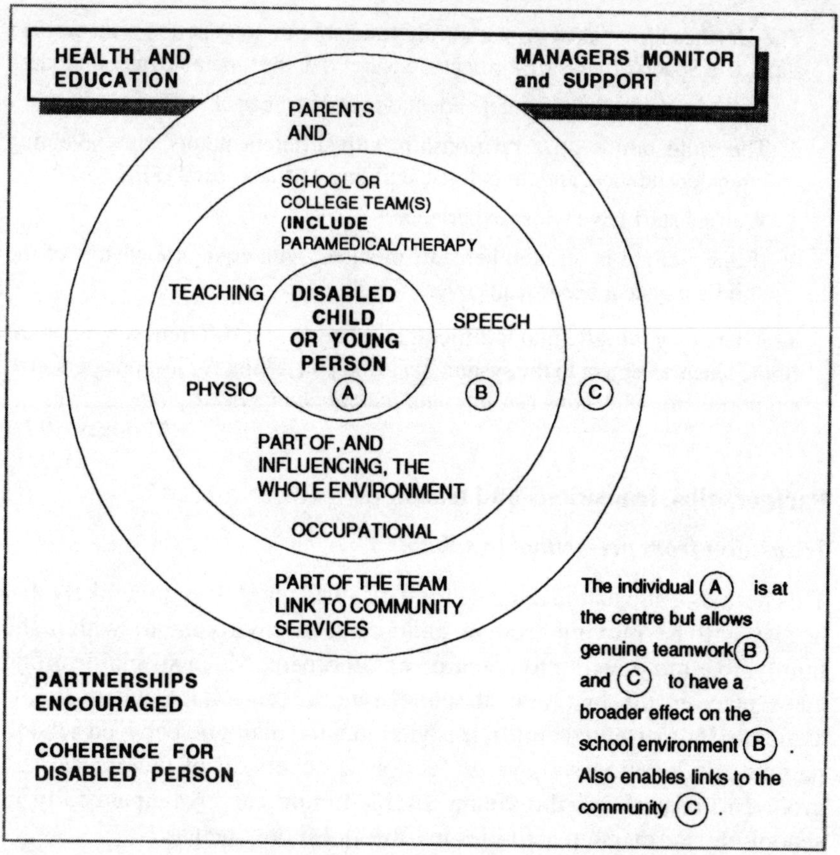

Figure 6.9 The SCOPE model of partnership

Michael Jones (1992) in observing practices, gives a good example of partnerships that keep the child at the centre. It recognises the child's independence and need to control the help given, rather than be taken over by it.

> This JMI school has a number of special needs children; 2 have physical disabilities.
>
> Both disabled children attend out-of-borough settings for physiotherapy. One, aged 5, goes to the Hornsey Centre; another, aged 7, goes to the Bobath Centre. Both centres give different instructions for care and handling.
>
> The school does not adopt the traditional model of deploying support staff, i.e. a named adult for each child. Instead, the Headteacher and Special Needs Co-ordinator have introduced a system whereby the welfare staff (4 in total) rotate their duties throughout each week, so that each welfare will work with a different child every day, or different children during each day.

The Headteacher makes up the termly timetable in conjunction with welfare staff. The Special Needs Co-ordinator ensures that the timetable runs smoothly.

1. Children do not become dependent on one member of staff.
2. The child builds up a relationship with different adults, thus avoiding inter-dependence, and, hopefully, building self-advocacy skills.
3. Welfare staff have wider experience.
4. If one welfare is off, another staff member, with equal knowledge of the child's physical needs, can cover.

Teachers may initially find it difficult to relate to four different support staff. Some teachers object to the system, on principle, asking for just one person to support them. *This, however, does not put the child's needs first.*

(M. Jones, 1992)

Partnerships, transitions and transfers

Transition from pre-school to school

This heralds a substantial change for a disabled child. It is quite likely that he/she will be moving from a child-centred environment, within the family, to a more institution-centred environment. Much special learning takes place in the first year at school (and at pre-school, where this is available for a disabled child). It is vital that the dialogue between school, parents and learning support professionals covers all of the appropriate ground to ensure that the young disabled child can participate fully in school life. Partnership activities involve questions such as:

- Can the pupil spend break times in the playground?
  Need this be supported? By whom?
  If they can't, what arrangements will be made to alter the situation so they can?
- Can the pupil eat lunch in the hall/dining room?
  Need this be supported? By whom?
  If not, what arrangements and physical alterations will be undertaken to facilitate this?
- Are there appropriate arrangements for emergencies or fire drills?
  Written up and circulated so all are aware.
- Are there appropriate, and suitably private, arrangements for using the toilet?
  What are they? Who needs to be involved? How?
  Are they available/planned for? What supplies are needed?
- Are all areas of the school fully accessible to the pupil?
  Is there need for help? By whom?
- What are the arrangements for therapy?

Before, after or in school time? Integrated into learning activities? Planning time (with parents) available? Catch-up time planned for?

- Any specific advice needed for PE?
  Medical or paramedical advice? Alternative activity planned that does not marginalise (Brown, 1987).
- Any are special transport arrangements needed?
  How will this affect the pupil's school day (e.g. fatigue)?
- Have arrangements been made for pre-school therapy and teaching staff to meet with reception teacher?
  Equipment, communication aids, enhanced teaching support, integrated activities, possible time away for treatments, special writing equipment, orthoses (ankle/foot), etc. . .
- Will parents be involved? How?
  Regular review meetings? Ongoing planning with multi-disciplinary team?
- Any other learning needs or advice to take into account?
  Statement, IEPs, particular forms of differentiation, perceptual (motor) or sensory disabilities?

Transitions, by their nature, require additional transitory partnerships with all concerned so that information can be passed on and continuity preserved. If the transitory arrangements are unsatisfactory, then the new team will either waste time trying to assess all over again or their expectations and strategies may be inappropriate. This is in addition to the fact that occasionally the quality of information passed on leaves much to be desired and may itself be misleading! Meeting face to face does much to remove these sources of error and misunderstanding.

The transition from primary to secondary

This transition is equally fraught with possible problems and is often a daunting prospect for the young person, disabled or non-disabled. Secondary school is bigger, more complicated and has additional pressures. All of the above questions apply (in the transfer to primary) but there are some additional considerations.

Check points for the transition to secondary education:

- Has early liaison between primary and secondary been established?
  Are parents involved? Contact teacher identified? Visits arranged prior to transition?
- Will the accessibility, aids and equipment be matched in secondary school?
  Including access to learning and social facilities.
- Is there a 'contact teacher' designated for regular dialogue with the disabled pupil?

Is there an accessible room available for meeting? How often will the contact person be available? On what basis?

- Will the pupil/student be able to use equipment effectively?
  In all areas of school? How will it be maintained? By whom?
- Has contact been made with each subject/department?
  To ascertain that all facilities are available? To discuss enhancement and differentiation of curriculum? Check on additional resources needed? Pupil's achievements in primary education correctly passed on?
- Are the school/college management team aware of (potential) needs?
  Resource allocation/requests. Facilities or additions or alterations needed. SEN and EO policies reviewed and adhered to throughout school.

The transition from school to college (further or higher education)

This transition again heralds many changes. For a student, the environments may become less supportive, requiring greater degrees of independence at each stage. A student who is disabled will have to contend with the same academic changes in this respect but will also have to contend with the change in physical and social environment. They may stand out in the new environment and have to 'battle anew' against prejudice, lack of awareness and hostile physical surroundings. It is still true, though, that a disabled student would wish to be treated like any other – to be listened to when there are problems and to be given the best opportunity to succeed as a result of their own effort and achievement. To this end, and *in addition to all the previous checks*, there are further questions to ask.

Check points for transition to further and higher education

- Check college guidebook and information to see about accessibility and opportunity.
  Course choices, access to facilities, social opportunities and academic requirements. Architecture of campus?
- Is there some form of learning or student support available?
  Learning support unit for equipment, aids and facilities? Counselling available if needed? Accommodation and enablers/facilitators?
- Will the student be needing work experience or activities off campus?
  How will these be arranged? Any special arrangements needed?
- Is there a careers or specialist careers service available?
  Contacts with local community and services? Links with employment and business? Involvement of other professionals for advice (e.g. health, psychologist, careers officers, etc. . . .)? Does student have

particular aspirations to discuss?

- Will special arrangements (need to) be made for exams and assessment of work?
  Who will be involved? Use of technology or specific electronic aids? Time allowed to complete?
- Are any subjects/courses unavailable because of lack of physical access, adaptation or equipment?
  Special arrangements or alterations made? Department staff aware of changed needed?
- Are any social activities not available?
  Either through physical or personal access problems? Support needed in forming social relationships?

Partnership roles and responsibility in the secondary school

Children move from a primary environment that is nurturing into a secondary environment at eleven that requires altogether more independence and confidence. It has always been a mystery why the age of eleven years was chosen for transition from primary to secondary education. It does not bear any relation to natural or physical development into adulthood or any marked social changes in a wider context. The secondary environment is complex and attention needs to be paid to establishing working partnerships with a disabled student. However, it is right to mention that at twelve, thirteen and fourteen years, teenagers will become busy making their own 'partnerships' and their peer culture is extremely important to them. Our society (that is Western or the 'developed countries') has tended, in this century, to separate childhood and adulthood in a somewhat arbitrary and adult-oriented way. Many disabled people have not really been allowed to grow up. They have been kept in a child-like state of 'adult dependence', in a state of powerlessness, unable to develop their own peer cultures and adult personalities. Primary education plays a crucial role in fostering and supporting the characteristics that will lead to confident, independent, adult to adult relationships into secondary school and later life.

Chapter 4 looked at the role and responsibility of the school or college management team in clarifying expectations and roles, and also in delegating responsibilities and actively generating policies for SEN and equal opportunities. The identification of a 'contact person', particularly in secondary education, is a partnership that will enable a disabled student to deal with the first two years of secondary education and gradually become emancipated into an adult culture.

The 'contact' teacher could delegate some of the tasks, but be the 'curator' of information and agent for collection and dissemination of information. The 'contact' teacher's (or SENCO or key person's) roles might include some or all of the following:

a) Gathering, storing, disseminating and updating information on their educational, physical and social needs with pupils or students who are physically disabled (or their parents/carers).

b) Constructing a database of information on managing the consequences of specific impairments, including ways of managing the curriculum of pupils with physical disabilities and sources of help and advice for pupils and the school.

c) Assessing the school or college's physical provision, comparing it with the individual pupil's needs and reporting to the senior management team on action needed.

d) Assessing the school or college's resources, comparing them with the individual pupil's needs and reporting to the senior management team on action needed, after consultation with course leaders, subject departments or class teachers.

e) Creating a mechanism for regular contact with pupil, home, auxiliary or nursing staff, doctors and therapists for management of physical care with a view to setting independence targets.

f) Establishing a support group, if required, for the management and monitoring of personal needs, hygiene or incontinence.

g) Creating a framework for regular contact with home, school or college departments, special needs adviser, medical or paramedical advice, educational psychologists (as required) for the ongoing review of the pupil's educational needs.

h) Training of and partnerships with learning support staff within the school or college. Some in-service training for teaching staff is useful outlining the pros and cons for teachers and pupils of having auxiliary help for individual pupils within the framework of independence targets set for pupils.

i) Creating a framework for developing the negotiating and independence skills of individual pupil/student who is disabled.

There is no time when the quality of the partnerships involved has greater relevance than the transition from school into adulthood and, hopefully, the wider community. At this time, the levels of partnership necessary also typify those that need to exist at other times in a person's educational experience.

Management partnerships in higher education

The HEFCE 'Widening Participation . . .' initiative involved nine categories of disability, four which were directly concerned with physical disability or medical conditions. In February 1993 the HEFCE agreed to allocate £3 million to this project in 1993–94. The projects developed would be 'exemplars which built upon existing good practice'. In other words, to 'pump prime new projects located at centres of excellence and experience' from institutions that could demonstrate existing commitment. Undoubtedly much useful experience has come from this project and the projects undertaken could act as a starting point for other institutions who have not developed and are not as committed. Nevertheless, out of the thirty-seven projects undertaken only eleven directly focused on (or included) the needs of students coming under the four (out of nine) categories relating to physical disability or medical conditions (approximately 30 per cent). This clearly shows the current trend in access for students with sensory disabilities and learning disabilities (mainly 'dyslexia'), sometimes described as 'print disabled'.

There seem to be continuing barriers to dealing with the fundamental issues of choice and opportunity in Higher Education through making all parts physically accessible. Whether these stem from college management's unwillingness to take financial responsibility without substantial support, or whether it is the apparent scale of modification to existing poorly designed campuses, is not clear. The financial scope of the HEFCE project, at £10,000 an institution, would certainly cover only the most minimal physical alterations, except where the college 'matches' HEFCE grants and supports financially. It seems from the individual reporting of physically disabled students that many, many Higher Education campuses are still off-putting and largely inaccessible to potential students.

Some issues thrown up by the project

- Compensatory marking and differential assessment – some academics felt this was devaluing the academic process.
- Should prospective employers know that the degree was awarded differently?
- Gaining agreement within institutions and departments when the extent of special arrangements was on a regular basis (i.e. went beyond examination arrangements).
- Any improvements must be embedded in and permeate all other activities of the institution (e.g. modular provision or assessment and methods).

Higher Education institutions, being much larger, work on a more formal basis than, say, nursery or primary schools. There is no reason, though, why the frameworks set up in a college cannot encourage partnership and teamwork. This has been proven in industry by proper delegation of authority and responsibility. It is surprising that in HE, where the boundaries of knowledge are being pushed forward, often the management of the institution itself is outdated, authoritarian and over-formal.

The HEFCE Project highlighted attitudes towards disabled students in Higher Education (HE) (1993–94).

- Challenging perceptions of disabled students within an institution was seen as crucial to forcing it to implement good practice across the board through changed attitudes.
- Descriptions and terminology used about disability was an issue for academic and service staff.
- Students themselves identified the barrier of the 'medical model' (e.g. 'struggling to cope' against the odds). *Successful initiatives* were based on the premise that '*difference is normal*'.

Further Education (FE) and HE institutions, because of their size and the diversity of people within them, are a microcosm of society in general. They also perform an important role as the 'seed bed' of new ideas in social as well as academic terms. It is this capacity to explore and experiment with new social and academic ideas that could provide an enormous drive to change attitudes in society generally.

Needs of disabled students in Higher Education

- The methods used to award Disabled Student Allowance (DSA) by LEAs gave rise to serious reservations by students and staff.
- DSA not available to part-time or access students, preventing many disabled people from entering Higher Education.
- Good quality support for learning and physically disabled students improved the general quality of the teaching and administrative systems (e.g. teaching materials better quality, equal opportunities implemented, lecture presentations planned better).

Why do partnerships count for so much?

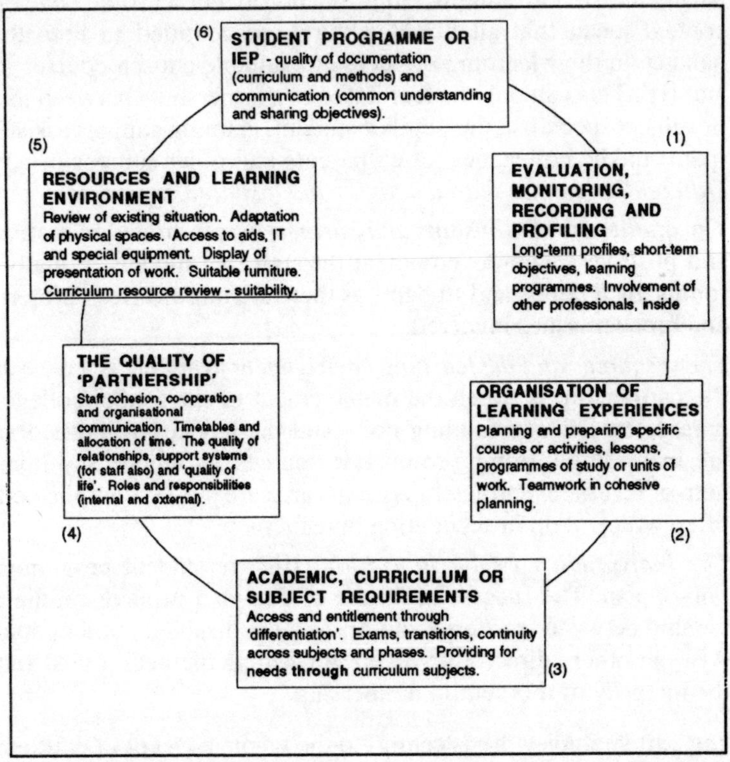

Figure 6.10 Putting programmes into action – a partnership

The quality of the partnerships involved will affect a physically disabled youngster at all phases of his/her education. At any stage, there are likely to be more people involved, at least in planning, and often in delivery, of learning programmes. I include social development and therapy programmes under this umbrella. From the diagram, figure 6.10, it is evident that, there are specific benefits that flow from effective partnerships and professional collaboration.

(1) Monitoring and evaluation involves a wider range of views, perceptions and values. *Increased objectivity*. Programme objectives developed, communicated and shared more effectively. Clearly linked to a broad understanding of needs and abilities. More likely to show progress when *observations are shared*.

(2) Programmes of study or units of work are more coherent and consistent across activities or subject areas when *joint planning is involved*. Lessons or work activities are more creative and interesting

when ideas are shared and developed.

(3) Academic or curriculum requirements in our current educational context mean that all disabled pupils are entitled to breadth and balance in their learning or access to suitable/chosen courses in FE and HE. This can only be facilitated by partnerships between teacher or subject specialist, the pupil or student, learning support assistance, (para) medic colleagues, often parents and other sources of advice. *Differentiation is a shared activity and a shared experience.*

(4) *The quality of relationships and partnerships* is crucial to motivation and positive social development through role models. Equally true for disabled pupils and students as there are more varied partnerships and broader issues involved.

(5) *The resources and the learning environment* available is a measure of the partnership between the management of the school/college, the parent, the LEA or funding body and the advice available. Parents are increasingly turning to outside sources for advice and financial help or leverage. Partnerships in this area are messy, complicated and often wrapped up in accounting bureaucracy.

(6) *The Individualised Education Plan* (IEP) or student programme is only a plan. The success of failure of this plan depends on the partnership between teachers/lecturers and the disabled pupil or student. Also on others directly involved in its implementation who rely on the integrity of this central partnership.

Making partnerships work is central to the whole concept of entitlement, choice and opportunity for pupils and students in any area of the education system. It is crucial to all pupils but more so for pupils and students who are physically disabled because of the variety, complexity and sheer amount of people that become part of the whole process of educating. The processes of group life, teamwork, relationships, communication and the collaborative or inter-personal skills involved have been ignored too long in education. The task-oriented approach, with minimal reference to the team or the individual (Adair, 1986) is pushing towards a mechanistic, bureaucratic and sterile appearance to educational practice. Within a bureaucratic, over-pressurised and ill-defined educational framework, relationships suffer and choice, opportunity and entitlement will wither on the vine. A more open, creative and visionary educational framework will acknowledge the human resource involved and allow these partnerships to thrive. Teachers, lecturers and their pupils or students, disabled and non-disabled, will then be able to seize the opportunities available to them and created by them.

CHAPTER 7

Parents' Expertise and Integrity

Working with parents and families

The role of partnerships and inter-personal skills was explored in the previous chapter in the context of professional collaboration. They are even more vital in positively handling the relationships between professionals and families. Further consideration of this aspect inevitably leads to fundamental issues for discussion and the following stories raise these in real and certain terms. The need for communication, coaching or counselling skills, and a framework for professional development for those who are at the first point of contact with families who have a disabled child, has been highlighted (Hornby, 1994). This is perhaps one of the more sensitive areas for professionals to handle and it is still common that parents, clients and other service users undergo far more negative experiences than should be necessary. It is generally acknowledged that the first five years of a child's life are highly formative. This is true of the physical skills that could be developed, to achiever greater access to experience, but it is also true in terms of the internal relationships within a family, the expectations that they have or can develop and the relationship between the family and the services they may need to access over an extended period of time.

A second important area is the wider context of the child and family in the community. The recurrent theme of raising public and professional awareness of the consequences of physical disability and medical conditions, in terms of social change, is a constant reminder of the great distance we still need to go in fostering realistic and affirmative actions. Whilst work is going on through the media and in large organisations, it is at the point of personal contact and interaction that changes in attitude and the development of effective partnerships can most readily show immediate benefit.

Thirdly, there is the whole question of what educational and other services are available, how they can be accessed and the ensuing decisions that have to be made by families. Again, it is the formative years from birth to five which play an enormous part in setting the scene for subsequent developments. Another milestone for the young adult and a crucial time for parents is the progress towards, and decisions involved in, in moving on from full-time education in school to college placement and then into adult life. In this area also there are often immense difficulties, not least brought on by having to make enormously difficult choices between few real alternatives.

The whole subject of provision for children with physical disabilities still has so many unanswered questions. How far do local services reflect the needs and wishes of children and their families? Do they have real choices or are the pathways generally prescribed by policy makers' decisions? How much are the choices available to parents limited by policy makers and what part of the country the child happens to live in? Parents often have to make very difficult decisions for their children, the consequences of which, one way or another, may lead to the temporary or permanent break up of the family. Shouldn't all local authorities be committed to providing a proper range of educational, residential, fostering or respite services particularly for all children with more severe or complex physical disabilities? How much do current local authority resources and financing severely limit the options for effective education for pupils who are physically disabled?

The variability and gaps in the quality, amount and type of services, up and down the country, for children who are disabled is an answer in itself. Children with physical disabilities are often catered for in settings which are either not really designed for them or take 'pot luck' in integrated circumstances where the ground has not been fully prepared for their specific needs. How much choice is really available to pupils who are physically disabled when compared with their non-disabled peers and their families?

> Imagine . . . in such a society, families which have a child with a disability would indeed be ordinary, everyday families . . . that their disabilities or learning difficulties were respected with dignity, as being part of the 'ordinary' human experience . . .
> The legal rights and the right to equal opportunity and choice is severely curtailed on many fronts for families with a disabled child. Families with young disabled children tend to be isolated with strictly limited financial support and services which are often separate from those received by other families. The extent to which disability controls the families' lives depends not only on the actual degree of physical or learning difficulty but on the philosophy, education and prejudice of other people in the family as well as fieldworkers, policy makers, statutory and voluntary agencies. The family's ability to become part of the community depends to a large extent on the sensitivity, consideration and dignity with which choices of services are offered to them.
>
> (Interlink – MENCAP, 1990)

The following three stories, written by parents of children who are physically disabled, puts the rest of this book, and the substantial material involved, sharply into focus. They were written separately with no reference to each other and yet the common themes are plain to see. They clearly show how the massive professional edifice that has been erected under the title 'special (educational) needs' impacts upon the lives of families, children and young people.

A PERFECT BABY AND A MUCH WANTED SON
by Liz Hirstle

Our family and our idea of an 'expert'

I am wheelchair bound. My husband is wheelchair bound. Our daughter is wheelchair bound and so is our son. In truth it is only our son who needs the aid of a wheelchair, but it might just as well be the whole family. The effect of having a severely disabled child affects the family. Everything is geared around his needs and his disabilities.

Jonathan was born a perfect baby. A much wanted son. At nine weeks he contracted an adult strain of meningitis. The spinal disease re-occurred three times. It became clear that Jonathan had brain damage. With the aid of the latest techniques of modern medical scanning we were able to see for ourselves the extent of the lost brain tissue. It was to leave him without the power of movement in all four limbs and with spasticity that made it almost impossible to communicate verbally. No movement and no speech. The doctors gave him a medical label 'cerebral palsy'. These two words will dog Jonathan's progress throughout his life.

One child in every 400 is born with cerebral palsy. That is approximately 30 babies every week. We do not have accurate figures for those children who end up brain damaged after birth but around another 30 children are injured in road accidents, or contract childhood diseases every week leading to cerebral palsy. And yet if you ask people 'What is cerebral palsy?' they will look blankly, unable to digest the medical term for brain damage. Cerebral palsy is the loss of brain parts.

No two people with cerebral palsy have the same brain damage. The term is used to cover a multitude of conditions from the clumsy to the severely disabled. *For a child with cerebral palsy there will always be conflicts between their medical, social, and educational needs.*

However, the biggest handicap facing people with cerebral palsy is not the brain damage itself but our attitude towards it. What frightens our family most, is not the attitude of the average person in the street, but the attitude of professional people who encounter brain damaged people in their ordinary working lives. The doctors, social workers, teachers and last, but far from least, the dreaded 'therapists' whose numbers seem to outweigh the knowledge necessary to assist those most in need. Notice the lack of reference to nurses and carers. These professionals are fortunately a breed apart, able to look beyond a disability to find the real person behind. Carers, the unfortunate people who are not considered worthy of a professional title, are all too often the only real contact with the outside world beyond the family, yet they give their badly paid time to assist us when we need a rest, with an insight into our problems that is constantly overlooked by those with more professional qualifications.

As a family we can only look at the medical, social and educational needs of our son's life from a personal perspective. The term 'expert' has to be the most misused word in the English language. Let me give you our family version of an 'expert'. It is not someone with letters after their name. It is someone with the ability to listen, someone who can communicate, a person with understanding and the intelligence to help solve problems. An expert is a person with a common sense approach. A person who understands how deeply involved a family are in loving their child and who wants only the best for the future. If this were the introduction to any course which would eventually lead to the profession of helping those who need 'an expert'; if these were made the most important features of any training, then, and only then, would we get the right kind of assistance.

A child is not a fad or an object

Medical people are a law unto themselves. After six months hospitalisation, and several brain operations later, we were told we could take our son home. The consultant asked to see us before we left the hospital. He explained in technical detail about the re-occurrence of certain things that we should look for and added, almost as an afterthought, that Jonathan had Cerebral Palsy. There was no explanation as to what cerebral palsy was, or how it would physically affect our son. *There was no offer of support. There was no emphasis on how this condition just might change the lives of our family for ever.*

Since our son's transfer to a residential school we have been involved with brilliant professionals: those people who have dedicated their lives to helping our children, with the expertise built up over years of specialisation. But things were not always so. In naivety, we asked as all parents do, our child being one year of age, when he might have the chance of walking, with an aid if necessary. 'Oh, he'll never walk' was the crushing reply. No mention of remedial help. No thought given as to how such an insensitive statement might affect our family, and no hint that anything other than the bare minimum of help would be needed to keep Jonathan even slightly mobile.

All professionals must learn the repercussions of any information that they may pass on to a parent. There must be a form of collective responsibility on behalf of these groups. *Expertise cannot be utilised fully unless this privileged group of trained people learn to talk to us, the parents, and, as importantly, to each other.* We have to break down the barriers of job description.

The professionals who work with us, the parents, in the first years of a disabled child's life, are involved in shaping his, or her, future, to a far greater extent than they could imagine. If they give a negative message to parents, the effect is often that parents turn to alternatives, such as, in the case of a child with cerebral palsy, 'Conductive Education', imported from Hungary. This form of aid is both ambitious and contentious.

We took this alternative route with Jonathan. A local 'Special School' he attended tried the method, but the staff were poorly trained, and the whole idea came to a halt after one year. A child is not a fad. You cannot change education and training as if it were wallpaper. We took as much knowledge as we could glean, from various sources, and began our own 24 hour programme at home.

We tried involving professionals, but most thought us cranks, outside the normal system, and if they did not avoid us altogether, gave us short shrift when we did see them. There was no basis for accumulating a responsive pathway for our son's future, but rather a tendency for interdepartmental bickering about the family who had rejected them.

When Jonathan reached the age of eleven it became clear that he would benefit more from contact with a world beyond his own immediate family. It was also clear that by dedicating ourselves to fighting for a better future for our son, the rest of our family was being torn apart. We began looking for a school where Jonathan would be seen as an individual, rather than just another disabled child to be processed through an overworked, dilapidated system, which seemed to be falling apart at the seams. We wanted somewhere that had the expertise of reliable, informed teachers, nurses, care staff, doctors, physiotherapists, speech therapists, psychologists and so on. It was like searching for an undiscovered planet. But, we did have help from what seemed, at the time, an unlikely source: the Spastics Society (now SCOPE). They were, at the time, beginning massive changes of their own, having come to realise that parents were demanding more for their disabled children.

Eventually we chose a school in another county. It meant that Jonathan would have to leave a loving home to compete alongside his peers at a boarding school. This was an agonising decision. To leave our son for at least one week at a time, knowing that he was unable to function without the help of carers on a 24 hour basis. The school was wonderful. It was obvious from our first visit that Jonathan was itching to start a new life. We, the parents, were given lessons as well, staying a few nights in parent accommodation, at the school, being taught about our children's condition. Things that no-one had bothered to tell us before. We discovered just how cerebral palsy affects the body. We discovered other parents willing to learn and share their similar experiences. But most of all we found the confidence to leave our son in their capable hands, knowing that we had found 'real' experts.

We are lucky. The school our son attends has every discipline under one roof. No one professional is more important than the other. We are consulted and informed regularly about all aspects of Jonathan's life and education.

Treat others as you would like to be treated

Children who have such a variety of medical and educational complications cannot be taught within our mainstream primary and secondary system, for the very reasons outlined in the previous paragraphs. It is our belief that if a time should ever come when the possibility of mainstream education were to become available on these terms, *schools as we now know them will have ceased to exist*. With computer technology will come the onset of partial home tuition. Far from a community joining together, there will be alienation. The family unit will have changed, and be either a more positive influence, or non-existent, leaving many children, especially those like Jonathan, in a definite two-tier society.

No-one asks for a child with disabilities out of choice. The strain placed on families with such children is considerable, although we cannot measure it. We do need help. Unfortunately we are often told what help we need, rather than actually receiving it from the professionals.

Our son is now a teenager, soon to be an adult. We have had to fight our way through the medical and educational systems in order to find the right route for his future welfare and happiness. We will have to continue the fight after his eighteenth birthday. He will be beyond the education system then, and, as always, passed to a different set of professionals who do not know, or we suspect, really care, what his quality of life will be. He will, in effect, be just another adult statistic for governmental aid. The fight goes one. We would say to all those lucky enough to be in a professional position: 'Please remember to treat others as you yourselves would like to be treated.'

EXPERIENCES OF A PARENT WITH A DYSPRAXIC CHILD

by Georges Dussart

(In this case, dyspraxia is taken to be synonymous with the terms clumsy child syndrome, minimal motor impairment and motor co-ordination deficit).

Babyhood

From the birth of AJ, his parents felt that there was something unusual about him. Having had one healthy female child three years earlier, they were not naive parents and were not in the habit of seeking medical and other assessments. However, within forty eight hours of the birth of AJ in a Cottage Hospital, they had requested that the GP visit the child at home in order to check on his development, since both parents had noticed some broken veins under the skin between his shoulders and felt uneasy about this health. The GP carefully examined the baby and declared that everything seemed fine but noted a slight scoliosis of the lower cervical part of the spine and made arrangements for a check-up at the local hospital. An intensive investigation by the paediatrician did not reveal anything to cause concern. In fact, the birth had not been simple: the midwife had caught her finger between the baby's head and the pelvis during one of the early pushing phases of the birth and it had been necessary to send for the GP in the nearby surgery to come to help deliver the baby. AJ was born blue, with the umbilical cord round his neck, though he started breathing immediately.

Despite these initial problems, AJ proved to be a model baby in that, from the first night at home, he slept all night and in fact had to be wakened to feed. On feeding, he consumed milk readily at the breast and appeared to be maturing normally although he did tend to be rather 'floppy' when held. At age thirteen months, he had a serious case of gastro-enteritis and, having been a chubby baby, now became emaciated; he stayed thin into adulthood. He was somewhat late in walking and did not really move through the normal phases of lying, crawling and walking. Indeed, he missed out the crawling phase altogether and moved himself around for a considerable time in a baby walker. He was a happy, contented and quiet child, who took some time to learn to speak and, to the parents' frustration, seemed to have some problems in differentiating between the meanings of 'yes' and 'no', although this did eventually develop satisfactorily.

The parents still felt that there was something odd about his behaviour and at age four arranged for him to be seen by an Educational Psychologist.

Nothing significant came from this investigation and the Psychologist concluded that nothing could be concluded.

Primary school

At almost five years old, he was placed in the same primary school as his sister. The parents felt that both children settled in well into this new school, though there were occasional, but normal, problems. The school had been recommended by a range of people whose children had attended, and also by others with professional knowledge.

It gradually became evident, after the first years of AJ's schooling, that something was wrong with his progress. Although he was a capable reader, able to function somewhat above his expected age level, his performance in other areas, such as writing and drawing, was slow. Initially his ability to draw was at his age level, but did not develop or show any sign of significant progression. This lack of general progression was raised many times with the school and the most common response, which is well known to parents with children with this sort of disorder was, 'He is rather lazy. We can see this because his reading is all right; except for the laziness, there is nothing to worry about'.

In social terms, the parents encouraged their children to attend the church Cubs and Brownies, the whole family being regular church goers. The parents also encouraged both children to try to play musical instruments. As AJ's school career developed in primary school, he showed reluctance to become involved in school activities. For example, he was reluctant to go on school trips. Throughout his school career he was somewhat overshadowed by his sister, who was a popular high achiever and successful in all activities of the school, including academic, sporting and playground performances. On a number of occasions his sister intervened on his behalf, both in the playground and within the timetable. On one occasion, when he was being taken to see the Headmaster, his sister insisted on going with him and, upon being admonished by the Head, she stood between the Head and AJ and, with fists clenched, defended him.

In the first three years of primary school, AJ showed almost no progress except in the area of reading, much of this having been achieved in reading with his parents at home. At parents' evenings, it was usual for the parents to hear that he was 'rather lazy, had a very poor attention span, and was inclined to have a rather difficult nature including a rather bad temper'. However, since there was nothing wrong with his reading, *his intellectual development seemed to be OK, except for the behaviour*.

Diagnosis

In the first two years of his primary schooling, he had been taught by middle-aged experienced teachers, but in the fourth year of his primary school he was given a newly qualified, although mature, student teacher. After some time with this teacher, she contacted the parents to say that she was not happy with his development and felt there was something wrong. This confirmed the feelings of the parents, who had noticed that AJ was finding difficulty not just in academic work but also in certain things like dressing himself. He needed to be dressed in the mornings and was constantly having to be nagged to do things and urged to feed himself. In discussion with the parents, the teacher arranged for AJ to see the school nurse, who identified an ear problem. This diagnosis was confirmed as 'glue ear' or 'fluid in the middle ear'. AJ had an ear operation to drain the ears and insert grommets to improve drainage of the middle ear. To all intents and purposes, so far as the medical staff, the teaching staff and the family were concerned, the problem had been solved.

At seven years old, AJ was sent for special remedial English lessons for the Remedial Reading Service of the Local Authority. These comprised a single joint lesson with other children, some of whom were slow learners, in a different school within the town. It should be noted that although he was a good reader, he read substantially from context. It was stressed by the specialist staff that these were remedial readings sessions, and it was evident that they did not address his needs for help with writing. AJ appeared to agree since his behaviour in these sessions left something to be desired: he would hide in the toilets to avoid the minibus which would take him to the session.

At age nine, the parents were now seriously worried about AJ's development. One year earlier they had been told by the school that AJ would be referred to the County Educational Psychologist, but this assessment did not take place. The parents reasoned that if his innate ability remained unmeasured, it would be difficult to know whether he was reaching his potential. They were not particularly concerned whether his potential was low or high, but were concerned whether it was being realised or not. Consequently, they took him independently to an Educational Psychologist to have an assessment; he came into the top twenty five percentile on the Wechsler Revised Scale.

AJ eventually moved into another class with a mature and experienced teacher. After one term in this class the teacher told the parents at a parents' evening that she was concerned about the performance of the boy and felt that something other than an ear problem was causing difficulties. She raised the possibility that there could be some malfunction of hand-eye co-ordination, in particular a possible reference-eye problem. As it happened, there was a special unit at the nearby hospital which was concerned with this kind of eye-hand malfunction and AJ was referred to this clinic for assessment.

Remediation

Following the assessment for the laterality of hand-eye co-ordination at the hospital and its failure to identify a reference-eye problem, the child was referred to a Paediatric Occupational Therapy Unit which specialised particularly in physical ability.

The assessors at this unit requested that the parents be present at the assessment. Here AJ was given a specific battery of tests which revealed a serious physical co-ordination problem, sometimes called motor impairment, dyspraxia, motor co-ordination deficit or clumsy child syndrome. The assessors said that this was quite a common problem but that it was little known among teaching and medical staff. The parents of the child were surprised to learn of the existence of this problem and astonished to see the extent of the handicap in their child. After the assessment, the local authority arranged for AJ to have a course of treatment at this clinic, comprising a one hour visit, weekly for two terms.

AJ and his father attended these occupational therapy sessions assiduously and the staff gave a list of exercises for AJ to the father. They advised that these exercises should be conducted at home, as it would be impossible to achieve any real remediation in a period as short as one hour. The father instigated regular morning exercises which lasted no longer than fifteen minutes and in which AJ, at first willingly but later much more reluctantly, took part. Eventually, when AJ became intransigent, the father stopped this exercise regime rather than unduly forcing it on him.

From a very early age it had been customary for AJ to spend a lot of his sleeping time talking, shouting and screaming and it had become a family joke that no-one could share a bedroom with him; it had been presumed by the family to be another one of his idiosyncrasies. However, after the diagnosis, *his father carefully explained his motor impairment problem to him in terms he could understand*. The father began by saying that he (AJ) was like a wonderful sports car which was having trouble moving because it needed some fuel – and the exercises would be the fuel. Together, father and child made a cardboard cutout car with a stylised petrol tank. Every time they did some exercise, 'fuel' (coloured sticky paper) was stuck on the tank. Immediately, from then on, the child never spent another night shouting or screaming and both he and the rest of the household slept soundly. For the next few years father and son maintained the exercise routine, but with no obvious benefits in physical performance.

Problems of communication

The major problem experienced by the family was the inability of the educational system to respond to the diagnosis of the problem, or even the needs of the child. In particular, although the child was eventually accurately diagnosed and his needs well understood, the teaching staff appeared to lack both time and inclination to deal with his problem. He had, during the previous years, developed strategies for avoiding putting himself into difficult or trying situations. He would not put up his hand to respond to questions and would not involve himself in the playground if at all possible. As long as he provided no problem to the teachers, and as long as his reading ability continued to be good, the teachers seemed to be satisfied.

> At home he would sit on a small stool and watch the washing machine operate in preference to watching the television. Later on he took an inordinate interest in electrical and then nuclear power. At the age of ten he was avidly reading *Atom*, the journal of the Nuclear Power industry, with some degree of understanding. It is possible that, given the lack of development of a sense of body-rhythm and sequencing in motor co-ordination, the cyclical processes of washing machines, power supply and later railway networks would offer him the security of patterns and rhythmicity lacking from his own body.

Although it was never diagnosed, his problems may have been compounded with a degree of mild autism or Asperger's syndrome.

One of the continually difficult problems faced by the parents both in primary and secondary school was the need to advise each new teacher of his medical and behavioural circumstances. The parents gained the impression that in both school levels teachers did not refer to the records of the children in their new classes. For example, parents' evenings would usually take place towards the end of the first term in December and it would be at these meetings that the parents would always have to point out to the teacher the problems faced by AJ. *Year after year the teachers would express great surprise at the fact that AJ had a problem* and would then assure the parents that 'something would be done' in terms of teaching. However, the parents rarely gained the impression that anything special was being done.

This problem of one teacher not letting another teacher know the situation became much more difficult and serious once AJ began to attend secondary school since he would now, on a daily basis, be dealing with many different teachers. He soon gained a reputation for being rather weird, and only recently have the parents come to think that bullying, which had begun in the primary school, continued in secondary school. By this time the parents had understood the vagaries of the school system and made a significant point of contacting and informing all possible personnel who might have any dealings with their son during his school day, from the Deputy Head downwards.

Statement of special needs

From the time of the recognition of the motor impairment problem when AJ was nine years old, the parents had tried to have a statement of special needs invoked but it took four years of continual harassment of the authorities before a statement was produced. The psychological assessment, which was part of this statement, took place five years after it had originally been promised. When the statement arrived, the parents found it inadequate in its generalities and banalities, and insisted on the statement being rewritten with specific commitments. Getting the statement re-worded also took a considerable time and the parents felt that the re-write was an excuse for the authorities to delay implementation. Indeed, the parents had the distinct impression that delay was a strategy of the Local Authority, such that the child would have grown up and left the system before anything would have been done.

The final version also contained some questionable statements. In meeting the Local Authority doctor, AJ said he liked long-distance running which, to all who knew him, was of doubtful veracity. If he did like such an activity, it was probably because it took him out of the reach of nagging authority and he could move at his own pace. Nevertheless, this statement was repeated in many of the reports from other specialists and in re-writes of the statement. The parents did not feel inclined to try to correct these and other minor and harmless errors in case the corrections were used as another cause for delay.

As a result of a statement, the school would be entitled to extra resources. The secondary school sent several letters in support of the many letters and visits made by the parents to the Special Needs Department of the Local Authority. Part of the statement had suggested there should be some support in terms of information technology and the father had already bought a word processor for home use, with which AJ rapidly became adept. Indeed, by the age of twelve, he started to write what had been the account of a dream, but which soon turned into an enormous story, several hundred pages in length. No machine was provided for class use though AJ had access to word processors at lunch times in the Information Technology (IT) room. He was offered a portable machine but at the time these were bulky and he did not want to be made more conspicuous.

> Writing his story became almost addictive but the parents felt that this might be his opportunity to express some of his many problems. Despite his wide general knowledge and accomplishment in writing, he was still seen by many staff in the secondary school as being dull, troublesome, and lazy. Again on many occasions, when passing this impression to the parents during parents' evenings, the staff concerned were surprised to find that the child had a problem or had in fact been statemented.

The situation was always better when there was a responsible and caring Special Needs Co-ordinator who understood AJ and was prepared to work on his behalf, especially in terms of liaising with other staff. The parents feel quite strongly that the lack of liaison was one of the most serious problems involved in coping with AJ's problems but understand that this lack of liaison is almost certainly predicated on lack of time, which itself is based on lack of resources such as manpower and money. This also explains the length of time taken to produce the initially banal statement of special needs and the need to provoke the Local Authority into providing a proper statement.

As a result of the statement, AJ was given significant help in the school classroom but some of this help was based on the fact that both school and parents had stressed the importance of safety, that is, a motor impaired child might be at risk in science, home economics and other lessons. He was therefore given support in these lessons. Physical education was an area in which he should have received quite specific support but received none, other than being excused the lesson. The statement included a bland suggestion that the PE staff should liaise with the special orthopaedic clinic which AJ had attended. This reflected many of the other parts of the statement in that no resources were assigned and, consequently, nothing was done.

Positive suggestions

The parents had now found out indirectly through AJ's sister (now twenty years old) that in fact AJ was bullied throughout his school career. The parents had seen no signs of this in terms of school refusal, and while it had always been seen as a possibility, they had not been given any inkling. AJ, however, had often found refuge in school buildings and spent his lunchtimes in the IT building where students had access to computers. If AJ's example is typical, it seems that it is important to give this type of child some sort of refuge from the feeling of threat posed by other children.

Since children with motor impairment have to concentrate on any and every aspect of their physical activity just to keep moving, they can get very tired. It might have been valuable if this could have been taken into account in a structured way throughout his school career. Formal rest periods might have been organised for him rather than his being allowed to spend his whole day under the teacher's chair in primary school.

Adult irresponsibility

In certain circumstances AJ was unhappy, usually when an adult had not taken their responsibilities seriously enough. For example, a sports day had been arranged for the Cub Scouts, including the group in which AJ was a member. Although AJ was reluctant to take part the father visited the Scout Leader and, pointing out the problems faced by the child, received the assurance that the child would be well taken care of. On the day in question, the father took the child to the Cub meeting from which the Cubs went by minibus to the sports ground in a local school. The father, having had many assurances from teachers and others in the past, decided to go to the sports ground too. He observed the following scenario:

> The children were broken up into groups and initially these groups involved children from a range of different Cub packs. Almost immediately, some children took his rucksack and started throwing it around between them in such a way that he could not catch it. He sat on the ground and removed a shoe and started picking at the lace. The children then took the shoe and, having played the same game with the shoe, threw it some distance away into bushes. No adults took care of the child while this was going on.

AJ was encouraged to take part in a variety of physical activities but his motor problems led to ridicule of which he was painfully aware. Other examples concerned a gymnastic club in which jeering children were not controlled by responsible adults, and a visit to a children's section of a local Rugby Club where he had his nose broken on his second visit.

Because children with such an impairment are not successful in the classroom in terms of writing, are not successful in terms of art, are not successful in the playground and are probably perpetually nagged to hurry up at home, especially with eating and dressing, it is possible that *they do not have a significant social refuge*. A dyslexic child may have a refuge in art or in sport. A child in a wheelchair is easily understood to have a disability and can find the opportunity to develop in the classroom. The parents felt that throughout his childhood it was firstly the lack of recognition of the seriousness of his problem that exacerbated some of his difficulties. Secondly, even where the problem was recognised by certain individuals in the system, there was a serious lack of adequate communication between the responsible adults. Children with motor impairment may have never learnt the intrinsic rhythms and sequence of their own bodies, and may consequently have problems in sequencing actions. For example, a hard-pressed classroom teacher or parent might give the children a sequence of two or three tasks. Most normal children can accomplish this easily but a motor impaired child may forget the sequence or get it completely out of order, to the frustration of the teacher, parent and workmates.*

WE WERE NEVER GIVEN THE FULL STORY

by Avril Mulligan

Tact, diplomacy and basic human respect from professionals

My experience in dealing with professionals from education, social services, health and the voluntary sector over the last eight years continues to astound me. The range of emotions my family and I have had to cope with: from frustration, anger, disillusionment, makes me wonder whether having a child with cerebral palsy has made us stronger or weaker people. That is not to say that we are condemning of all professionals. We have befriended those who empathise and understand our situation.

Alexandra will soon be nine years old and, as my first child, my introduction to motherhood was left somewhat wanting! Alexandra has cerebral palsy as a result of medical negligence at birth. An uneventful pregnancy ended in a fraught and harrowing labour. Obviously our concerns after Alexandra's birth were whether she would live or die and what her possible problems would be. The answers to these questions were never forthcoming and *coping with telling the truth is something the medical profession have yet to learn, especially if the truth is bad news.* It wasn't that we were lied to but more that we were never given the full story, only bits of information were allowed to filter through to us. When we did eventually get a clearer picture, Alexandra was six months old. Those six months had been unpleasant and stressful, not quite how I imagined being a mother would be!

The final label was given to Alexandra after a variety of scans and tests

---

Footnote

*As a footnote, it is worth saying that during the later school years AJ developed his own interests in model railways and railway renovation. He developed his own network of friends who again had to be advised through the parents about his problems. Once this advice had been given there were no significant problems within the context of these clubs. This type of club is run by volunteers.

had been carried out on her at a London hospital. I feel the way that parents are told of their child's diagnosis and prognosis is extremely important. It surely affects how we come to terms with the problems and how we may feel about our child in the future. The delivery of this information to us I felt could not have been worse – although I know there are other parents who have had equally unpleasant experiences. We were told in no uncertain terms that 'the input you give your child will not be worth the output you receive from her'. I still wonder if that neurologist had ever had lessons in tact and diplomacy. What I found difficult to understand was, this statement was being made about my daughter. She is my child first and foremost, and her cerebral palsy surely must come after that. When will doctors learn to look at their patients as human beings and not just as a set of medical problems that come through their doors?

Professional judgement and allocation of services

We encountered a range of problems when dealing with professionals from various services. My biggest bone of contention is with those bright sparks that love to pass judgement on their clients without being in full knowledge of the facts. This particularly applies to most social workers. Common sense and tact are abilities few seem to have, especially those who happily label mother as 'neurotic, over-wrought, creating problems for herself'. Who wouldn't be when you have a child who can't feed, who doesn't respond to any visual stimulus, who doesn't sleep, and who constantly screams and twitches. Surely we are the ones who do the caring 24 hours a day. Are we not the experts in judging our child's difficulties? I might add that we do now have an excellent social worker, not that we get to see him that often. He has listened and taken note of what we feel our needs are, as a family, and he has tried to accommodate those needs into what provision is available.

After Alexandra, I went on and had two more children, Ailsa is six and Andrew is four. My son has communication problems. His label is 'verbal dyspraxia'. He understands spoken language but has major difficulties in forming words and speaking. Why I have brought Andrew into this is the ludicrous fashion in which services are provided. When Alexandra started special school it was nigh impossible to get speech therapy provision for her on any regular basis as the speech therapist was in school for one day a week for 75 children. Not hard to see what her problems were. Alexandra is unable to communicate by spoken language, appears to have a good degree of understanding, and she has severe spastic quadriplegia, so has very poor oral control with feeding and drinking being a major problem. Andrew on the other hand can feed himself, has no problems with eating or drinking, is independent but just can't say very much. Yet from the age of two he has received weekly speech therapy. In effect, we feel that children are categorised on the basis of whether they are worth putting the effort in (i.e. will they eventually contribute financially to society?)

Fragmented, disjointed and unrealistic service provision

Medical litigation has been, to say the least, an experience for us. It certainly opened our eyes to the indiscretions and inadequacies of the 'system' that is supposed to support our child. Suing a health authority is not a job undertaken lightly. It requires courage, determination and effort in all those involved. The first hurdle is to find a solicitor well experienced in the field of medical negligence. The next stage is to prove you have a case. This took us nearly two years to accomplish. A time we found stressful, emotionally draining and time-consuming. This was also a time when I had had my second child and was dealing with the various traumas that Alexandra kept presenting us with. Once it was acknowledged that the health authority had been responsible for Alexandra's problems, we then had to go to court to prove liability. Having never been to a court case before, we were unsure of what would be the sequence of events but nothing had prepared us for the sheer mental pain and exhaustion. My feelings now are the legal profession have a lot to answer for, especially the way barristers and QC's can twist and turn words and statements against you. After the first hearing we left court feeling as if we were the guilty party. Fortunately, liability against the health authority was accepted. We at least then felt we were making progress. Over the next 2–3 years, demands on our time became increasingly more and more as I then had our third child. We were also tackling the education provision for Alexandra, having proved the school she was at was unable to meet her needs, *and her statement of special educational needs was so vague it could have applied to any number of children*.

Whilst all this was going on, I continued to work as a physiotherapist, specialising in paediatrics, in special schools and in hospital. There were times when I found it difficult not to break my professional code of ethics. Being a mother of a child with cerebral palsy and being a professional dealing with parents and carers of disabled children often brought me to question the quality and quantity of the service being provided to these families. My conclusions were often condemning of my profession and other health professionals. I strongly feel *the service being provided is fragmented, disjointed and quite often unrealistic*. I would also question why some doctors cannot be truthful to parents at a baby's birth when it is obvious that a child has major problems. Why should a baby be 'kept going' for an extra week because the doctor failed to tell the parents that their baby was dying, therefore allowing them time to come to terms with the news? Giving bad news to parents is never easy but surely professionals must realise the need to be frank and honest at the outset about difficult situations. Giving false hope is a very cruel thing to do to any parent. Giving realistic hope and advice is right. Brushing it under the carpet only creates further pain and suffering for parents and families.

Valuing people with disabilities

Another contentious area for me is the way professionals decide what is right for people with disabilities and their carers. It is a rare event for us as parents to be asked what we would like and an even rarer event for anyone to consider what Alexandra would like. As we approach the year 2000 I wonder if our society is any nearer to valuing people with disabilities. Most professionals I meet see Alexandra as a burden on our family. Surely the time has come for people to accept each other for what they are and not be prejudiced against their inabilities. I also wish that professionals, such as paediatricians, physiotherapists and occupational therapists, would stop seeing Alexandra's disabilities and problems first but would see her as my daughter and a child. It has always been the aim of my husband and I to give Alexandra the best quality of life we could. Also that her siblings understand and respect her as a human being and as their sister. We have never forced them to be involved in her care or would wish to ram her disability down their throats. Young though they are, they have more understanding of their sister's needs than any professional I have met. A comment passed by Ailsa last year still sticks in my mind. It was after we had won the appeal against the education authority, Ailsa commented that surely we knew what Alexandra needed because all the other people didn't know her or hadn't even met her!

I am sure, along the corridors of power, there are few people who care about the real plight of families but along the corridors of petty officialdom and bureaucracy there are people who may cringe at hearing our name, probably none more than the LEA. Whilst Alexandra's litigation case was ongoing, we took a long hard look at her education as various incidents and problems kept surfacing. It took the LEA nearly 3 years to issue a draft statement of her SEN's. During this time we had some very confrontational meetings and case conferences with professionals. The attitude towards us by certain people was at times rude and ignorant. If we didn't fit into their pattern of working and provision then we were considered awkward, rebellious and unrealistic. We eventually took Alexandra's case to appeal and won. But did the LEA want to work in partnership with us? No chance! They chose to ignore the Appeal Panel's recommendations and didn't even have the courtesy to inform us. What also came out during the assessments of Alexandra was the amazing way in which professionals complied with the LEA's restrictions, the fact that they are willing to take part in the process of rationing support for the disabled or who are too cowardly to stand up for the rights and needs of the very people they are trained to support. Following the Appeal, we took the case to the Secretary of State. A year later Alexandra's case is still to be investigated but I am assured by a very nice lady at the DFE it will soon be sorted out! Whilst all the dispute over Alexandra's education was going on, we managed to conclude her medical negligence case and she was duly awarded compensation.

Not just another child with problems

This enabled us to move her from the LEA school to a SCOPE school more suited to her needs and where she has flourished, obviously enjoying her new challenges. A huge plus about her new school is that she is seen very much as an individual and not another child with problems in an environment that is under-resourced, over-worked and over-whelmed. The wonderful thing about Alexandra's new school is that everything from physiotherapy, care, education and communication is co-ordinated and integrated with all the professionals under one roof. It makes a refreshing change not to have to juggle advice from several different sources and sort out a workable timetable to fit in around my family. What a difference to be listened to when you have concerns about your child and to actually have those concerns acted upon. It's taken some adjustment on the part of our family to 'hand over' Alexandra's welfare to the school, having been so heavily involved in her previous school. We have actually begun to relax about her school for the first time in five years. We now have our evenings back for leisure rather than supplementing what was missing from her education. Education for Alexandra must be the holistic approach where no professional is more important than another and they work together rather than against each other as we have found commonplace in the past.

It is difficult not to feel cynical and disillusioned about what has happened over the last eight years but I always hope that out of our fight for our daughter's needs and rights, future families and carers of the disabled will have an easier ride than we have had. The providers of services for the disabled must recognise and listen to what the real issues are and provide the amenities and services we need. To be treated and respected as an individual and not as yet another statistical dilemma. Having Alexandra has taught us to appreciate the contribution she makes to our family, her wickedly evil sense of humour and how, despite her profound difficulties, she gets her own back on her brother and sister. I would never claim that it is easy having Alexandra. We do get tired, upset and frustrated but not at Alexandra, it is the system we are fed-up with. I don't suppose for one minute that things will get any easier the older Alexandra gets but we are fortunate that she is financially secure, which gives us peace of mind; something I am sure a lot of parents must be concerned about.

These parents writing their stories, in common with tens of thousands of other parents of disabled and non-disabled youngsters, are looking beyond the confines of their own family circle. They are asking 'What kind of a world do we want to live in? What kind of a world do we want for our children when they grow up?' These parents are not prepared to adopt a subservient position and accept the morsels dished out by a system that exists within an 'exclusive' society. Many parents are also professionals in these services and they realise that there are so many conflicting forces at work. The goodwill, commitment and knowledge of some is cancelled out by the arrogance, lack of care and ignorance of others. The campaign goes on and Micheline Mason (1994), a disability equality trainer, and 'proud parent of a disabled child' sees some light at the end of the tunnel.

> These parents, of course, pose the biggest challenge because they are after something which requires commitment and change, both of which bring up fear in most people. These parents, more than any others, find themselves locked into bitter battles with schools and LEAs, because it has never been acknowledged that both parties have different value systems, and different goals.
>
> The Code of Practice has as its aim getting a better deal for vulnerable children and their parents. It gives everyone a chance to re-evaluate the whole approach to 'Special Educational Needs'.
>
> (Mason, 1994)

The Code of Practice, which emerged from the 1993 Education Act, will certainly make a difference and has energised schools and colleges to take 'special educational needs' (SEN) very seriously. There are certain duties on schools that have emerged such as a published annual report on meeting SEN (screening and assessment, teaching strategies and resources) or if your child has no statement a parent has a right to know what the school is doing to meet his/her needs. In particular though, there is the development of the independent, regional special needs tribunals. These are required to be set up to hear parent's appeals against Local Education Authority (LEA) decisions. Unlike the former legislation and even the particular intervention of the Secretary of State for Education, their decisions will be legally binding upon LEAs. In addition to this, the actual grounds for appeal have been increased and made more specific to support the parents in getting their child's needs reckoned with. The grounds are:

- if LEA refuses request for an assessment;
- if LEA decides *not* to issue a statement following assessment;
- if LEA has not named the school you want when SEN is finalised;
- if LEA has not named any school;
- if you disagree with the description of your child's SEN in Section II;
- if you disagree with the special education provision set out in Section III;
- if LEA refuses to comply with your (annual) request for a change of the school named on the statement;
- if the LEA amends Section II or III or changes the named school;
- if the LEA ceases to maintain the statement.

Finally, my own experience tells me that the battles will continue to rage simply because too many educators and administrators fear the honesty, commitment and individual demands being placed on them, both personally and professionally. There is, of course, an out-of-date, overworked and overburdened education system and facilities, with classes that are still too large, that also militates against positive change. Nevertheless, the persistence, tenacity and 'people power' of such families should not be underestimated. It has wrought change and will continue to do so. I leave this chapter with Micheline Mason's words (1994) about this establishment fear of change and growth:

> These families are your most precious resource, not your biggest enemy. They are the pioneers of a new beginning for many disadvantaged young people. Alongside these people are their allies, disabled adults skilled in the kind of training needed by a fearful and confused non-disabled world. And alongside them are the many professionals, especially teachers, who are longing to use their skills to help build safe, caring environments for all children to learn together the real meaning of community.

CHAPTER 8

Codes and the Sharing of Practice

Treatment, education and methodological 'drum beating'

The legislated 'Code of Practice' (1994) defines positive teaching intervention or the setting up of *positive learning environments* and experiences through the Individual(ised) Education Plans (IEPs). Sadly, some are interpreting it as a charter of deficit descriptions and categorisations in the rush to justify increased finance or resourcing. We have already seen how the concept of 'special need' as a category, separate from so-called or implicit 'normal need', is not conducive to inclusion and opportunity (Chapter 3, 'Disabling Schools and Colleges'; Chapter 2, 'A Healthy Perspective?'; Chapter 4, 'The Challenge of Inclusion'). The present chapter attempts to review and understand the variety of approaches that have evolved from psychological, educational, social and paramedical sources. Professional practice in education and health could benefit from greater co-operation, sharing of views, issues and knowledge that would enrich multi-disciplinary practice (see Chapter 6, 'Making Partnership a Reality') and extract effective principles from each other's methods.

> Matthew is 7 years old. He attends a 'designated' mainstream primary school. He has cerebral palsy affecting his limbs with mobility (walking) problems. He has a small dose of physiotherapy each week at school (approx. 1 hour) with some additional work through the week, supervised by the support assistant. His parents, keen that he should have optimum opportunity to overcome and work on his walking and movement, took him to a local centre based on the 'Peto' (Conductive Education) method. The school physiotherapist immediately withdrew her services from Matthew at school, refused to work with or discuss his case with the centre (and another physiotherapist). Matthew cannot choose to take advantage of both opportunities and the school physiotherapy is far too limited to have a major impact.

The above story exemplifies the problems professionals have co-operating around the child's needs and choices. Although different in effect and delivery, there are also differences between the underlying principles of different methods (e.g. Bobath and Conductive Education). A combination or succession of these methods, after joint discussion and planning by those involved, could well cater more successfully for an individual. After all, the anatomy, physiology and mechanics of the body are what they are. They do not not change to suit the professionals or methods involved.

> Professional demarcation and an unwillingness to work co-operatively with others has denied this child both choice and opportunity. This is not uncommon.

So, what of the Code of Practice for schools and our Code of Practice in this chapter? The national code aims to provide a framework to enable mainstream teachers in schools and colleges to provide education for pupils who are experiencing special educational needs. Alongside this 'Code of Practice' are the 1992 Further Education Act for Colleges (see Chapter 1), and the 'Code of Practice' for taking GCSE Exams. The new 'Code of Practice', under the 1993 Education Act, is a welcome start to the process of recognising the diverse needs of children in our education system. It provides a framework of guidance that at least recognises, on a practical level, some of the difficulties faced by children and young people who are disabled. It provides a starting point and basic parameters for identification of needs under the categories of 'physical disability' and 'medical conditions'. The next step is to re-visit the many possibilities for incorporating methods, approaches and some of the principles that underlie these into making the curriculum accessible and ongoing monitoring possible.

This can be done effectively through the Individualised Education Plans (IEPs). The efficiency of both the 'Code of Practice' and the implementation of its IEPs is highly dependent on the whole school ethos (as examined in Chapter 3 and Chapter 4). Success also depends on the systems that exist to allocate resources and teacher support in each school or college. The latter factors are considered in Chapter 4 ('The Challenge of Inclusion'). It is also important to question whether the IEP exists to satisfy administrative (or even financial) requirements or whether it is a genuine step towards positive intervention and inclusion into education.

Supporting learning

> A major controversy surrounding the choice of motor activities concerns the issue of whether we should teach skills or, alternatively, teach basic movement patterns that are assumed to assist performance in a wide range of skills.
>
> (Haskell and Barrett, 1977)

In a sense, the above dilemma is limiting the debate to a narrow view of 'physical skill', if you like. As we are discovering through sport psychology, a person's ability to improve their physical abilities revolves around their whole personality, circumstances, their attitude and that of significant others around them, the nature of their physical development and ability at the outset. The current problem in supporting learning (or living) for children and young people who are disabled comes back to the recurrent theme of 'competing ideologies'.

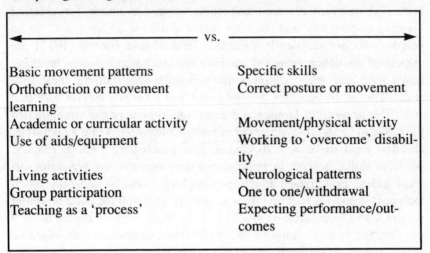

←	vs. →
Basic movement patterns	Specific skills
Orthofunction or movement learning	Correct posture or movement
Academic or curricular activity	Movement/physical activity
Use of aids/equipment	Working to 'overcome' disability
Living activities	Neurological patterns
Group participation	One to one/withdrawal
Teaching as a 'process'	Expecting performance/outcomes

Figure 8.1 Tensions and 'madness' in supporting learning

Movement and development

There are a number of reasons why the study of motor learning and physical development is important for those interested in the education of children and young people who are physically disabled. Babies' and young infants' movements and responses provide evidence of development and useful functioning of the nervous system. Movement responses, such as reflexes, are useful tools in the early monitoring of motor and perceptual abilities. In the years prior to adolescence, activity such as exploring the physical properties of the environment and of objects in it, is vital for learning fundamental concepts such as weight, shape, size, speed and spatial relationships. The third important area is that of independence. It is not enough to assert that motor skills are required for basic social functioning such as feeding, dressing and cleanliness. Independence has as much to do with communication skills, attitudes and sociability as it does with discrete movement 'skill' groups. Finally, leisure, recreation and physical education activities are important for a person's physical and social development (Jowsey, 1994).

Each of these areas of interest has its own body of literature and procedures for instruction and evaluation. In this section a broad discussion of movement, learning and development looks at a number of fundamental principles and concepts. The whole chapter looks to discuss the relationship between movement and learning and to describe some of the principles underlying the learning and continued acquisition of motor skills. It is an attempt to extract straightforward principles based on bodies of relevant research and some current methods for creating learning opportunity and teaching motor skills for children and young people who are physically disabled. Haskell and Barrett (1977) are critical of the deficit remedial teaching approach that involves breaking down goals and larger outcomes into sub-skills and 'training' these sub-skills. The 'skill' becomes the end result, not *what you can do with that skill.* The upsurge of laptops and palm top computers has strengthened the move towards enabling environments (Chapter 9). As far as possible, children need to be able to choose how much they wish to practise physical skills, bearing in mind social development, the physiological 'cost index' or fatigue factor (see Chapters 2 and 5) and how much technical support is required. It is absolutely vital that the child or young person learns to exercise *as much choice as possible* with regard to both physical (or motor) learning and the additional equipment they might be able to use to access learning and life experiences.

One-to-One vs. group work

It has been commonly held (particularly by those who work with the most severely disabled children) that one-to-one work is the most efficacious way of teaching, particularly if a child or young person has complex or specific difficulties. This assumption should be questioned on individual, social and educational grounds (Caswell and Portsmouth, 1989). One-to-one teaching is certainly not a universal panacea and has masqueraded as the most effective practice because it looks, on the surface, to be a solution. Children and young people who are disabled, usually because of practical or organisational considerations, can end up in one-to-one situations for the following reasons:

- **communication needs** (e.g. talking keyboard, E-Tran frame);
- **pace of work** needed is different from that of peers;
- **physical therapy** sometimes dictates withdrawal;
- **'catch up' sessions** if the child or young person falls behind.

The practical arrangements for intensive or one-to-one situations should bear in mind some of the potential consequences for the learner:

- inflexibility and narrowing of the curriculum;
- assumptions that the problems are child-centred and through child weaknesses alone;

- difficulties in transferring learning into group or more complex situations;
- lack of continuity with the child's daily experience and normal curriculum;
- increased pressure and intrusiveness experienced by the learner;
- an increased perception of 'differentness' that pushes the child outside his or her social group.

(Caswell and Portsmouth, 1989)

Once learning support through withdrawal has been decided upon, it tends to set in motion all kinds of practical problems related to timetable and staffing arrangements, the end result being sessions more often than not organised when they can be fitted in. The move into *and out of* individual work needs to be carefully planned with social and educational objectives kept clearly in mind.

The fundamental principles of good teaching (and quality of learning) apply in the same measure to group and individual sessions. For example, positive relationships, precise target setting, close monitoring of progress and clear feedback that enhances self-esteem. In short, a genuinely good relationship between a leader and a group, coupled with effective teaching practices and individualised knowledge (and planning) is every bit as effective as one-to-one work. It is hard to see what are the real benefits are of removing a child or young person from their group for any length of time. It often has more to do with the needs of the adults involved than of the child or young person. To take it further, there are longer term considerations making it important that a child or young person is *not* removed from their peers, other than for reasons that any person might be (e.g. if their behaviour is dangerous or they genuinely need personal privacy).

> If these curriculum principles are more consistently applied in the classroom then the narrowness of the one-to-one option will become apparent: it will also ensure that where it does operate the process is likely to be more productive and less patronising.
>
> (Caswell and Portsmouth, 1989)

Self-esteem enhancement

Following the brief discussion in Chapter 2 on self-esteem, it is interesting to note the common ground between current humanistic psychology and Professor Peto, the founder of conductive education, nearly 50 years ago. Peto laid an emphasis on active learning, the urge for self-development, self-esteem and spontaneity, the importance of an environment suitable for learning, and on the connection between thought, language and action. He epitomised a struggle against the tyranny of 'scholasticism', defined as exercise without meaning. The classic research by Rosenthal and Jacobson (1968) called the 'Pygmalion effect' illustrates very clearly the impact that a teacher (or other significant adult) can have on the child's self-concept, expectations, cognitive style and motivation, in short, on the whole of a child's academic or learning abilities in school. More recently, in 1993, Charlton and Hunt have been developing the Enhancement Approaches to Self-Image 'EASI teaching programme' aimed at self-image enhancement for pupils. This programme was, in turn, launched from previous research (Aspy and Roebuck, 1983) which clearly indicated that teachers who had undergone a 'humanistic training programme' behaved differently towards their pupils in 3 main ways:

(1) Proficient at empathising.
(2) Became congruent. Genuine relationships and rapport established.
(3) Unconditional positive regard. Treating pupils with greater respect for their individuality and ability.

(Adapted from Charlton and Hunt, 1993)

The changes in pupils taught by these teachers included increased self-esteem, more positive self-image development, gains in academic achievement and even increased IQ scores.

Establishing the importance of teacher or adult behaviour towards pupils is very much related to the idea of motivating or activating, and to its converse, learned helplessness or disaffection. In previous chapters we have considered the effects of negative social and cultural models that children who are disabled currently have to grow up with. To counter the negative stereotypes or absence of role models, teachers, parents and other adults who work with disabled children and young people need to be aware of the importance of enhancing self-image, not by telling children 'how brave' they are or by disingenuous attempts to engineer unrealistic positive outcomes all the time, but simply by applying the points (1) to (3) above. *Genuine empathy, respect and good relationships can do more for all children, including disabled children, than any amount of remote, impersonal or pseudo-scientifically constructed programmes.* This must be the first and most efficacious intervention strategy before the application of other approaches or techniques. It is interesting to note that there will be some approaches and some professionals that regard the above as outside the realm of their professional brief. My answer to that is, get wise and get properly trained! Chapter 5 also explores the use of the school curriculum in promoting positive and inclusive social and cultural models.

Extracts from 'Body Shopping'
by Simon Brisenden

I was arrested, it was a fair cop
for loitering with intent inside the Body Shop
I entered innocently hoping to find
the perfect body and the perfect mind . . .

held in the vice of their rubber gloves
I begged for my release
they laughed and said there's no escape
once you're caught by the body police . . .

they sentenced me to be spotty and fat
so everyone will treat me like a door-mat
they sentenced me to have an arse like a sack
they sentenced me to be black
they sentenced me not to walk or run
and never to appear on page 3 of The Sun . . .

Conductive Education and Bobath

Conductive Education is not a treatment or therapy and offers no cure. It is a system of special education, for children and adults with motor disorders. When people first become aware of Conductive Education they usually emphasise the system's apparent success at teaching children and adults to develop greater bodily control. Although this is a central concern, as a system of education (rather than simply exercises or training) it not only aims to improve motor skills and functions but also transforms development as a whole including emotional and intellectual aspects.

(Source: Foundation for Conductive Education, 1989)

Professor Andras Peto's ideas can be traced back to the 1940's to some of his early experiences and to current research or knowledge at the time. A parallel movement, exemplified by Vygotsky (1962), explored the relationship between thought and language; language as an abstract and symbolic framework for organising thinking and problem-solving. It seems that Peto (a Hungarian neurologist), quite logically injected the idea of movement and its organisation into the thought, language and problem-solving relationship. This came to be known as Conductive Education. This seemingly simple equation was developed by Peto into a system that claims to be centred around the person's individual learning processes and unique potential. This is superficially at odds with the way in which it has been 'imported' into this country as a system whose activities revolve around 'set pieces', physical functioning through fixed skills, group chanting and controlled movement on demanding pieces of wooden (and very hard) furniture. The image of rigidity has been compounded by an interpretation, in this country, that disabled people shouldn't have to use special aids or equipment. There are many issues here of cultural translation and narrow professional (or practitioner) interpretation or even misinterpretation.

It was an over simplistic description of the elements of Conductive Education that heralded the problems of translating it into practice in this country. It was as if the superficial appearance of Conductive Education had been imported at the expense of the original and underlying principles and ethics. In a sense, the problems generated by its transplantation indicated larger problems that are still associated with our educational and medical practices, such as inflexibility, the search for solutions not principles, the 'treatment' (or doing to) ethic, grouping people by disabilities (in every sense) or a view of the disabled person as a passive recipient of a 'programme'. It has to be said that, despite the laudable principles later outlined, the Hungarian (medical and educational) system *in practice* probably falls short of its own principles and in the clinical setting falls short of the ethics of choice and opportunity. Many disabled groups consider the way in which it has come to be imposed upon individuals as an infringement of rights.

Karel and Bertha Bobath, on the other hand, developed a system that was directly concerned with therapeutic intervention at the level of physical movement and posture.

The Bobath treatment aims to give the child the experience of more normal posture and movement. Through specialised ways of handling, stiffness can be reduced, muscle control against gravity can be increased and fluctuating muscle activity can be stabilised. Depending on the severity of the condition, the child is better able to learn how to sit up and use his hands, to stand up and walk. Ideally the treatment is an integral part of all of the management programmes for that child.

The assessment of the individual child's pattern of movement and pattern of muscle tone is critical to the regime provided. Many unwanted reflexes from the lower part of the brain are no longer inhibited from the higher levels due to brain damage and these greatly influence the pattern of the child. Paying attention to these reflexes, it is possible to observe patterns of abnormal movement that interfere with the child's or young person's ability to grasp, move objects, concentrate on things in front and many more. For example, when the child turns his head, all the limbs on the face side of the child extend, and all the limbs on the skull side flex (bend). This immediately leads to an unbalanced body posture and usually one side becomes dominant (a symmetrical tonic neck reflex).

Orthofunction (in *Conductive Education*) is more than just achieving the skills of 'daily living' as a set of 'performance goals'. It is concerned with the 'organisation' of skills and the way they are used to anticipate or solve problems in real life situations. The ability to adapt what we do to changing circumstances (active intelligence) has been at the heart of our own endeavours with pupils who are both learning and physically disabled.

> ORTHOFUNCTION: . . . learning does not just consist of copying, and letting oneself be carried along by the intervention of the teacher . . . it is very important for the person learning to have a clear perception of 'what it is all about', to abandon passivity and to reconstruct the implicit content . . . this reconstruction must not be accomplished by merely adding together the fragments . . . It must be possible to anticipate the ultimate aim of the action . . .
>
> (Hari, 1988)

Step by step and precision teaching techniques have been developed through task analysis and targetted steps for people with learning disabilities. Thinking or problem solving approaches involve both the teacher (as mediator) and the learner in exploring the way a person 'organises' his/her thoughts to achieve a goal. It involves the learner in the process and arms him/her with the ability to take on new challenges with confidence. The teacher does not provide the learner with the answers or the skills but simply establishes the conditions in which the learner can move more freely to achieve his/her own objectives. Unfortunately, the achievement of explicitly stated and externally 'fixed' objectives has become the major activity of education, including the current national curriculum. A child may achieve a whole variety of alternative objectives and still 'fail'.

> The teacher, the conductor, is merely a catalyst. The conductor does not, himself, construct the pupil's orthofunction"
>
> (Hari, 1988)

In other words, Dr. Hari's expression of educational principle states that it is not up to the teacher to define the child's objectives but to assist the child in achieving *his or her own objectives* in movement.

The aims of *Bobath treatment* are influenced by several factors such as the age of the child, the severity of their disability and their motivation and these aims are developed by the physiotherapist. Treatment is planned for each child by observing how the child is moving. Why is the child moving abnormally? What are the patterns of movement? What is the child not doing that is appropriate for its age? What can the child do? What is the child's posture? All these questions are used to assess the child's ability for movement.

Depending on which reflexes are dominant, a certain pattern will show, and may give asymmetry (an unbalanced posture), or even already show contractures (muscle groups becoming permanently tight). Some children have unbalanced posture regularly and symmetry (getting a balanced posture) is vital. They move in and out of patterns and have less contractures during early life. Whereas other children who are physically disabled may have more static or dominant patterns and these can quickly lead to contractures. When the muscles become tight they will tend to shorten and may be painful to extend. Once contractures develop, the pattern has more of a complete hold and the normal pattern is extremely dificult to regain.

In Bobath treatment, the physiotherapist has to develop patterns of movement with the child that combine elements of flexion and extension. Hands on treatment is essential, otherwise effort will increase the abnormal or rigid patterns and the child will not be able to succeed.

In effect, the intention of Bobath is to by-pass conscious involvement of a child in the movement. This is done to reduce the effect that anxiety has in triggering off more unwanted reflexes. This is in contrast to the principles of Conductive Education.

In contrast to the Bobath method, the construct of 'intention' in movement also seems to be very important in the practice of Conductive Education. It is central to motivation and cohesion of effort within an individual.

> THE ORIGIN OF INTENTION: The conductor must allow someone to reach his goal without helping him directly, at the same time keeping the link with the person active, while not interfering directly with the function that should be modified . . . Conductive Education seeks to change intention rather than performance.
> The inner reorganisation is the reorganisation of intention . . . an action becomes effective only after having been organised orthofunctionally.
> By unifying and co-ordinating these specialisations (psychology and physiology) it is the person himself that is won and given the means to use the power of his brain. In this way conduction allows the achievement of the highest results. It is a true education.
>
> (Hari, 1988)

> THE ORGANISATION OF CO-ORDINATION: If the teacher wishes to change the dysfunction of the nervous system . . . he must find objectives which are near enough and which are accessible only by establishing a new internal organisation. (The possibility of functional reorganisation, of flexibility and plasticity is known today) . . . one learns more by actions than by passive response or by simple repeated connections.
>
> (Hari, 1988)

The organisation of co-ordination is important to Conductive Education (C.E.), whereas positioning is very important to Bobath treatment. Correct positioning helps movements become normal and can discourage abnormal movements. A child's position can be changed frequently to achieve this. Handling the child using key points on the child's body is also important for correct positioning. In this way, the Bobath therapist manipulates the child to correct abnormal movements. Help is given with movements like chewing, handling objects, moving about, sitting or lying down. Even when a child is being carried, using correct positioning and handling key points on the child's body is very important. This is the essence of the skill of the physiotherapist who can then 'train' others such as carers and parents to provide this support.

The Bobath therapist works with the child's family to teach them how to handle and position the child properly at home so therapy can be continued to encourage and facilitate normal movements. Many children do not like physiotherapy because being placed in 'correct' positions seems 'unnatural' to the way the body is used to moving. Both the child and the parent need to be encouraged by the therapist, and Bobath, like any other therapy, requires effort and practice in order to achieve benefits.

Can we use the principles of CE in this country? These are no more (or less) than effective and holistic teaching principles that have been in use in this country for many years. Peto's ideas may go back 60 or so years, but this was also a time when many parallel ideas in learning theory were developing in Europe and the United States. They did not develop in a vacuum and neither did our current learning theories in this country. Other learning theories and theorists which have influenced our practice were also influenced by the same research and its application, more often than not by the same people in the 1930's, 40's and 50's (Vygotsky, Luria, Kelly, Skinner, Bruner, Piaget, Dewey, Maslow, Broadbent, Vernon). It is not something utterly new, its principles already existed in this country under many different guises.

Professor Peto organised some of these underlying theories into a cohesive and practical programme mainly designed for children under five, who have moderate to severe physical disability with few complicating or associated disabilities (such as cognitive, degenerative or sensory). However, the problem still remains with the various ways that Bobath and CE have been incorporated into units, schools and institutions in this country; the way that groups of professionals have hijacked the activities and kept their own principles to themselves; or the technical or mechanical aspects of Bobath and CE could be fulfilled but without real understanding of the individual and personal nature of the interactions involved.

The professional debate between Bobath and Conductive Education has served a purpose by drawing attention to the right of children and young people to have their physical needs considered in a positive and educational manner. The ethics, issues and principles involved for all the so-called

TABLE I

	PETO and CONDUCTIVE EDUCATION (CE)	BEHAVIOURAL	BOBATH	DOMAN-DELACATO
LANGUAGE/ COMMUNICATION	Verbalised/rhythmical intention. Singing and speech linked to movement. Also counting until child achieves aim. **Development of the internal language of active movement. The child is assisted in 'organising' their own movement** (they are not physically/passively moved). The neurological links between language and movement are exploited.	Varies on degree of formality of siutation or approach. In the very formal, **minimal and highly regulated use of language.** Precision teaching requires the setting of clearly expressed (and shared) targets. **Communication can become stilted and limited by fixed and limited responses or by mechanistic types of interaction.** This lack of sophistication often puts children off entirely.	Spoken in appropriate based language of body parts and movement. Depends to a large extent on the therapist and the relationship(s) involved. **Language is not seen as an important part of physical or movement development**. The neurological links between language, feelings, cognition and movement or posture don't seem to be acknowledged.	It is very hard to guage what kind of communication is actually going on. It certainly does not look like 2-way communication. The language seems to be **highly defined by the 'therapist' or adult and not flexibly explored/used by child. Purports to treat the brain directly on the basis that the brain, like a muscle, will grow when exercise in specific patterns.**
TRAINING/ PROFESSIONALS INVOLVED	Conductors. Professional training plus theoretical courses in education, psychology, biology, physiotherapy, speech and language. All included in a 4 year teacher training course. **They are 'educators' not therapists. A more holistic and transdisciplinary approach in that the 'conductor' is a trans-disciplinary professional.** Restricted access to knowledge, it has been maintained within Peto or associate organisations	Varies enormously. Can be quite intensive and structured, e.g. EDY training package or Assertive Discipline. **Teachers often have a 'grounding in behavioural psychology.** Behavioural approaches currently favoured by many educational psychologists but not for PD pupiils. The effect of behaviour and other's responses on self-esteem is a more productive avenue to follow for pupils who are PD.	**Pysiotherapists domain**. Bobath training course – held Bobath Centre (and possibly others now). Exclusive and limited access to training and knowledge base. Held specifically within the physiotherpay profession although there are books on the method. **Requires hands on. Physiotherapists will use otehr adults to train as additional 'hands' in some cases.**	**"Parents main participants in therapy treatment"** (The Director of Knowle Hall). parents receive instruction and training. The **methods then have to be passed onto many volunteers** who work in teams, engaging in very precise and structured activity. Kerland – 1 day both parents or one parent and one volunteer. **Assessment with families and links with medical and educational services.** BIBIC – two and half days.
INVOLVEMENT OF PARENTS	'Schools for Parents' teachers and supports management of child at home. This includes how to activate and motivate your child. Toddlers with mothers working in groups. **Continuity at home encour-aged through daily living skills and carefully struc-tured programmes. Parents encouraged and guided in handling their child and gain in confidence.**	Varies enormously. Parents and other adults (consciously or unconsciously) 'shape' their children's behaviour with negative or positive feedback. **This feedback is often very subtle and not knowingly transmitted. This is particularly important for the child's self-esteem, self-image and self-concept.** Attitudes and feelings are often unconsciously transmitted.	Detailed training (when situation allows it) in early **physical development, correct positioning, handling and giving correct sensory input. Parents become involved in handling and positioning** with professional when there is the facility to do so. The limitations have mainly to do with the way that services are managed and delivered.	Very important (see above). **Parents are taught about brain function** and given intensive programmes to work through with their off spring. These are **classic "hot housing" techniques** for children range across the intellectual and physical ability spectrum. **Tendency to set up expectations by parents that are not always realistic or avhievable**.

INTERACTIVE	SPORT PSYCHOLOGY	NATIONAL CURRICULUM	SURGICAL INTERVENTION	
The language of relationships and sophisticated sensitive communication signals. Two way communication (rather than professional or adult to child/client/passive recipient). **Communication process vital both parties alter their actions, language, responses or behaviour with the other**. Different from expecting performance from the recipient of the treatment. High degree of skill to support and guide.	**FEEDBACK** (visual and verbal) is seen as a vital component of encouraging motor learning. The language of physical skill, movement, success, motivation, visualisation and personal achievement encourages a positive self-image.	When applied carefully the **breadth of language picked up should match the richness of the curriculum content.** Communication in the true sense has been severely compromised by pressure and restrictions of content delivery and time. Sadly, the emphasis is on **written language** (for testing) not on oral and problem-solving language.	Lack of proper communication involvement of and decision-making by the child or young person can have a detrimental effect on their self-image. Questions need to be asked to help **individual feel part of the process and active in decision-making**. Language used is often unnecessarily obscured and specialised (e.g. "Physiological Cost Index – Gait Analysis").	**LANG. & COMM.**
Spoken in appropriate based language of body parts and movement. Depends to a large extend on the protagonists and the relationship(s) involved. A high degree of skill necessary but has not been formalised, packaged or 'taken over' by one group of professionals (thankfully!). For use with individuals or with groups.	**Emphasis on choice and responsibility. Learner takes full control of, and involvement in, his/her own learning.** This leads to ACTIVITY not PASSIVITY. Activation, goal setting, motor learning, attriubtion and anxiety reduction are all features.	The emphasis is still on **prescription and bureaucracy to maintain the nC and differentiation for SEN.** A model based on extended professional training with increased autonomy would be preferable. At the moment it relies on bureaucratic accountability – a nonsense!	The combination of **medical and paramedica views should provide the basis for CHOICE by the client (or parent).** Highly complex techniques and procedures are not always successful. Balances need to be struck between the needs of the highly trained professional and the personal/social needs of the client.	**TRAINING**
The result of early parenting skills involving sensitive response and active interaction with the child's developing personality and abilities. **Puts parent knowledge and expertise at the forefront.** Promotes the view of **learning as interaction not performance**.	Greater understanding of the role of the whole personality of the child in motor and other learning. This empowers everybody to assist in the **learner's own effeorts**, not to impose wild or unncessary anxieties on them.	Greater degree of parential involvement is intended by policy but **still elusive in practice.** Parents are still very much excluded from new NC jargon which has set up 'competitiveness'. The latch **on to obscure definitions of "success".**	**Some parents will hold to the 'normalising' effects of some surgical intervention.** Other parents or young people may opt for it out of choice or because they are **not offered any choices.** Some parents **are told** and not given the whole story.	**PARENTS**

TABLE I	PETO and CONDUCTIVE EDUCATION (CE)	BEHAVIOURAL	BOBATH	DOMAN-DELACATO
LEARNING TAKING PLACE (including breadth and balance)	**Emphasis on physical development, through group work on academic or curricular skills.** It is debatable how much space there is for individual's interests and skills. There are large cultural differences between European and UK perception of 'education' and delivery of curriculum. More academic curriculum centres on 3Rs and NC? Dr. Hari says – **not a therapy but a pedagogical method.**	**Applicable to behaviour and skills training or to reducing extreme or antisocial behaviour.** Less applicable to applied more academic, abstrct or complex learning situations. Behavioural 'targets' can be come very narrow, denying choice and opportunity. Problems generalising skills and behaviour into wider, more complex or more sophisticated situations.	**Follows (usually) developmental milestones** – will not progress unless child has been through milestones. **There is little concept of the breadth of learning or of applying skills in a wide range of situations.** Skills application may broaden from posture/movement depending upon the child, situation and invidivdual therapists.	2–3 hours, five days a week. Programmes on visual, auditory, tactile, mobility, language, manual dexterity, therefore seems faily broad. The **basic principles that are not yet proven to be correct (e.g. patterning).** Preservation of the myth of 'cures'. Research indicates rapid increase in learning over short periods (1–2 years) but little overall increased over longer periods (5+ years). Strict developmental approach.
FREQUENCY OF LEARNING EXPERIENCES OR 'TREATMENT'	**Whole working day. In purest form, throughout waking hours.** Wide diversity in this country. Original method taken and apllied in widely different contexts, for example, CE groups for 1/2 hour, 1 hour sessions to full time in day/residential settings. In Hungary varies between full time intensive programmes to short courses. Holism and consistency achieved solely by use of one person as the key – the 'conductor'.	At any time the behaviour occurs **or** whenever the skills is to be enhanced. **Consistency and progression must be involved, hence co-operation and teamwork.** Behavioural techniques, to some extent, **encourage the learner to depend upon the 'structure' of their environment and others' responses. Can be a problem in applying these skills in less structured environments.** Cognitive assimilation and involvement are necessary.	1 or possibly 2 sessions a week and home treatment by parents. As often as possible – usually 1–2 sessions per week. Parents trained in handling. Often **delivered as 'remedial' or withdrawal sessions, losing continuity and cohesion.** Bobath principles **can be very much part of daily living and curricular activity** (given the necessary co-operation) between professionals.	Regularly throughout the day. **Very intensive and prolonged intervention that sometimes treats the recipient as an 'object'.** Personal involvement in the process neither thought necessary or desirable. Ethically questionable in it sintensity and personal intrusiveness. Many parents feel their children have benefitted and there are positive side effects ofr the recipient and family.
EQUIPMENT OR SPECIALISED ENVIRONMENT	Wooden plinth, ladder back sets, boxes and foot stnads, rings, sticks. All furniture and equipment made of wood. No metal or 'high tech.' equipment. An environment that is simple and without undue visual or auditory stimuli (seen as perceptual clutter). Is this a response to the lack of high tech. facilities in Hungary? Equipment encourages child to be responsble for movement and posture.	The use of equipment is not usually associated with behavioural techniques. Teaching machines and some IT equipment provides **contingent and immediate feedback to reinforce attempts at movement** (see Chapter 9). Used appropriately, technology and electronic controls encourage and stimulative active attempts to control and organise movement for specific and individual purposes (e.g. writing and environmental control.)	Therapy balls, wedges, side lying boards, arm splints, standing frames, supportive chairs, fibre glass "moulds". **Equipment is intended to 'place and maintain the child or young person in a correct posture in order that they can then exhibit (or be encouraged to initiate) controlled movements.** Intention to reduce and remove unintentional movements or postures.	Nothing appears to be singularly identified with Doman-Delecato methods. **Tables or flat surfaces used for 'patterning' exercises.** Volunteers move the child's limbs endlessly to achieve some kind of motor development or neurological response. **Children are masked or hung upside down from the ceiling and spun.**

INTERACTIVE	SPORT PSYCHOLOGY	NATIONAL CURRICULUM	SURGICAL INTERVENTION	
A **child learns**, through forming relationships, **sophisticated language and communication skills.** These skills are very much at the interpersonal level but can be extended into more formal communication. **An individual learns how to exercise choice** with others.	All movement training and motor learning can be seen as a 'means to an end' – not an end in itself. Can then be integrated into academic and learning activity.	Should read **'broad, balanced and impossible curriculum'.** Until recent modifications was too big to be applied in practice. Has caused adverse reaction to those experiencing SEN. PD pupils still regarded as burden on teaching load by many.	On the positive side, **h patient may learn more about themselves in the process and about the disability.** Negative views transmitted by attempts at 'becoming normal'. Positive benefits from a 'Health Education' approach.	**B & B C**
An interactive approach will **optimise every opportunity to extend knowledge and understanding.** Does not rely on stilted and limited formalisation of learning by outcome. **More likely to produce "skilled performance"** than formal or didactic methods.	The 'coaching' model can be seen as selected by the learner, or at school, integrated into daily teaching/learning activities. **Choice and control mean the learner will select level of activity.**	During whole school experience. The big issues here have to do with **'entitlement' through 'access' to the curriculum.** This is where the overlap with other methods that support **'access' to having experience through physical support.**	Once embarked upon a course of surgical correction, it may involve a great amount of time and repeated visits to and stays in hospital. Some surgical interventions can **carry on for a number of years with social and personal consequences.**	**F R E Q.**
No equipment or specialised environments are specified. This 'interactive approach' has more to do with relationships and changing or developing understnading. **Anything and everything can be used to facilitate interaction.**	**Equipment to facilitate the development of physical skills and abilities is seen as enhancing the individual's motivation and self-esteem.** Even the most accomplished athlete needs some equipment to enhance performance.	Some definition of areas to be covered has led to **improved targeting of teaching materials and equipment.** It remains to be seen whether materials and equipment will be readily available to support curricular access specifically for PD pupils and students.	Occupational therapy will support sometimes very large expenditure on domestic alterations and equipment. This is patchy, means tested and under-resourced. **Tremendous benefit can ensue from environmental alterations.**	**E Q U I P.**

TABLE I	PETO and CONDUCTIVE EDUCATION (CE)	BEHAVIOURAL	BOBATH	DOMAN-DELACATO
MISCELLANEOUS	Professor Peto based much of his method on the applications of principles developed by Luria (----_ and Vygotsky (1962). Theories of internal language and mediation in the orgnisation of movement, proximal zones of development and encouraging problem solving are **still very relevant in all areas of education today.** Peto took these principles and used them with children who experienced movement disabilities.	**Most other methods described have 'behavioural components' in them** (e.g. 'target setting' in CE or contingent sensory feedback in Ayers interactive) or the, often vain, attempt at massive physical 'programming' of Doman-Delecato or Kerland approach. The problem is that it defines learning by outcomes or skills, not necessarily the processing and wider use of these skills.	The "Bobath" method received this label through Karel and Bertha Bobath's work to base physiotherapy practice on the early development of movement and posture. **Contains a wealth of important principles but the direct application of intervention to remedy bits that have gone wrong is limiting to the child** and causes problems in other areas of learning and development. Needs to be placed into a daily living and learning domain (not clinical).	The links between **brain strcuture and specific functions have not yet been proven**, neither has the efficacy of these methods, in the long term. Controls tend to catch up after 5+ years and the extent of **adverse effects on holistic or general development have not been sufficiently investigated.** Sometimes has more to do with the ambitions of parents rather than the needs of the child. Some unusual treatments involved.
COST (Financial and human)	Prior to CE Assessment Centre at Fitzroy Square, London, the cost of taking a child to Hungary (financial and to family life) was considerable (up to £8,000 for short assessment period0. Cost now depends on provider, location (UK or Hungary) and intensity of programmes (**Peto Institute is still expensive due to heavy world wide demand).**	School age facilities for pupils who are **physically disabled and experience significant emotional or behavioural problems are extremely expensive (around £700–£800 per week).** Behavioural approaches do get 'packaged', like conductive education or Bobath but not specifically for children who are physically disabled.	Training for paramedics only. Specific treatment costs will depend on the cost of the physiotherapist (£0–£80 per hour) and can be paid for by Health Authority or privately. No specific time limits to lengths of treatment. Cost in terms of time taken from other facets of development should be considered against physical (development or skill) benefits in the long term.	(British Institute for brain Injured Children – BIBIC). BIBIC: Initial interview £25. 4 day initial assessment £500. Monthly contribution £75. KERLAND: 2 day assessment £320. Subsequent 1 day re-assessment £160. 3 hours per day over 5 or 6 weeks. (These figures are circa 1992 so may well be out of date).

INTERACTIVE	SPORT PSYCHOLOGY	NATIONAL CURRICULUM	SURGICAL INTERVENTION	
The term 'interactive approach' was coined (Nind and Hewitt, 19--) but this highly sophisticated analysis is more a result of **observing and utilising natural phenomena. The natural human interplay between two or more people serves as a base for developing all skills and knowledge.**	The role of **stress and anxiety** are acknowledged. There is special stress and pressure attached to motor learning and ability. It is inherently tied into our personality and self-image. Recognition of the personal involvement leads to more sensitive activity programmes and expectations.	The net effect of the introduction of NC has been to promote more 'specialisation' of attitudes, re-sources and approaches. **Truly inclusive education systems should regard IEP's, accessibility and involvement of PD pupils in all school life as a completely ordinary,** and for all.	Surgery is **often proferred as the only solution to physical problems when it is not.** Careful consideration should always be given to social and environmental intervention.	**M I S C.**
The cost resides mainly in leaving behind formalised, rigid or 'highly packaged' approaches and getting down to shaping and using personal interaction well.	Ranging from **participation in school PE and sport,** through to having a personal (and perhaps expensive) coach (or coaching team). Lesson from sport psychology is that **PHYSICAL SKILLS SHOULD NOT BE DEVELOPED AT THE COST OF OTHER AREAS OF DEVELOPMENT AND PERSONAL SATISFACTION.**	The NC has cost children and young people by wasting a lot of teacher time and effort. Children and young people who are PD have been **locationally integrated but educationally marginalised.**	Usually the cost is absorbed by the Health Service. What is the cost of lost 'education' times though for medical treatments? It should be assessed. What is the cost and benefits in human terms of surgical intervention?	**C O S T**

different methods should be up for wider professional debate and I therefore make no excuse for using Bobath and CE as prime examples.

Common principles

Table I is an attempt to draw out some of the valuable work that contributes to teaching and learning generally but specifically to the great variety of methods that are noted. It aims to offer the reader an opportunity to compare the range of approaches and principles. There are many derivatives from these under different names such as 'Unified Approaches' or 'Functional Language and Movement Programmes'. It is not possible or desirable to go into all of them in greater detail. The search here is for the basic underlying principles, extracted from the combined knowledge and understanding to date. A proper functional 'Code of Practice' or body of knowledge should be built on such principles and cannot afford to ignore *any aspect* of the child or young person. Sadly, we have in existence, a plethora of discontinuous 'practices' whose components depend not upon the needs of a child or young person but upon which professional perspective (education, health or social) you are looking from. It is all very well to produce an educational 'Code of Practice' but where it interfaces with other services and parents it is patently not working, at the moment. This is due to various factors of policy and management discussed in Chapters 1, 4 and 6.

Returning to Table I, it is not sensible to suggest that each of the methods referred to are exclusive of each other, despite the way they might be packaged and promoted. For example, Professor Peto based his methods on the work of psychologists Luria (1966 and 1970) and Vygotsky (1962) whose theories of language, problem-solving, internal language and proximal zones of development or learning are common to many western cultures and educational practices. Behavioural psychology underpins much practice in education but there are still ethical questions to be answered, for example, about the process of 'target setting' (used in behaviour programmes, conductive education and in precision teaching programmes for those experiencing minimal physical or learning disabilities). Whose targets are being set and to what purpose or eventual end? Are they goals that are meaningful, useful or capable of extension into real life or are they simply to satisfy some preconception of the adults concerned? Table I also illustrates the overlaps between methods used. It is important that we move the debate from a medical perspective through into an educational model. Following Table I, the contribution of sport psychology is an attempt to put forward a possible framework within which the learner is able to exercise choice and control. He or she is not done to, but is actively involved in the process.

Sport psychology

Improved motor performance is one of the main goals of 'Sport Psychology' and it is worth considering the ways in which this is achieved. Athletes are constantly striving to improve their own physical abilities and push themselves to greater feats, whilst learning to understand their own limitations. The key factor in this is that it is centred on the individual, who takes responsibility and is motivated. Sport psychology is a positive way to look upon the learning and development of physical skills because the learner takes full responsibility for, and has full involvement in, his or her own learning. In this sense we are dealing with ACTIVITY in its fullest sense and rejecting PASSIVITY as detrimental to short and long term success and fulfilment.

Positive and ongoing feedback plays an important role in directing attention to problems associated with movement skills. These are related to real, everyday events and activities that have general meaning to the learner. This also involves, in a major way, both the personality and thought processes of the learner, in correcting less useful movements/actions, in understanding the consequences of certain actions and in planning more useful sequences of movement or sub-routines to practise.

The setting of specific and realistic goals or targets that represent a proper challenge are more useful than vague, easy or non-existent goals.

> Goals give direction to the attention, they 'mobilise' the person, increase the powers of persistence and make the development of a strategy easier (Locke et al, 1981, p.125).
>
> (In: Bakker, Whiting and van der Brug, 1990)

In addition to this, the positive feedback given, once a skill has been worked on through others watching your programme, has a beneficial effect on that performance.

Attention and activation are increased when the learner is given the opportunity to prepare properly for activities or physical movement. He or she also develops an awareness of relevant uses to movement and can increasingly learn what to expect (and reduce anxiety or tension). It is clear from sport psychology and physiology that anxiety causes tension in conflicting muscle blocks (agonist and antagonist) and thus increases effort for less movement 'pay off'. Children and young people are constantly subjected to this kind of physical tension and stress by the living and learning environment we have created. The relationship between anxiety and physical performance is an important one. One of the major causes of tension and stress is powerlessness. That is, where the movement learner is not involved in decisions about what he or she is about to do.

> Under low levels of stress and physiological arousal performance should improve as stress increases up to a certain critical threshold. At this point the performer begins to perceive an imbalance between the demands of the situation and his capability to match them. Anxiety occurs and performance suddenly and dramatically falls . . .
>
> (Jones and Hardy, 1989)

The term 'raising action potential' in certain muscle groups has some importance where the physical disability is associated with neurological problems or damage. It says that such things as practise, experience, anticipation and developing physical control and skill are related to cognitive, problem solving or, more simply, intellectual or thought processes. In applying these principles, care must be taken to *allow the learner to guide*. A disabled child or person is the one who makes the decision to try movement and is activated by their own (not other's) motivation and anticipation. These include the emotional factors already outlined. This is important because it tends to unite the existing divisions that exist between academic, physical and practical activity.

We also suffer from a tyranny of academic status, defined narrowly by those whose interests are served by this definition. It has already been argued that the 'scholastic' or 'academic' emphasis placed on education, in its most limited form, acts against the acceptance of diversity (and hence diverse physical needs) in our schools, colleges and society generally. We seem to be further away than many countries (e.g. USA and Japan) from acknowledging the 'scholasticism' of physical endeavour and the variety of ways that a person can express their intelligence. Professor Stephen Hawking is an example of an intellectually gifted individual who is able to communicate his thoughts through advanced technology. The Candoco Dance Company is an example of disabled and non-disabled people putting together visually stunning, emotionally evocative and physically astonishing dance programmes. Candoco are working in the physical domain, as creative artists and athletes, both disabled and non-disabled. Admiration for dance and creative skill is equally due to all members of that company as it is due to the intellectual activity of Professor Hawking.

To sum up, then, sport psychology has some specific lessons for all professions who work on specific or 'packaged' methods that have to do with 'motor learning'. It also has some lessons for the way in which education and paramedical services are delivered to children and young people who are disabled. The choice and opportunities for learning should be largely controlled by the learner, and this has particular benefits when a disabled child or young person is treated with the same respect as an athlete:

- shares or makes the decisions about the goals and objectives to be achieved;
- becomes more aware of stresses and strains generated or imposed;
- chooses from a range of possible activities and methods;
- active planning and problem-solving is involved;
- chooses how, when and where he or she practises and performs;
- learner has optional preparation for physical demands;
- takes responsibility for his or her own motivation and enthusiasm;
- learner becomes more aware of own abilities and needs;
- decides who they wish to or can involve in their activities;
- raises 'action potentials' in specific muscle groups;
- learning is related to real, everyday and personalised goals;
- anxiety is reduced through positivity and quantity of experience;
- learner is able to develop their own 'action plans' to combat physical problems.

Including pupils and students

From talking to pupils and parents or guardians in schools in eight education authorities in Scotland (Scottish Education Council, 1990), it was clear that they were largely enthusiastic about the experience of being in mainstream schools. The pupils welcomed the chance to mix with their non-disabled peers in and out of the classroom and to have a full range of curricular choices. Teachers also spoke of the benefits to staff and non-disabled pupils of integration, such as sharing in the lives of people who are disabled, understanding some of the problems they face in many areas of daily life and opportunities for developing friendships.

These are some of the problems discussed by pupils who are physically disabled, as they grow up:

- Being regarded as children incapable of making decisions, or as objects of pity and over-protection.
- Being the objects of charitable giving, however necessary.
- Relying on help from parents for dressing, styling hair and applying make up when school friends can experiment alone.
- Finding difficulties in dressing fashionably when in a wheel chair, or wearing callipers, or using an appliance for incontinence, or being very short or stout.
- Spending too much time on static pursuits such as watching television and reading magazines, where emphasis is placed on bodily perfection and measuring appearance against this may be depressing for those

with physical disabilities.

- Finding difficulties with access and transport to places where young people meet socially, and often having to involve help from parents when others go alone.
- Listening to stated medical policy on pre-natal screening and elective termination of pregnancy for such conditions as spina bifida and muscular dystrophy, when growing up with them.
- Finding difficulties in obtaining confidential advice on sexual relationships and family planning.
- Having restricted opportunities for living independently if adapted accommodation or care staff are needed.
- Having restricted options on leaving school if adapted access or support with daily living is needed.

(Adapted from Scottish Education Council, 1990)

The above points will have a significant impact on the young person's motivation, self-image, school life, academic achievement and ability to form relationships at school or college.

Developing specific motor skills is not worthwhile for an individual unless he or she will be able to use them in real and everyday settings, or they have something to look forward to in exercising these skills in real life.

Control and choice

When teachers and professionals talk about 'control and choice', it is generally acknowledged that they are vitally important in the development of an individual. Removing control and choice from any human being can have a catastrophic effect on motivation, passivity, the will to live, to communicate, to learn and to function generally as a social and sociable human being. Children, on the whole, are often denied control and choice, except within carefully defined limits, until they reach adolescence, where the transition can be traumatic.

> 'The transition from living a life as others want (dependence) to living it as the adolescent wants to live (independence) is extraordinarily difficult for most teenagers and their families. The difficulty is compounded in the case of adolescents with disabilities'.
> (Students as Controllers of their Help – Fenton and Hughes, 1989). (In: Webber, A. 1991).

In practical terms, though, control and choice are often denied to children and young people who are are disabled. Why is this?

- People are sometimes over eager and too anxious to help;
- there is pressure to complete activities within time limits;
- there is lack of awareness or willingness to explore a variety of options about how to proceed;
- there is lack of acceptance of the child's or young person's ability to make choices, even at a very basic level;
- there is no real human relationship or partnership between the disabled and the non-disabled person;
- a lack of understanding of the meaning of independence, that it is always relative, for all of us;
- the perception of disability as a burden on non-disabled persons.

Inability to accept another's disability (or even differing ability and understanding) is a key factor in undermining choice and control for people who are disabled. This could be extended to cover a general inability to accept different or diverse abilities both within the education system and society generally. (See Figure 8.2).

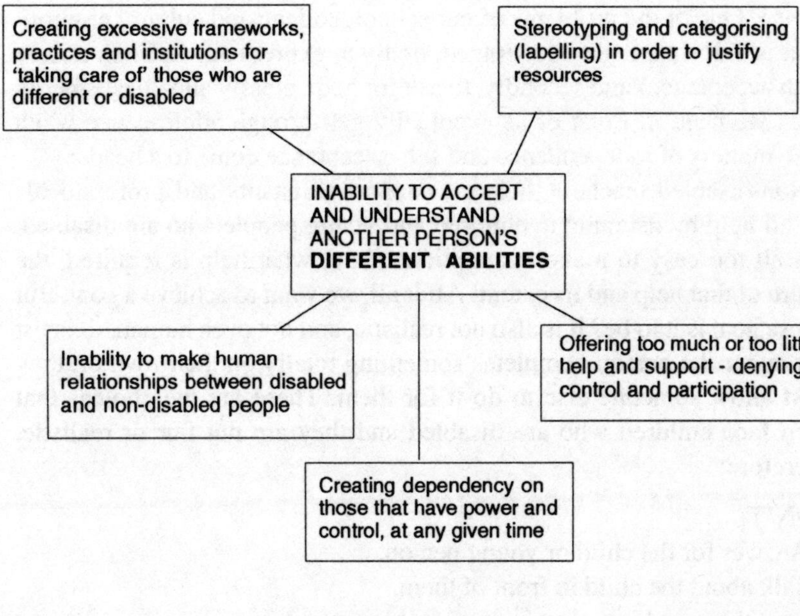

Figure 8.2 Diverse abilities

> . . . key to independence which is CHOICE: choosing to complete physical tasks without assistance or choosing to complete physical tasks with assistance whilst being in control of how and when that assistance is offered.
>
> (Fenton and Hughes, 1989)

Aileen Webber's (1991) *Independence and Integration* series, based on previous work such as that cited above, offers a wealth of material for working with students who are disabled. However, the principles of involvement, choice and control are just as relevant at all ages. The differences are the type of choice and extent of control not differences in the quality of control and choice.

> The main goal for all helpers of adolescents with disabilities is to work with the individual towards the student being able to:
>
> DIRECT AND MANAGE THEIR CARERS
>
> as efficiently and politely as possible . . .
>
> (GOAL, from Webber, 1991)

It is important, right from nursery age, that a child begins to learn how to direct and control others successfully. Obviously, this is only one aspect of human communication and use of language, but it is an important one. A child learns that it can direct its mother when it wants a feed or a nappy change. One of the problems of our school, college and cultural environment is that we are not encouraged, firstly to express our feelings clearly (with acceptance) and secondly, to ask for help, clearly and unashamedly when we need it. Most of us eventually get through adolescence when these matters of independence and self-acceptance come to a head.

Non-disabled teachers, helpers, support assistants and professionals can all help by listening to children and young people who are disabled. It is all too easy to make assumptions about what help is required, the nature of that help and its extent. After all, we want to achieve a goal. But whose goal is it to be? It is also not realistic, and not even human, to insist that either the person completes something totally on their own or, they must allow someone else to do it for them. These are the choices that often face children who are disabled and they are not fair or realistic. Therefore:

DON'T:

- Answer for the child or young person.
- Talk about the child in front of them.
- Stop them making mistakes – we all learn by our mistakes.
- Be too bossy or unnaturally cheery (*treat them like a child*).
- Anticipate what they want you to do. *Ask what to do next*.

- Do the work or complete the task for the child or young person.
- Leave out the person who is disabled when you ask questions - even if their speech is unclear.
- Speak loudly or oversimplify your language (*patronise*).
- Sort out the student's wheelchair without asking him/her first, push them without asking or leave them in an inappropriate place (e.g. facing the wall!)

DO:

- Let a child or young person make mistakes, *but support by asking relevant questions (e.g. 'Was that what you wanted?' 'Has it worked?')*.
- Ask how they would like to be helped – today.
- Wait – to be asked to help, when possible. *Comply accurately to help the other person gauge their accuracy in giving instructions.*
- Wait – for their replies and for any attempts at communicating.
- Read through what the students have said themselves. *General good practice.*
- Be prepared to discuss and negotiate, even with very young children – it does both of you good!
- *Let the pupil/student anticipate and prepare for physical, social and educational activity.*

These are some practical do's and don't's in helping children and young people who are disabled, adapted from Webber (1991) – compiled from comments made by adults and adolescents who are disabled. (*With author's additions in italics*).

In the early years a child will begin to learn to cope with having others mediate for them or being able to achieve certain things with special aids or equipment. It is important that they should be able to gain the same self-respect, whether they have produced something directly or through a medium or through another person; that they should be able to feel that they have directed and controlled events that lead to the production of the task outcome, piece of artwork or other product or skill.

It could be churlish not to acknowledge that much of this discussion about 'choice and control' would not seem to apply to young children up to secondary age in our school system. It is only when reaching secondary schools and colleges that issues of being 'in control' and 'exercising choice' become something that, in educational terms, are considered. At the pre-school level up to year 5, 'choosing' is a function of mobility, dexterity and timetable (or time allowed). A child who is disabled is reliant on others to make 'choice' a real possibility. He or she cannot necessarily explore (physically) and thus choose activity, toys or tasks as a mobile child can. Children at a young age are very much self-motivating and develop their intellectual and physical skills through exploration and seizing informal opportunity. There is a great deal of pressure on adults working with young children who are disabled to apply programmes of learning or remediation. The concept of 'early intervention' has become a race to see how much can be done by the time the child who is disabled reaches school. This has led to immensely over-prescriptive and over-complex programmes, implemented by a variety of professionals, over a period of two to three years. The very complexity of some of these programmes can make them a fragmented experience for both the young child and his or her parents. It can have the effect of marginalising or reducing the involvement of both parents and the child. This has to be balanced against a situation where a young child's difficulties have not been acknowledged and may thus lead to lack of compensatory actions and activities all round (Chapter 7, 'Parents' Expertise' AJ's story).

> **DO NOT ASSUME WHAT KIND OF HELP THE CHILD OR YOUNG PERSON WANTS, AS THIS WILL TAKE AWAY HIS/HER CONTROL AND FORCE HIM/HER INTO A PASSIVE ROLE.**
>
> If you have already negotiated with the child or young person how s/he wishes to be helped – then you only need to check that s/he wants the same help as last time. The level of help is therefore flexible, not fixed. The principle also applies at whatever age. A young child may wish to direct the splashing of paint on a piece of paper; the student may wish to direct the progress of a college survey.
>
> (Extended from Webber, 1991, *Integration and Independence Series*)

When working with a child or young person who is disabled on any task, it is necessary to explore together the possible ways of helping. The child or young person, whenever possible, can then choose for this task, with this help, on this day, in this context, at this time how much help she wants. Some children or young people may ask for more help than they really need.

Steps to take

1) WAIT AND BE SENSITIVE TO 'CUES FOR HELP'
   They may not need help – or may organise you to help in a particular way. If the child has difficulty communicating, it it important sometimes to let them initiate.
2) POSE A CHOICE OF 2 OPTIONS TO ENCOURAGE CHOICE
   e.g. 'Would you like me to cut this out for you, or shall I help you to do it?'

3) IF NO HELP NEEDED, DON'T PUSH IT
   Move away. You could say, e.g. 'if there is anything you need later, could you ask me, please?'
4) SEE IF ADVICE OR EQUIPMENT WILL HELP
   e.g. 'Would you like us to ask someone else to help with this?' Or, 'Should we ask someone about other ways of doing this, or equipment that might help? We could ask another helper, Occupational Therapist or a teacher'.
5) PUPIL OR STUDENT DIRECTS HELP
   Prompt: e.g. 'How do you want me to help with this, today?' 'Can you tell me the best way of doing this, please?' (e.g. helping with a coat) or 'I'm not sure what would be the best way for you to use my help. Can you tell me what you want me to do, please?'
6) FUTURE OCCASIONS
   When you have worked out together a way of helping for a particular task, it is not necessary to keep on asking.

Be aware that colleagues (e.g. the therapist staff) may have specific goals for the student that you should take into account, e.g. a child with Cerebral Palsy, Hemiplegia, etc., may need encouraging to use his/her damaged hand as much as possible.

It is also important that whatever communication method or aids are being used, these reflect the above strategies to encourage choice and decision-making at all levels.

(Source: Webber, 1991)

At this stage, if the reader wishes to read more, I can do no better than recommend Aileen Webber's set of photocopiable materials for use in schools and colleges (see Webber, 1991d). A number of other useful sources can be found in the Bibliography at the back. This chapter has dealt with a number of issues and tried to come to the heart of basic principles that should really underpin a proper 'Code of Practice' for pupils and students who are physically disabled or have medical conditions. The principle of choice and control is not new and it is not always easy to put into practice. I can already hear the 'let out' excuses being formulated. 'He/she is too dependent/disabled to make choices' or, 'We have to deliver a therapeutic/curricular programme of "set" activities that offer no choice' or, 'There isn't time to wait for individuals to make choices in our busy schedule'.

My own teaching experience, the best practice I have observed and discussions with disabled and non-disabled colleagues, leads me to assert that *it is always possible to offer involvement, choice and control* no matter how extensive the impairment or how busy, pressured or even hostile is the educational environment. The amount of choice and control may have to be balanced against many factors, such as how much choice and control does any pupil or student have? A school or college that is able to support diversity, creativity and acceptance of ability, manifested in unusual or diverse ways, will be a richer educational environment for all.

CHAPTER 9

Enabling Technologies for Communication and Learning

Mike Blamires

Enabling the enabling technologies

What are the enabling technologies? As I write using this word processor I am able to organise and reorganise my thoughts on the screen without worrying overmuch about my misspellings and typing errors which can be sorted out at a later stage of proofing. Like many others the software on my computer is a prosthetic which enables me to write but I hope I am not so dependent upon this technology that I will not be able to make use of pen and paper technology if my computer fails to work or the electricity gets cut off. So much for the enabling technologies! You always need a back up whether it is a disc, access to another machine or an alternative means of communication. Will technology ever become reliable? Will I ever have to stop buying replacement ball point pens or borrowing them from someone else?

As life is unpredictable, you will always need some alternative whether it is a disc, access to another machine or an alternative means of communication. People who rely on portable communication aids will often have a signing board in case the communication aid stops working.

The key point is that people use everything within their means in order to communicate. Words are just not enough. We use body orientation and posture, pointing, eye contact, visual orientation, tone of voice, intensity of utterance and repetition to get to message across and to respond to messages we receive in the same way. It is a game that we are all playing when we are in proximity with people and our skills in the game dictate how well we make contact. Sometimes we do not play it well because we are tired or we are unsure of the subtleties of play at that moment.

> A child can communicate to his father by context and inference that he would like a young visitor to his house to join him on a prospective weekend outing. He does this by leaning towards the visitor, making an utterance and then leaning back towards his father. Without having said anything to his father,

his father then voices the question to the child.

We use whatever methods of communication are available to us to get the message across. Technology can only be enabling when it is viewed as part of the development of a whole range of communication skills. A technological device may be only part of the kit we need in order to play the game of communication.

Jenny Taylor (1990) has listed some of the things that an unaided communicator has to learn and be aware of. These can be summarised thus:

Learn to wait
The average rate for an aided communicator is only about 12 words a minute. Because this can be frustrating and uncomfortable for people used to standard communication, there is a tendency to jump in and redirect conversation.

Respond to all signals
Not just the ones the aided communicator makes with the communication aid.

Time responses
In addition to waiting, the speaker needs to respond at the appropriate speed reinforcing what has been said and allowing the chance of further initiation.

Follow the non-speaker's lead
A difficult bit of self-control but wait to be guided as to what the aided communicator wants to converse about.

Think about where you need to be
Where is the best place to be without infringing on personal space?

Make the communication real
Often we ask questions that do not really need answers especially in educational settings. Conversation aids social interaction for real purposes.

Therefore the choices that the aided communicator can select from should include things that lead to real changes happening. Communication helps us to influence the world around us.

So what access devices are available?

The choice of devices to control a computer is not only dictated by the physical constraints of the learner. Their own personal preferences may involve self concept and long term ease of use and robustness and availability of support and technical backup. To this end there are a variety of professionals who may be involved in the process of selection of a communication aid. These include occupational therapists and or physiotherapists concerned with positioning and movement issues, the speech and language therapist concerned with language and speech development including the development of augmentative and symbolic communication, medical physicists, advisory teacher, parent, teacher, children or young person. This is clearly recognised in the English Code of Practice and expressed in the expectation that they will have trained the child, teacher, relevant staff and, where appropriate, the parents.

The problem can often focus upon the child and the device rather than the environment that the child needs to function in – the classic special needs issue. The assessment model focuses on accommodating the child to the environment rather than how the institution or school has to change in order to accommodate the child. Both the child and the institution have to change but how often does the assessment give equal weight to the environment which that the child is in? In a recent conference Professor Steven Hawking declared that the right to freedom of speech should be augmented by the right to the freedom to speak. Such entitlement should therefore be properly resourced not as a act of charity but as a right. A recent survey (ACE Centre,1995) found that about a third of the people they assessed as requiring a communication aid were unable to get one. This ignores all the people who have not formally been assessed who might also be in need.

For over a decade all but a few Education and Health authorities have got their act together to provide funding for assessments and for allocation of equipment. The recent initiative for communication aids centres (ICAC,1993–94) provided some guidelines for collaborative projects based on the few successful case studies available. Successful schemes would only be the first step. Some form of economic model needs to be applied so that the person who needs a communication aid is a regarded as having the power of a consumer with real choice rather than a charity case. The advent of life style magazines available on supermarket shelves aimed at disability consumer issues is a positive step forward. However, the first copy of *Chariot Magazine* I picked up (Output UK Publishing), was on a shelf not accessible to a wheelchair user!

Specialised communication aids

A number of specialised portable communication aids are available. These are robust dedicated machines with a lot of backup, as you would expect from the companies that develop such potentially enabling devices.

These can be configured to generate text, synthetic speech and/or digital speech in response to a range of input choices. The user might use a switch or switches to choose an item by scanning through a matrix of images or words. Alternatively this might be selecting by touch, a joystick or a head mounted light pointer. Synthetic speech is produced by translating written speech into phonemes using phonic rules. This electronic sound is being improved all the time through the use of higher quality sampling of the phonemes which can be done on the newer machines plus the addition of stress and frequency change so that the voice is less monotone. The advantage of synthetic speech is that it does not take up much space on a computer in comparison to digitised speech which is a direct reproduction of a digitally recorded voice. This is of a higher quality as it is natural speech but communication aids can only store a few minutes of it with current technology. Examples of portable communication devices include the Intro Talker, Orac, Light Talker and Touch Talker. Some of these devices can, in turn, be attached to a computer so that the communication aid can be used as the keyboard for controlling the computer.

Recently the trend has been towards systems that adapt standard computers to produce flexible systems that can be configured to individual communication needs and at the same time enable access to a wide range of curriculum or business software. An example of such a device is 'The Chameleon', an adapted lap top computer with customised software and input devices that are mounted into the user's wheelchair.

Making the ordinary computer special

The mouse is the main way that computers are controlled, especially when Windows programs are used. The mouse is a small creature that can be pushed and pulled to move a pointer on the screen and to press buttons on the screen using the buttons on the mouse. The main actions used with mouse control are the double click to start a program and dragging to draw, paint or select a number of objects on the screen. Double Clicking involves pointing at a desired object on the screen and pressing a button on the mouse twice in quick succession while dragging requires the same button to be pressed down while at the same time moving the mouse. Clearly these functions can cause problems but they may be overcome by the use of mice with extra buttons which can be set to emulate the double click or act as a latching button so that when it is pressed down it remains down until the button is pressed again.

It may be too obvious to state but one of the simplest devices that you can get for anyone using a standard mouse is a mouse mat which provides a firm surface with a bit of friction to turn the ball under the mouse. It also keeps the ball clean so that the pointer can be controlled properly.

Mouse mutations

You can get a wide variety of alternatives to the mouse which just plug into the same place on your computer and will work straight away with your programs on the M & S series computer. You can obtain a wide range of mice with different shapes and sizes of body and buttons including a mouse that looks like a proper mouse for young children.

Trackballs and joysticks

Track balls are basically upside down mice where a mounted ball is moved by the hand. It means that less gross hand and arm movement is required. A large trackball with a billiard sized ball plus an extra middle button is available. Some track balls are available which have control over vertical and horizontal movement plus extra toggle switches for holding the left and right buttons down. They are also available as joysticks. A foot operated trackball is also produced.

Ball point mouse

This is a portable mouse which can be mounted on the edge of a notebook keyboard and controlled by the thumb and first finger or held in the palm of a hand. Although slightly strange to use at first it can become very intuitive. There are also left and right handed mice as well as thumb operated mini trackballs that provide palm support.

Alternatives to the mouse

These include:

Stylus or mouse pen

This is a stylus with a ball in its tip or a graphics tablet so that the mouse pointer will move in response to the pen's movement. It is useless for people with gross and fine motor difficulties in the arm or hand but in any case, many other people would not use anything other than a mouse. Having a range of alternative input devices is not only necessary but a matter of personal preference, self-image and style.

Mouse keys

This enables the keyboard arrows to pretend to be a mouse. This is standard on Macintosh computers but is readily available on other computers. It can be very useful for someone who uses a head pointer or key-guard who might find it difficult or impossible to use a mouse.

Touch screens

This is a transparent membrane which can be fixed over a monitor screen so that programs can be controlled by pointing, thus mimicking the action of a mouse. It is particularly useful with early learning software but needs carefully positioning so that the user does not become fatigued.

Headmaster

This is a head set coupled with a suck and blow switch or other preferred switch so that the mouse pointer can be controlled by moving the head. Typing can be done in Windows or on the Mac using a configurable on-screen keyboard.

Switches

A user's preferred switch or switches and switch action can be used to control the majority of all of the new computers. For example, Switch Access to Windows (SAW from ACE), GUS, Switch Clicker for the Acorn A, and Kenx for the Mac. These are very flexible pieces of software that can be used to produce a wide range of scanning templates to control educational and other programs found on these machines.

The principle of switches is very simple. Two connections are mechanically brought into contact or moved apart. However, there is a vast range of ways in which they can be made and triggered.

Switches can be produced to be triggered by a vast range of pressures dependent upon the preference and capability of the user. These include switches responsive to eye blinks, proximity, sucking, blowing, heavy gross movement of a limb or very fine movement of a finger, palm or head. The operation of a switch may vary according to the requirements of its use. It may be triggered by pressing or letting go. It might be a latching switch that, once triggered, remains on or off until it is pressed again.

Because the ability of the user to control the switch may vary, software working with switches has to be configurable to take into account accidental or incidental pressing of the switch. Some of the parameters to consider when customising switch controls to the individual are :

- **Acceptance delay** – How long does a switch have to be held down before a valid switch press can be assumed ?
- **Repeat delay** – How long after a switch press is accepted does the switch have to be held down before a repeat switch press can be assumed ?
- **Post acceptance response delay** – How long must switch presses be ignored after a valid switch press ?

There are also a host of sophisticated ways in which a switch user can control software:

1) Direct entry

The triggering of a switch initiates a discrete action such as the turning of a page on the screen or the display or building of an image or cartoons. The latter is most appropriate for switch training and /or as early learning software.

2) Scanning and area selection

There is a wide range of scanning options. These include basic scanning where a picture, icon or word in a grid is highlighted in turn; column or row scan where a line of the matrix is highlighted for selection and then each cell is the line is scanned through, and area scanning where the matrix is divided into groups of cells possibly according to action or function and each area is then highlighted in turn for possible selection and subsequent individual scanning of cells. Hierarchies of matrices can be created for or by the user. With the newer machines, these can be selection sets for identified pieces of software.

During scanning with a single switch each cell is highlighted in turn for a specified amount of time so that the user has to wait until the desired cell is highlighted. With two switches, the second switch can be pressed to move onto the next cell so that the process is speeded up. Also alternations of switch presses can be used for editing actions such as starting to scan from the beginning again.

3) Encoded

This is the most demanding but probably most efficient. The code which might be Morse based or specifically devised indicates a selection or action. An example of such a system is Minspeak in which a sequence of images has a unique message or action attached to them. For example, the selection of a symbol for the user, a heart and the symbol for tree could result in the production of the utterance, 'I want to go the park'.

A more involved and graphic account of these important issues can be found in the ACE booklet, *A Guide to Switches And Their Use*.

Despite the wide range of switch access routes, switch access is time consuming and can be frustrating for the user and for the listener. It is probably the last resort after all other keyboard substitutes have been considered.

Hand co-ordination

A learner may have poor hand control which manifests itself in a number of ways for any number of reasons. Alternative access to a keyboard may help in managing this difficulty. It may be that the keyboard repeat speed should be disabled using a utility such as Access DOS or Access Windows or the control panel on the Mac. There may also be a need for a keyguard (a metal platform with holes which fits over a standard keyboard) to give support and guidance to the fingers. Alternatively, those with large gross movements may consider using an Overlay Keyboard with a perspex keyguard or an Enlarged Keyboard both of which can have control keys spread over a large area. A learner with a limited range of movement might be able to use a smaller sized keyboard such as the one on a notebook computer or may find that they need to use a mini keyboard or even the keyboard on a pocket organiser such as the Psion which can be used with a computer instead of the standard keyboard.

Enabling keyboard use

The advent of repetitive strain injury (RSI) has focused the minds of hardware and software developers on the individual needs of users. Principles of flexibility and customisation which have been widespread in software design are now becoming applied to hardware used to control the software. Both Apple and Microsoft have recently produced 'ergonomic' keyboards in response to this. They are reminiscent of the Maltron ergonomic keyboard which has been in production for more than ten years. Why has it taken so long to learn that standard keyboards may be a bad idea? This is the beginning of a promising trend. A recent yuppie computer magazine bemoaned the lack of configurability of the standard keyboard layout. This will probably be responded to by the computer industry but has already been met to some extent by the overlay keyboard (see below).

- **Sticky keys**

  Access DOS and Windows Access (Trace freely copiable) cut out the automatic repeat that standard keyboards have so that a learner with poor co-ordination can press hard on a key when it is located without a hundred key presses occurring. These utilities also enable a single finger or head pointer to generate 'shift' or 'control' key presses.

- **Keyguards**
  These are available for all the main computers including notebook computers and in some cases overlay keyboards (see below).
- **Enlarged and mini keyboards**
  Enlarged versions of the standard keyboard with single key auto shift and key accept and response delay are available for users with good control of gross movement. The Tash Maxi Keyboard with an alternative keyboard layout is also available as is a mini keyboard from CAC (M and S Series).
- **External control**
  Many portable communication aids such as Orac (Mardis), Light and Touch Talker (Liberator) can be used to control programs computers in the place of the standard keyboard. This requires the use of a serial link to the computer and the use of ACCESS Dos or Windows ACCESS to redirect control to the serial link. Notebooks and laptops can also be used in the same way to control another computer.
  Matchmaker is a device which enables a range of devices such as a switch, overlay keyboard, joy-stick to be connected to the computer without any modification which can then control the computer (SRS).
- **Voice control**
  This is no longer science fiction. It does not require the user to have good quality spoken English, whatever that might be, but it does require the ability to make a wide range of utterances that are differentiated from one another. There are basically two levels:
  Voice navigation: The Microsoft sound card and Sound Blaster Cards allow some control over Windows programs while Voice Navigator can be used in conjunction with Mac computers. These have limited vocabularies which have to be trained for each program that you use. You can allocate voice commands to often repeated actions such as printing a document or selecting a menu item. You cannot write a document with them other than by using the old Radio Alphabet, e.g. Allocating the utterance 'Oscar' to the letter 'o', 'Charlie' to the letter 'c' and so on.
  Voice dictation: This is full voice control in which what you say appears on the screen as text. The price of such systems has dropped dramatically over the last five years from thousands to hundreds. The software works by making guesses and learning your vocabulary as you work. With a headset it is reliable.

Overlay keyboards

The overlay keyboard is now the generic term for the concept keyboard. It is probably the most versatile and widely used device for meeting special educational needs in many different contexts. Its value – as an add on device which enables activities to be structured and presented in interesting and appealing ways – is widely recognised, so much so that it is used with learners of all abilities.

The overlay keyboard provides a flat surface which contains a grid of touch sensitive keys onto which a paper overlay can be placed containing words, pictures and even different textures. The number of cells on the matrix can range from 128 keys arranged in a grid of 16 by 8 up to thousands of cells. It can be used in conjunction with or as an alternative to the standard keyboard.

The newer software can be used to assign words, speech and pictures to the overlay keyboard. The overlay keyboard can be pressed in various combinations and areas and the required information sent to most existing programs. The possibilities are almost endless. The overlay keyboard can be used as a word bank containing lists of words for consideration in the write up of an outing in conjunction with a simple word processor. Alternatively, the piece of paper on the overlay could be a diagram or photograph. The learner can investigate them by pressing on the different areas of the overlay keyboard and then reading a message displayed on the screen.

The overlay keyboard can be a relatively inexpensive means of making a multi media computer into a communication aid.

Multi media

The fact that the newer computers have multi-media capability, so that they can readily display high quality images and produce synthetic speech as well as digital speech, means that they can produce powerful presentations and communications. This capability is now being built into laptops and notebooks computers. The distinction between communication aid and standard technology is getting murkier. This is good for value and for progress. Access materials can be produced using leading edge development tools and peripherals devices. For example more digitised speech can be used within a communication system because of the development of file compression techniques for speech. 'Gus' for a Windows machine with sound card and 'Kenx' for the Mac are examples of communication aids that are based on multi media computers.

The nature of enabling technology

In a 'Techno Heaven', where there were enough trains and they all ran on time and they were accessible to wheel chairs, it might be possible to have a system where people who needed a technological aid would have ready access to a multi-disciplinary assessment where a group of experts assessed needs and prescribed the device or devices required. It would be just like going to the opticians to get a pair of glasses, you are assessed and then a prescription is made which should stand you in good stead for a significant period of time.

However, this medical model has widely been abandoned for a number of reasons:

- It was a medical model which assumed that technology could be doled out like medicine.
- It was based upon the model of assessment which views people as recipients with little consumer power or entitlement.
- The resources to implement it were never there despite a great deal of commitment from the centres and advisory staff and the usual 'pump priming' from central government.
- It did not take into account that people change and may have a longer term view of their needs than many of the professionals.

Note the language in use here. 'I have a word processor, you have a communication aid.' I have a bicycle but do I have a mobility aid if there are no cycle paths along the busy roads I need to use in my town?

The move towards an ecological perspective

Due to the work of centres such as the Access, CENMACH and the ACE centres a more appropriate methodology of allocation of devices has occurred which has moved away from a fix it model towards one based upon personal growth and change facilitated by the increase in confidence and expertise of parents and professionals.

What will be the enabling technologies?

Special technology is becoming less special and more invisible. Information technology pervades everybody's everyday life. Overlay keyboards which were once only found on the drilling platforms of oil rigs or attached to BBC computers in special schools are now to be found attached to the tills in MacDonalds and other renowned cafeteria checkouts. By picking up a phone we are attaching ourselves to numerous computer systems. One of the first requirements of the new English national curriculum for Information Technology, for six and seven year olds, is to be able to control a video recorder remote control. This is a part of information technology which is also in the vast majority of homes. It is also something that makes the vast majority of adults disabled – admittedly to a trivial but very frustrating extent. The CD player, microwave, washing machine, answer phone, photo copier and fax machine are all examples of clever gadgets which are part of the growth of information technology which can have a prosthetic effect on our lives but we need to be in control of them and choose when and when not to make use of them. Steve Jobs, when he explained the design principles of the first Mac computers, stated that he didn't see the need for user groups for the Mac because the aim was to produce a computer that would be as easy to use as any household gadget. He summarised his point by claiming that 'You don't find user groups for the Hoover Vacuum Cleaners, do you?' In the years since this statement was made, household devices have grown in capability and complexity, they can now even talk to each other. Perhaps we do need a Hoover user group after all ?

At the present time, there is currently a lot of hype about the Internet which promises to connect everyone with a computer to everybody else. The potential of such a system for enabling communication between people is vast. One of the main proponents of electronic mail systems as a tool for meeting communication needs was Tom Holloway who had a vision of its use back in the mid eighties when most people working with technology to meet special needs were fixated on the wonders or otherwise of individual computers, particularly the BBC. While myself and others were at the very least doubtful, Tom began to get electronic mail access for children with physical disabilities through the 'Chatback' project so that they could send and receive electronic messages without being labelled by their looks or writing speed. The benefits of such an innovative project were never formally assessed but it is clear that there is much that can be built upon. Claims are now made that society's institutions and decision making will move onto the net. It is threatened that you will have to be part of it or be disenfranchised. I am concerned that children and adults will have hundreds of friends or acquaintances on the internet but not have any outside in the street or school. Will these be merely cyber mates, pen pals or just virtual friendships ?

Further, there are levels of participation

The information superhighway is a consumer revolution in technology that is dependent upon your spending power. If you have a job or have the money to be a student then you are able to take part. Despite widespread claims to the contrary the information on the information super highway is not free. You have to pay to access it by paying for the machinery and telephone/cable link that gives you access. Even if you use a cybercafe where access is provided, you still have to pay your cafe bill! There are also levels of access, the Internet is solely text orientated with access dependent on the ability to type in convoluted names linked with "\" (the back slash key). There has been a backslash backlash resulting in another level of access which is not solely text based called 'Word Wide Web' which has a point and click mouse orientation posing problems yet again for non mouse users but none the less it is a great improvement and has made some use of iconic and pictorial presentation of information. Another factor in your level of participation in the information super highway is how much information can be sent down the cable to your computer. If you are one of the lucky people connected to a high bandwidth cable, you will be able to do such things as watch a real time video of the Coca Cola machine at the Massachusetts Institute of Technology without having to wait a long, long time. If you are one of the great majority then interactive multi media on your computer will be a long way off. Interactive communication with these cables is as slow as communicating with someone with a communication aid. Perhaps we all would be better off improving our own interpersonal communication?

Summary

The technology is changing, offering more possibilities. These possibilities must be supported by funding for the entitlement to communication in which institutions and individuals are enabled to include users of enabling technology.

For further information or sources

1. See the Bibliography at the end of this book.
2. Contact Mike Blamires (Senior Lecturer, SEN/IT) at the Special Needs Research and Development Centre, Canterbury Christ Church College, North Holmes Road, Canterbury, Kent CT1 1QU. (01227) 767700 Extention 395.

CHAPTER 10

Opportunity and Change – Inclusive or Exclusive Education?

At the start of this book I mentioned the House of Commons debate on the Civil Rights (Disabled Persons) Bill in 1994 – the last attempt to introduce legislation for disabled people: the Government claimed that it would cost £17 billion a year. As well as being a reason for inaction, the Government's figures were an over-estimate. The true figure would probably be less than a third of this. The Government, in its Cost Compliance Assessment, in which this figure was announced, admitted that it was based on speculation, *each a worst case scenario.* It was described by a prominent member of Parliament as 'the worst quality document to come out of the Civil Service for many years' (TUC, 1995). The Cost Compliance Assessment did not account for the fact that the Civil Rights Bill allowed for the phasing in of measures such as making buildings accessible, and some items were counted twice. The Access Committee for England (1994) commented that the £10 billion estimate for making buildings accessible was 'a gross over-estimation of the true costs'. This Parliamentary process did not allow for the savings from the anti-discrimination legislation. If disabled people got jobs because of such legislation, they would pay taxes, and not have to rely on benefits. This alone could produce net savings of £5 billion a year (Rights Now, 1994 in TUC, 1995).

There are many critics of a general move towards including disabled people more fully into our society. They emphasise the cost but ignore the fact that it would not only be disabled people who would benefit from it. Elderly people and women with children would also benefit from a more accessible environment. The impact of wider social and cultural traditions and attitudes is also apparent in education.

- Two studies in 1986 found that most local education authorities were failing to publicise key elements of the procedures for assessing children's special educational needs, despite being required to provide this information by the Education Act 1981.
- Report on special schools by Her Majesty's Inspectorate rate accommodation and resources 'satisfactory' at best to 'downright dangerous'.

Other reports have found specialist science facilities rare in the smaller special schools. Special schools often have no teachers with expertise in important subjects, especially science and maths.

- Other official reports have looked at the position of disabled children in mainstream schools. In primary schools, most classrooms have insufficient space for children who use personal aids and equipment, many schools do not have accessible toilets or changing rooms. In most secondary schools where there are young people with physical impairments, few adaptations have been made. In many cases, inaccessibility prevented students being able to choose major subjects at GCSE.
- A 1987 survey of further education colleges found fewer than a third able to offer physical access in all teaching blocks, and more than a fifth said that they might have to reject a student 'with a physical handicap' because of poor access or inadequate support. A 1990 survey of universities and polytechnics found a similar picture.

(TUC, 1995)

In 1995, there were two Bills on rights for disabled people in Parliament: the Government's 'Disability Discrimination Bill' and Harry Barnes MP's 'Civil Rights (Disabled Persons) Bill'. Harry Barnes' Bill is a repeat of the previous (1994) Bill, wrecked in 1994 by back-bench stalling but which commanded wide support outside Parliament. In Australia, Canada and New Zealand they would be surprised to hear that anti-discrimination legislation for disabled people will not work in a common law system – their countries all have such legislation. It has had considerable impact on the quality of everybody's life without the dire financial consequences predicted by critics in this country.

In 1990 President Bush said: 'Let the shameful wall of exclusion finally come tumbling down'. The Americans with Disabilities Act, in the USA, has raised the profile of disabled people without causing any of the problems anticipated by critics. Half the adaptations employers have made as a result of the Act have cost less than $500! (TUC, 1995). If the Government's 'Disability Discrimination Bill' proves to be successful, at the expense of the Barnes Bill, it may prove far less effective in encouraging change because of omissions and 'weasel clauses'. Omissions and 'weasel' elements include:

- **The definition of disability** is too narrow, too medical and not worded carefully. It should be broadened.
- **The National Disability Council** has only an advisory capacity. A Commission with full powers to enforce the law is needed.
- **Small firms**, as well as large organisations, need to be encouraged to

enact the 'right of access to goods and services'.

- Education should not be excluded from a general 'right of **access to goods and services**'. After all, education is a fundamental right, indeed a legal requirement in our society.
- **Transport** should also be included in legislation to enable disabled people to access an individually empowering facility available to everyone else. This infrastructure is at the heart of contribution and participation in work.

In Britain, employers can discriminate against disabled people. Many disabled people live in institutions where many decisions are made by people over whom they have no control. The media subtly promote and introduce language and images which bolster prejudice against disabled people. Accompanying a disabled colleague, friend or family member on any excursion, from a trip to the corner shop, to a two-day conference, is an 'eye-opening', frustrating and usually stressful experience. My disabled colleagues and friends have learnt to deal with a hostile environment, I haven't yet.

We live in a society that worships youth, vigour, stereotypes of attractiveness and competitive success. Competition has its place but so does co-operation and personal achievement. The education system is no place for an all out competitive ethos. We don't want to generate losers. This is neither productive nor healthy for a society. Issues of choice, opportunity and learning inevitably require careful scrutiny of the political issues and current ethics that pervade our society and school communities. In Autumn 1992, the 'Special Educational Consortium' (under the aegis of the Council for Disabled Children) made the point that 'children who are vulnerable in the educational system . . . provide a good test for the quality of the system as a whole'. The process of developing a high quality education for all is actually supported by the process of acknowledging the need for choice, opportunity and improved learning activities to cater for the diversity of children in the system.

There are a number of specific points relating to pupils who are physically or movement disabled (or have medical conditions) that relate to the structure and organisation of our education system and some attitudes that underpin these.

- Every pupil everywhere does not have the same opportunity. *Children who are physically disabled or have medical conditions may not be able to attend their local school and access to under 5 provision will depend on where they live.*
- The market economy currently works against the proper education of children who are more costly in terms of money, time, exam results.
- Devolution of power and decision making to governors and parents does

not encourage schools to take a broad view of their responsibilities to all the children in their community.

- The diminishing role of the local education authority (LEA), with devolved management and budgets, threatens the provision of a coherent range of services for children with special educational needs.
- Introduction of the Funding Agency (FA) further confuses lines of responsibility, duplicates functions and creates particular problems of the co-ordination of special needs work.
- Lack of sound information base in a range of areas, for example *in physical disability and/or medical conditions (because of its inter-disciplinary basis), means that the challenges that face the education service in this area cannot be properly understood.*
- Lack of support to the development of under 5's services will undermine the learning of all children, will leave many young children with unrecognised and unmet needs and will leave those with recognised need in segregated provision.
- *Under 5's provision for children who are physically disabled is particularly 'polarised' into exclusive and inclusive due to the demands of remedial approaches and separated professional expertise.*
- Schools should have a policy on inclusion and long-term plans showing how this is to be achieved. These to be monitored under the new inspection arrangements.
- Schools should be given extra financial incentives to educate children who are expensive, *such as those who require adaptations and equipment. It also seems that the statutory services need financial incentives to co-operate more.*
- Value-added measures of school performance need to be developed to replace the publication of raw exam results.
- *The emphasis on narrow academic success should be reversed so as to include pupils who are now marginalised.*
- There needs to be monitoring of the school's admissions policy and practice through the new inspection arrangements.
- There needs to be detailed monitoring of the school's performance with the more challenging and more vulnerable pupils through the new inspection arrangements. *In particular, the school's arrangements to make the curriculum accessible to pupils.*

Under 5's provision:

- Proper support needs to be given to the development of provision for under 5's *generally. This is very patchy and in some counties does not exist at all.*

- Within under 5's provision there needs to be greater clarity about appropriate ways of identifying and providing for children who may have physical disabilities or medical conditions.

Specialisation and children who are disabled:

- Specialisation must not mean selection. Children with disabilities must be included in specialist schools, *even those with academic selection.*
- *Specialised 'approaches' or 'methods' can also have the effect of segregating children from their peers and community. Professionals offering exclusive or specialised treatments, methods or provision should show how this specialisation increases choice, opportunity or facilitates learning. They should be subject to OFSTED inspection by inspectors with appropriate qualifications and experience.*

Source: Adapted and extended from Special Education Consortium (Council for Disabled Children). (*Author's additions or adaptations in italics*).

Much of the responsibility for implementing the development of our educational and social systems has been placed upon the professionals concerned with the education and welfare of young people who are physically disabled. Excessively bureaucratic administration, professional ineptitude or even maladministration have hampered progress. This is not the solution or the way forward to achieve a long-term inclusive ethic in our schools and colleges (Barnes, 1991). The resolution of these problems lies in deeper and more wide-ranging areas that surround education and in a redefinition of the relationships between curriculum, learning and therapy.

The construction of disabled categories leading to the growth of separated provision, programmes and approaches is not a matter for medical or clinical judgements, nor is it a matter of pure educational considerations. It is also based on the ethos of our society and upon shorter term political considerations. This book has traced some aspects of these through legislation, current research, school and college ethos, the delivery of curriculum and the components of support. In many ways it is a broad and inadequate summary of these. There are inherent paradoxes in trying to provide some detail in reviewing current provision and approaches whilst trying to preserve an overview that maintains the philosophies of choice, opportunity and a fundamental appreciation of the learning process. This book also attempts to put forward some more detailed keys to combating the inadequacies of the current systems that professionals work within.

- **Legislation** that truly encapsulates proper rights, choice and equal opportunity for disabled people in the UK. Education legislation that protects the rights of the individual against the bureaucracy of accountability, discrimination by constructed 'groups' and the competitive ethos that makes undefined 'standards', academic tyranny and exclusivity its goal.

- **Affirmative action** based on enforceable legislation that will enable change and growth in our schools, colleges and other institutions. A positive view, based on a 'social model' of disability that allows everyone to be included in this growth and change, rather than the limited domain of certain professionals or experts.
- **Access to learning and curriculum** by encouraging and releasing the growing creative potential of teachers and colleagues within schools and colleges.
- **Effective partnership** through acknowledgement and appre-ciation of the role of human relationships, mediation and open, rather than hierarchical, management systems. The whole concept of partnership, at different levels, could be facilitated by inter-disciplinary training initiatives and an overhaul of the current separated management systems. Examples and precedents for this are already springing up in the UK.
- **Sharing benefits** by reducing professional sectarianism and vested interests in narrow methodological 'camps'. Where debate, discussion and shared knowledge exists, there is a more human and accessible body of knowledge. Parents and disabled people can become equal partners and co-ordinate the programmes that are, after all, *their programmes*.
- **Recognising expertise** that exists within parents in their holistic, intuitive knowledge of their child and within disabled people themselves (professional and non-professional). Their knowledge of their own abilities in relation to their living environment is unique.

Further education, the Funding Council and continuity

The Further Education Funding Council (FEFC) was established by the Further and Higher Education Act 1992 (the Act) which came into effect on 1 April 1993. The Act itself represents a significant development and is primarily concerned with changes to the legal and financial status of further education colleges. It also places important duties on the Council with respect to students aged 16–25 who are disabled.

Section 4 of the Act outlines the requirement for the FEFC to secure facilities for further education for all students aged over 16. This includes securing provision at day and residential institutions outside the maintained sector.

Guidance to Further Education Funding Council (FEFC)

This requires that:

- Disabilities do not prevent access to further education.
- Students with statements at sixth-form colleges enjoy continuity of provision through their transition to the new FE section in 1993–94.
- Specialist advice is obtained where this is not available from within the Funding Council's own resources.
- Adequate arrangements exist for assessing the needs of students who are disabled and identifying appropriate provision.
- Account is taken of the role of other agencies involved in the provision of advice and support to students, and inter-agency collaboration encouraged.
- Provision is made to secure the support services required to meet needs in the new sector.
- When allocating funds to colleges, account is taken of the additional cost of making provision for students who are disabled, including any extra support that may be appropriate to enable the students to have access to the curriculum.

So what does Government planning mean for lecturers in both Further (FE) and Higher Education (HE)? Securing the facilities, as it is described, is only the start of the process. Equal opportunities experience in many contexts indicates that attitudes, partnerships, teamwork and planning are crucial no matter what the level of resourcing. Whilst there may be a cost in time, these important areas of development depend mainly on the people involved. The challenge of inclusion involves:

> Recognising, owning and describing diverse abilities accurately and objectively . . . setting up the right kind of expectations.
>
> Altering the learning environment (physical, linguistic and perceptual) for access-group and individual issues, differentiation and management.
>
> Planning learning or course programmes and frameworks. Monitoring progress effectively and involving the student, parents and/or outside facilitators/help.
>
> Developing whole college policy – joint ownership of this policy and recognition of everybody's worth. No 'bolt on additives'.

Professor Paul Black (1992) reflects on the implementation of the national curriculum and the way right wing think tanks (e.g. Centre for Policy Studies) have over-ridden the views of teachers and educationists since 1988.

> . . . if it is true that the judgements and experience of the whole so-called 'educational establishment' have to be dismissed, then we are really in profound trouble. If the teaching profession's practices and judgements are no longer to be trusted, then the fault cannot be corrected simply by giving them new orders. They are not robots. All who care for education should not want them to be robots. To treat them as if they were robots is to run the risk that they will start to behave as robots should.
>
> (Black, 1992)

Pundits promoting legislation directly to teachers as 'training' are often perceived to have 'sold themselves to the devil' and greeted with cynicism. This is not surprising when a lot of people and groups associated with the special needs bureaucracy in education have simply sought to impose and apply legislation, not to mediate, interpret or question its applicability and efficacy. The enormous plethora of 'this is how you should do it' handbooks and publications testifies to an over-simplistic and patronising approach to teachers, and their colleagues in schools.

A major characteristic of changes since 1985 is that most of the 'inclusive' activities that are going on have been initiated on a local or school and college basis. It is schools, colleges, teachers and other staff, alongside support staff, who have really created choice, opportunity and a suitable learning environment. This has often been in the face of exclusive, academically divisive and unclear directions or prescriptions from government legislation. They have also managed to preserve the relationship between teacher and learner, as an essential human interaction, despite the industry and bureaucracy that has found willing participants in forcing schools and colleges down a mechanistic and self-seeking pathway.

Putting theoretical perspectives into practice

One of the basic problems of research when applied to dynamic or living systems is the attempt to 'quantify rationality' (Hudson, 1972) by applying statistical or numerical techniques to constantly changing circumstances and events. The very attempt to control the circumstances (remove the variables involved) in order to measure a specific action or event, places that action in an unreal setting. What is more, the nature of the controls and limits placed on the experimental (including assessment and testing) context have to be decided by somebody. This is at best an act of expediency, trying to make the optimum match to reality and is a genuine problem of research and researchers, particularly in social and educational research. In doing so, it automatically creates a false situation whose parameters have been manipulated. At worst, it will reflect existing mind sets of the researchers or, even worse, it can become an act of social engineering and political manipulation designed to maintain the status quo or to promote specific policies already decided by political groups.

The teacher or special needs co-ordinator will consult and work with (para) medical colleagues, or an educational psychologist when available, but they do not have to hand over or deny responsibility for the education of that child *at any point*. There are also much wider social and educational perspectives that the teacher will bring to bear on learning, in addition to strict medical or psychological perspectives and progression of any physical condition. For any child, the knowledge required to teach that child does not begin and end with descriptions of the physical, psychological or medical impairment, or checklist of symptoms, or the condition. Education is not 'treatment'. The child is a 'whole person' who exists within a school, a community, a family and a society. S/he also has a viewpoint which is particularly unique and knows what it is like to be him or her. Children and young people who are disabled need more opportunity to take control of their lives through being given choice and through developing appropriate learning and academic skills. To achieve this there is much work to be done on attitudes, organisation, structures, school ethos, curriculum differentiation, equal opportunities and on the physical environment.

In short, we have examined areas that relate to an holistic view of the development of children, whether disabled or not.

- All professionals in health, education and social services need to **listen more to the wishes of children and young adults who are disabled**. Planning and provision of care and education, as well as community (residential, work, leisure) planning should be INFORMED BY THEIR JUDGEMENTS. Education and paramedical provision has been too driven by a prescriptive, remedial (deficit identification) ethic.
- Empowering environments require attention to **factors outside the medical definition of disability**. It requires us to adopt a problem-solving and contextual approach which does not bow to the 'tyranny' of self-adjustment, self-deprecation and loss of self-esteem.
- **Self-esteem** is a function of the 'ideal self' versus 'self-image'. Assumptions from non-disabled people that disabled people want to be like them are wrong.

Most of the statements I have made are nothing particularly new. The synthesis of viewpoints and approaches may generate some new ideas on a practical level. They do, however, continue to challenge some of the foundations upon which our current educational and social systems are based. It could be pointed out that much of what we call 'rights' and 'equal opportunity' apply to all children, young people and the staff who work in educational institutions. This is true. It has been pointed out by many researchers, writers and activists, for many years, that inclusion and equal opportunity are really about improving the quality of life *for all*, not just for the few.

Exclusion

People who actively promote exclusion and segregation 'blame the victim' for his/her own problems. The exclusion road creates new labels as old ones die. 'Learning disability' and 'attention deficit disorder' are current labels of choice. Exclusionists hold fast to the 'medical model' and still believe that IQ tests, diagnostic assessment and packaged programmes will save the day. They buy and sell solutions, and promote 'things' and 'medications' that will solve all our ills. This road has architects who build more prisons, institutions and sanitised homes for the aged.

Forest and Pearpoint (1991) illustrate the meaning of a policy of exclusion (in Canada) by a 'reliable' senior government official's retort when asked 'What should we do about those who aren't in the "mainstream"?' He responded partly in jest, partly in frustration: 'We train the best, and shoot the rest'. The comment was off-hand but identifies the dilemma. The unstated underlying assumptions of exclusion are, among others, that:

- We are not all equal in capacity or value. We therefore have to be measured against 'norms' and then subjected to limiting environments and professional responses.
- It is not feasible to give equal opportunity. Lack of concern, the skills to form partnerships and little will to problem solve make any kind of 'affirmative action' an impossibility.
- We must choose and thus train an elite who will take care of the 'rest'. Maintaining capability, arbitrary 'standards' and power become the predominant goals.
- 'They' will benefit through the trickle-down theory. Education for pupils who are substantially disabled becomes a 'watered down' and less important process than that offered to the 'academic elite'.

(Expanded from Forest and Pearpoint, 1991)

Inclusion

The road to inclusion is also a choice. People choosing inclusion look at whole systems and only label people by their names and their needs. The process of inclusion requires co-operation and collaboration to solve problems. It involves understanding and actively working on partnerships at many levels.

Inclusive educators, paramedic professionals and support staff know through experience that they can solve virtually any student problem by getting together with the student and brainstorming on the problem. The people who gather know the person involved intimately, and they care. The first label is citizen, then neighbour, relative or friend (some of whom may be psychologists and doctors). Inclusion proponents believe in technology and science which serves people and is not used to make profit or war at the expense of human beings (Forest and Pearpoint, 1991). The implications are that:

- We are unique in value; however, each has unique capacity.
- All people can learn. Social development, (academic) achievement, movement skills, therapeutic outcomes and successful partnerships are all part of a LEARNING PROCESS.
- All people have contributions to make. 'Entitlement' and 'access' are all about enabling disabled youngsters to make their contribution to the learning process.
- We have a responsibility and an opportunity to give every person the chance to make a contribution.

The road to INCLUSION is a MOVEMENT from:

The Disability Paradigm	**to**	**The Giftedness Paradigm**
isolation	to	community
rejection	to	acceptance
medical labels and stigmas	to	first names and citizenship
loneliness	to	friendship
being unwelcome	to	being welcome
competitiveness and individualism	to	co-operation and collaboration
blaming the victim	to	acknowledging systems failure
oppression and exploitation	to	full human rights and social justice

(Forest and Pearpoint, 1991)

There is, at the moment, something of a crisis in education. Debates about class sizes, resourcing issues, special needs co-ordinators having nervous breakdowns, parents' outcry at lack of proper choices and the demoralisation of the teaching profession, all contribute to this crisis. Nevertheless, a crisis is also an opportunity. An opportunity to scrutinise the educational values that are currently driving the system. An opportunity to use both legislation and social or political movements to make a

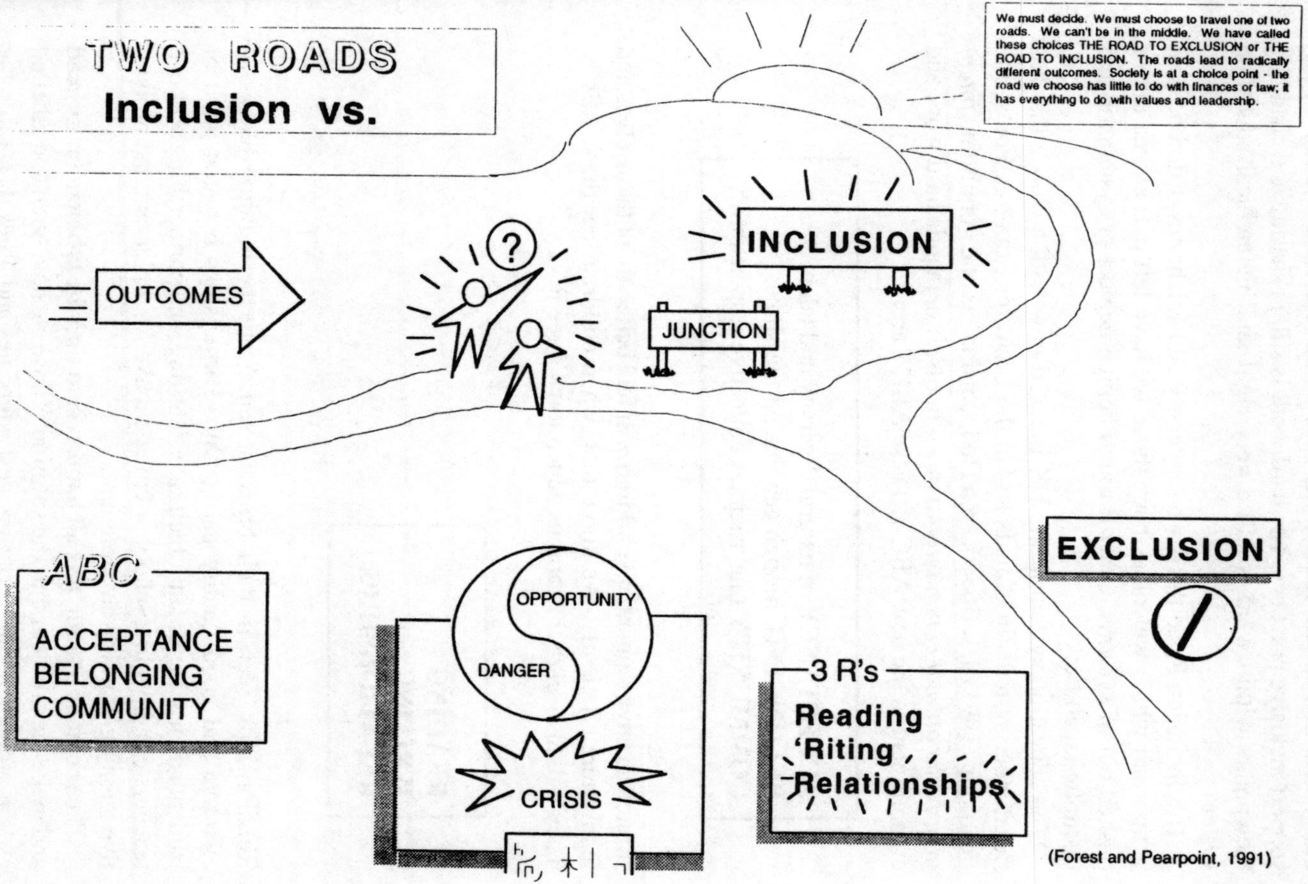

Figure 10.1 Which way?

clear definition of an educational viewpoint. Teachers, on the whole, support inclusive practices. The hard work is still in sharing and changing viewpoints within what is still a very rigid and hierarchical education system.

The Inclusion Road thrives on diversity and celebrates differences. It is the road which welcomes back those we have left out, kicked out or pushed out of systems, either through benign neglect or systematic and institutional abuse.

The education system in the UK is faced now with a choice that has faced other systems in Canada and in the USA, for example. Forest and Pearpoint (1991) describe 'the road to inclusion' as one of building *intentional educational community* in our schools. It demands hard work and commitment to the new ABC's. These ABC's are:

ACCEPTANCE of natural diversity and talent
BELONGING through genuine partnerships
COMMUNITY that assumes collective responsibility

In such an environment, all children will feel better about themselves and learn more efficiently. We know that, when children feel these ABC's. They will also learn the famous educational three R's:

READING
WRITING
RELATIONSHIPS

Relationships, seen in their broadest sense, are the building blocks of effective and good quality partnership. Partnerships between pupil or student and teacher or adult facilitates learning, and partnerships between teachers or adults in a school or college make for a pleasant and productive learning/working environment.

The secret of making this all happen is to turn the problem on its head and make the problem into the solution. Those we have seen and labelled as 'the problems' can be our greatest advocates and allies. It is often the 'drop-outs', the 'street kids', the people with disabilities, who have the most creative answers. They have the most to win or lose, and they have the most intimate knowledge of their own problems. Given an invitation to partner with skilled professional educators, this new team can truly resolve problems and change the system. It is not just 'experts' who can find positive solutions to complex and difficult problems. It is teachers and parents in their own schools and colleges who have grappled with these problems, over the past 10 years, and come up with amazing and creative solutions.

Road to Exclusion		**Road to Inclusion**
segregation	vs.	wholeness, harmony
brokenness		harmony
elitism		integration
group homes	vs.	life in real families
institutions		
special schools	vs.	quality school where
special classes		kids belong 'together'
ghettos, gangs	vs.	neighbours and friends
violence		
nursing homes/prisons	vs.	community options

(Forest and Pearpoint, 1991)

There is continuing debate about the 'continuum of special educational needs' and the need for choice in provision. The key questions that have kept appearing are:

- How much real choice is there?
- Who makes these limited choices?

A recent Master's degree study by one of my students made one fact clear: that the physically disabled students integrated into her school were reluctant to talk about their future. Not because they could not talk or communicate but because there wasn't much to talk about. The future for them looks rather grim at the moment. They may be integrated in school but will not be included in society, through productive work and respect for their place in the scheme of things. The views, or lack of views in some cases, of a small group of students tells us just as much about the nature of our society as complex, statistical and expensive research projects.

It is difficult to write a book, one of whose messages is that there is nothing special about special education.; that disabled people are people, that special is ordinary and ordinary is special. The obvious response is 'Why have you picked out this subject to write a book about?' Some of the answer to this lies purely in the circumstances of my life and career, some in the choices I have made, but most derive from a belief that the kind of society I want to live in and I want my growing children to live in, is an accepting, open and creative society. This has been eloquently expressed, and referred to here, by Marsha Forest and Jack Pearpoint. They manage to capture the wholeness of the issues surrounding choice, opportunity and disability in education. They also show clearly, as I have attempted to do, that the benefits of inclusion do not go just to disabled people. *The benefits are for everyone*. The concept of 'inclusion', rather than just integration (social, functional or location) is more than just a panacea for a minority group in the population. It is part of a way of life and it is having an effect at all levels of social and political activity. The movement towards open management, change as a permanent feature, information technologies and tremendous possibilities for communication are linked with the concepts of 'inclusion' and 'exclusion' that run through the book.

At the risk of the author being labelled as a 'whinger', the book has consistently returned to the idea of 'fragmenting' children through 'professionalisation of the problem'. I make no excuses for having done this. The personal consequences for a disabled child and his or her family are enormous. The effect of over-inflated opinion and larger than life experts on the child and family is enormous. A person's sense of identity, confidence and integration takes a downward spiral when a range of distant and diverse professionals become involved. To maintain self-esteem, a sense of integrity and competence, independence and confidence in the face of many unspoken messages of worthlessness, incompetence and 'being a problem' requires a personal survival strategy. This is to radically reduce the *significance* of these professionals and advice given in your life. This happens all the time and is a justifiable human reaction to the fragmentary service provision and impersonal treatment often handed out.

The current system of planning and managing support across the statutory services requires substantial review for everybody, and not just for disabled people. Despite the efforts of many bodies, groups and individuals, the management, training and research structures that currently exist, for the majority, are still not cohesive or trans-disciplinary in any sense. Training and research could provide important cornerstones in any attempt to build a more coherent and holistic approach.

Training and research

It has been acknowledged over the years by many sources (e.g. Mittler, 1989; Bowman, 1989; Haskell and Barrett, 1977; Tingle, 1990) that, in order to overcome separate conceptualisations of handicap, there is a great need for both pre-professional and in-service education and training to take place on an inter-disciplinary basis. In terms of integration it is often forgotten that teaching, particularly of children with special needs and most particularly those who have complex physical or movement disabilities, is a highly collaborative process. Hegarty (1989), for example, talks about curriculum intervention in schools. One could be forgiven for thinking it is the domain solely of the teacher. This can no longer be so. It must become a more collaborative exercise involving other professionals as well as the parents/family. The skills of teaching are no longer simply related to the teacher, subject or method and the class but now involve a far more complex equation, at the end of which is a total learning environment for pupils and students.

The initial problems of a multi-disciplinary group on the first pilot year of 'Children with Cerebral Palsy: Exploring their Special Educational Needs' (Cornwall, 1991) were outweighed by the positive work done to achieve a common consensus and the richness of contribution from the range of specialists. Education and in-service training provide valuable opportunities to explore common ground, to gain a better understanding of the theories that underpin other areas of professional endeavour and to get a better understanding of each other's professional and theoretical backgrounds. In fact, this is one of the keys to future progress in improving provision and services for children who are physically disabled or experience medical conditions.

In summary, the process of setting up and fostering a body of knowledge (for want of a better term) and an inter-disciplinary base or working framework could allow all who work in this field better access to relevant knowledge and enable them to work more effectively together. There is still a reluctance to 'grasp the nettle' of meaningful partnership, teamwork and co-operation. It appears that, particularly in education and health services, the approach to training is technocratic where knowledge about methods and approaches reigns supreme. Not enough consideration is yet given to both the process of implementing these methods and all the human interactions involved during the whole complex process. Similarly, in paramedical training, there is common ground with teaching in a more holistic approach that goes beyond the mechanical considerations of physical development, language construction, body 'mechanics' or 'manual dexterity'. There is a more holistic view of the person and this is increasingly shaping co-operative endeavours.

The general practice though is still without any proper guiding philosophies or ethics, hence the grasping for an apparently cohesive and self-contained system such as conductive education. All too often, the planning, communication and implementation of a complex individual programme founders on the rocks of 'people problems' (day-to-day communication and misunderstandings, communicating the whole view, lack of interpersonal or assertive skills, negative attitudes to other team members, lack of understanding of group life and effective sharing skills). People are unable to contribute positively to the partnership and the team is unable to get the best from its members. A lot of work that is done in schools, colleges, child development centres, and other places where children are physically and movement disabled with associated difficulties, could not really be called partnership or teamwork at all. This is the challenge that faces us in moving from multi-disciplinary and often fragmented work to a truly inter- or trans-disciplinary approach which can effectively enhance learning and provide a more consistent experience for clients and pupils.

Labelling and research

Our current labelling procedures also constrain the content and direction of research by psychologists, social workers, medical and paramedical colleagues and teachers themselves. How?

- It perpetuates the notion that there is a clear division between normal learners and 'special' learners. This is nonsense and is not consistent with a view of learning difficulties as a 'continuum' and part of normal development for that individual.
- It defines the problems of access to schools and learning activities as learning difficulties when we know perfectly well that children may not access the curriculum for physical reasons or reasons which have nothing to do with their own abilities.
- Once a pupil or student has been categorised, assumptions about more general abilities are often (and often incorrectly) made.
- It portrays difficulties as the properties of individuals rather than relationships or environmental factors. Hence the term should be pupils or students *experiencing special educational needs* not '*with* special educational needs'. They don't own them, they haven't bought them and they don't need to carry them around like a uniform.
- Organisations of disabled people have made it known that they prefer to be called *disabled people* and not people with disabilities. They are

not people *with* disabilities. They don't carry them around and they haven't purchased them at the supermarket. It is part of a positive identity and integral to the individual.

- There is currently, and due to the categorisations used, say, in the Code of Practice, a muddle between disability or impairment and the concept of learning difficulty related to access, choice and opportunity.

Terminology – what's in a name?

Different professional groups use different terms for what may essentially be similar concepts and classifications. Curriculum is apparently the domain of teachers but discussion shows that it is not always understood by therapists, teaching assistants, nurses or parents. 'Hand function' may be central to one professional as the key to other skills but, to another, 'dexterity' may be only a part of the overall curriculum. Similarly, the principles of encouraging useful patterns of movement and good posture may be central to even begin to access any learning experiences. To another, certain levels of physical skill and body awareness may be another basic milestone in development along with the first words or ability to discriminate shapes. The terms 'hand function', 'dexterity', 'manipulative (and tactile) skills', 'hand-eye co-ordination' all relate, in functional terms, to similar spheres of activity. However, this is not just semantics; each professional group will interpret the breadth and importance of any given term differently even if they are able to use the same terminology. Where the terminology is different it gives a sometimes confusing and often fragmentary picture of the child to the child, his or her parents and others. Parents of disabled children and disabled people often become trans-disciplinary experts in the jargon that surrounds them. By combining the areas of professional knowledge along with their own intuitive understanding and application to daily life, they become the real 'experts' in the equation. However, the jargon can lead to a fragmented programme for the child and a preoccupation with certain areas of development, sometimes at the expense of other areas of knowledge, skill or learning. Self-esteem to one professional will have to do with physical skills, to another with attainment in maths, and so on. The potential to fragment a young person's experience, because he or she is trying to 'do well' for each professional is immense unless it is given cohesion through planning or explanation.

Apart from the fact that insensitive use of language or jargon can be embarrassing and damaging, it has a *social meaning* which changes all the time. The language we use is indicative of overall social attitudes. These stem from the images or constructs that we use to discriminate between people and events that we encounter in our life. On an individual basis, it drives our behaviour. In turn, this affects our relationships and the planning of our social environments. Our language is not only indicative of our thinking patterns but it can influence, or even dictate, our thinking, planning and behaviour.

Giftedness – what is it? Who has it?

There are people in every generation who can run really well and do amazing physical feats. People like Ben Johnson, and Olympic divers and skaters. We say they are gifted. It is interesting that there are as many people like Ben Johnson as there are like me. But there is one profound difference. People really enjoy and value the fact that Ben can run, or that my classmate Beverley could dive. I don't understand what intrinsic use it is to be an Olympic class diver or runner.

For Bev to become an Olympic class diver, our society created thousands of gifts. We created opportunities for pool builders, coaches, pool cleaners, advertisers, swim suit manufacturers, etc. People got up at four o'clock every morning, travelled thousands of miles, raised tens of thousands of dollars. Thousands of people were involved in making this possible.

A person who is labelled disabled needs exactly the same support. I need people to set up organisations, to be friends, to tutor, to raise money, to set up special places to do governmental negotiations – exactly the same things that Beverly needed to become an Olympic class diver.

What is the difference? What prevents society from seeing me as important and exciting as Bev?

There was a serious mistake. Someone jumped the gun and labelled us (people with disabilities) a problem. Instead of seeing us as a gift and an opportunity, we are called problems and projects. We are not supported by 'the community'. We are serviced by staff. People's livelihood is determined by their fixation on fixing us. But this is crazy because we are not fixable. We never stop to think about that. Our society has created a billion dollar industry to fix people who are not fixable. It is destined to failure. It doesn't work, and there are tremendous costs both to society and to the people who cannot be fixed.

There is another cost. The community is denied the talents, gifts, contributions and opportunities of all the people who are excluded.

Extracts From 'A Reflection' by Judith Snow
(in Forest, M. and Pearpoint, J. 1991)

Towards a definition of disability which empowers everybody

Disability affects a large number of people in many different ways. Disabled people are often portrayed as being dependent and unable to make decisions about themselves, but this is inaccurate stereotyping. This is not just 'playing with words or being 'politically correct' to keep up with fashion. Defining disability in the right way opens up greater possibilities for everyone to be able to do something about civil rights, access and opportunity. The answers do not just lie with a limited group of professionals. It is not 'someone else's problem' (Moore and Morrison, 1989). The **Disabled People's International (DPI)** is a world-wide organisation, with national affiliations, which is run and controlled by disabled people, for disabled people. The DPI use two definitions:

Impairment the material condition of lacking all or part of a limb or having a defective limb, organ or mechanism of the body (including sensory impairments and learning difficulties).

Disability a disadvantage or restriction of any activity caused by the limitation placed on people with impairments by the environment, provision of second-class education, poor employment prospects, reduced social contact, low income and assumptions that are negative or patronising.

These definitions suggest a social model of disability as oppression rather than a problem of an individual. This model portrays disability as being constructed and maintained by the society which creates the environment we live in, therefore it can be destroyed by society changing its structures.

The World Health Organisation definitions use the terms 'normal' and 'abnormality' in the context of describing impairment and disability. Some disabled people and organisations would reject these terms and focus in on the environment as the disabler.

The language, concepts and classification systems of disability often fall into two groups:

- Those associated with medical disciplines and concerned with medical diagnosis, treatment and rehabilitation. These tend to focus on a particular condition of ill health or disability.
- Those associated with identifying functional impairment and used by professional associations involved in social or employment rehabilitation. These tend to focus on identifying a person's capabilities, as well as noting what they cannot do.

There should be a language, culture and classification system constructed that revolves around and focuses on what disabled people can do and achieve. This exists and as it comes into pre-eminence it will counteract the negative effects that have hitherto maintained the stereotype of disability.

Integration or inclusion?

It is possible to be physically integrated but remain socially or psychologically isolated. Inclusion is about having opportunities and choice, about participating in those activities that interest you, not just those which are offered to you or those which are physically accessible. It is about acceptance and meeting people on common ground. Inclusion is a subjective, interpersonal and institutional question and real incorporation of people who are disabled in the social community of the non-disabled can be located on a scale of possibilities, somewhere between acceptance and complete isolation.

Organisations often claim to integrate people with disabilities based on the theory that an integrated group is one in which one or more people who are disabled are involved in the same activity as those without. The relationship between the disabled and non-disabled members of the group is, both in name and in practice, that of disabled person and helper or pupil and teacher. A truly inclusive group is one in which everyone participates on equal terms. Normally, inclusion is rare and usually involves only the most able, privileged and educated people with disabilities. It becomes necessary to make a conscious effort or to use legislation in the hope that it will one day lead to inclusion motivated by human friendship rather than pity, guilt or any other reason.

Integration could be described as a three stage development for disabled and non-disabled people.

> The first stage for people who are disabled is the *stabilisation* of him/herself by realising that exclusion because of disability is not his/her own fault, but is a question of his/her environment and of social attitudes.
>
> The second stage is the *integration* of people who are disabled into the activities of organisations which allow a close interaction between disabled and non-disabled people.
>
> This leads finally to the third stage of active *participation* to initiate and to take part in the decision-making process.
>
> The same process in the reverse direction has to take place among non-disabled people.

In the first stage the non-disabled person will be confronted by people who are disabled. This may be a new and challenging situation. It requires a person to question the usual model of participation within society.

Through joining in common activities with people who are disabled, a non-disabled person has a first hand experience of inclusion which can give rise to a questioning of existing and accepted behaviour. This unsettling effect needs to be stabilised by the realisation that despite previous fears and ignorance, people who are disabled are just people with the same needs and aspirations as anybody else.

Changing attitudes

In order to provide access to education for disabled pupils and students it will be necessary for schools and colleges to recognise and value people's different capacities, and also to:

- change the *attitudes of those who are not disabled* that centre around fear and ignorance as well as over-protection by both parents and others dealing with people who are disabled;
- form an 'intentional education community' (Forest and Pearpoint, 1991) which offers a chance to disabled pupils and students who have internalised a perceived 'lack of ability' to prove to themselves and others what they can do.

In Disability Awareness in Action (DAA) literature there are many ways proposed for changing attitudes in a school or college.

An inter-cultural model: This is through social learning where the differences between the life experiences of disabled and non-disabled learners is explored with the aim of achieved tolerance, empathy and awareness through personal reflection. It provides many curricular possibilities (outlined in Chapter 5) for curricular activities in schools and colleges. It is achieved by:

- considering a disabled person as the 'expert' on his or her disability. This is useful to the teacher in any learning situation;
- considering carefully the terminology and language used;
- direct contact with disabled students, their publications and networks;
- through an enabler, carer or learning support assistant where appropriate; (INFORMATION SHARED – PARTNERSHIPS DEVELOPED)
- adequate preparation of those involved and of the learning environment;
- training;
- organisation and procedures examined in the light of feedback from disabled and non-disabled pupils and students.

How can my school achieve supported education?

- Understanding the change process.
- Teaming.
- Creative problem solving.

- Individualised planning.
- Using instructional strategies which benefit both students with and without disabilities.

SUPPORTED EDUCATION – an example from Oregon, USA (1993)

Choice and opportunity – a state of mind?

Equal opportunity (EO) is a concept that seems to be easy to avoid. Professionals working with people who are disabled can make assumptions that are as damaging to opportunity as many of the negative attitudes encountered in the community. On the other hand, the ability to listen and work with people who are disabled can do as much as formalised distant 'treatment' programmes. The vital spark that energises positive action and progress is, as usual, found in the relationship between user and service provider, doctor and patient, learner and learned, contrary to the much held belief that there is such a thing as a doctor : patient or teacher : pupil or provider : client. There cannot be a relationship, for example, between a 'body of knowledge' and 'lack of knowledge'. The relationship can only exist through the medium of human contact, communication and under-standing. Although EO is concerned mainly with gender, ethnic and disability issues, this book has been concerned with disability issues in the context of 'special needs' in education. The 'special' already marks out a minority group who are different in some way. The term education includes schools, units, hospitals, treatment units, residential units and facilities. It is also taken for granted that *EO issues apply to staff within an organisation and, if it is a 'service', to clients or customers.*

What is equal opportunity? Yes, there is legislation for women and ethnic minorities attached to EO but none for disability. There are concepts and constructs that can be monitored or used as yardsticks by which we measure progress towards or away from a society which accepts difference and is able to promote harmony whilst still challenging individuals to achieve their maximum potential.

To be more specific, why do organisations (small or large) have EO policies?

- To share and test our views about opportunity, integration and differences between people;
- to show that an organisation, community or society has some form of commitment to the well-being of the individuals within it;
- to provide a framework for investigating and identifying procedures and practices which create unnecessary and unfair barriers for people (for service organisations this is particularly pertinent in terms of client contact and care (or 'customer relations').

A teacher's story – planning for independence

The school has set aside an adapted room specially for pupils who are PD. To acknowledge the problems caused by physical management, the process involved school staff losing their staff room! and consultation with county architects to provide room for OT's, Physios, special activities and recreational/leisure facility. Due to the siting of accessible entrance/exit, the pupils are now able to independently wheel themselves out to taxis which couldn't happen before. They also have more privacy and opportunity to develop a greater level of independence, improving dignity and privacy for pupils who are disabled.

So, in focusing on EO in the context of pupils and students who are physically disabled or have medical conditions, what are the benefits of openly developing, sharing and operating EO policies? They can:

- ensure that no individuals or groups within a school or college are excluded, that they **are able to participate fully** and do not feel marginalised;
- help with flexibility, creativity and problem solving by bringing into the forum new perspectives, by breaking down myths and assumptions and **improving partnerships**;
- **raise the level of debate** from organisational 'detail', with limited impact, to important principles which will have **greater impact on practices and behaviour** throughout the school or college;
- help to ensure that the school or college shares and understands the values of the community and society around it. Keeping in touch is vital to its image, relevance and accessibility. There is a responsibility to prepare students for life beyond school and college.

The book has aimed to move on, so to speak, from the 'handy hints for teachers' or 'things you must know about physical disability before you can teach properly' schools of thought. As a teacher, I found these sometimes useful, sometimes patronising and sometimes unusable in practice. Teachers are professionals in their own right and should regard themselves as such. They have had, or should have, substantial professional training and this professional training should enable them, through sensitive observation, teaching and curricular assessment (yes, curricular assessment!) accompanying educational activity, to identify diverse abilities and needs. This would include broader or associated difficulties that may be associated with the diagnosis of a physical condition. Therefore, the material in this book is not intended to be presented at a simplistic level, which so often insults teachers' intelligence these days. It is intended to stimulate thought about broad issues, set up questions in the pursuit and sharing of effective and appropriate practices, provide interesting illustrative material throughout, and to raise the level of debate from narrow professional boundaries. It is not intended to be over-academic, nor is it a 'mindless teaching hints' manual.

There are many, many issues and arguments that are missing from this book, despite a genuine attempt to review, overview and analyse. I put this down to my own inability to organise, synthesise and present the simple and fundamental ethics and philosophy of 'inclusion' in practice in our complex society. This society is sophisticated and technologically advanced but is also primitive in its corporate attitudes and individual drives and responses. I can only hope that, despite any omissions or losses, something has been gained in the attempt to examine and re-examine (in true problem-solving mode) the nature of the task we face. The problem clearly lies not just with any individual, be they disabled, non-disabled, professional or parent, young or old, but with the systems we have built around the edifice of education. There is a collective responsibility to help our institutions and systems to grow to serve people not manipulate them. I offer this book to you as one, albeit humble, contribution to that process. It may even contain some useful and possibly thought-provoking material. I have, therefore, cast this pebble into the sea of knowledge. If you are still reading this then the modest ripples produced have, indeed, engaged your attention.

I'm so well adjusted
(a poem by the late Simon Brisenden)

I'm so well adjusted
in company I can be trusted
with my clenched teeth and my clenched heart
I won't fall apart

there's no need to be nervous
I shine upon the surface
like a vase I'm regularly dusted
to ensure I'm well adjusted

other people live in hell
but my adjustments are all well
so far as anyone can tell

but one day I'll be dead
and looking through the bullet hole
you will see inside my head
all the adjustments to my soul.

Bibliography

Adair, John (1986) *Effective Teambuilding*. Pan Books: England.

Audit Commission and HMI *Getting in on the Act: Provision for Pupils with Special Educational Needs: The National Picture*. HMSO: London.

Bairstow, Philip (1992) *Evaluation of Conductive Education: The Selection Process*. In Ed. Jones, P. R. and Crowley-Bainton, T., *Education and Child Psychology*, Vol. 9, No. 1.

Bakker, F.C., Whiting, H. T. A. and van der Brug, H. (1990) *Sport Psychology: Concepts Applications*, John Wiley & Sons.

Barnes, Colin (1991) *Disabled People in Britain and Discrimination: A Case for Anti-discrimination Legislation*. C.Hurst & Co., U.K.

Barnes, Colin (1992) Foreword to *Disability Equality in the Classroom: A Human Rights Issue*, *Disability Equality in Education*, 78 Mildmay Grove, London, N1 4PJ.

Barton, L. (Ed.) (1989) *Disability and Dependency*. Falmer Press: Lewes.

Bishop, Michael (1987) *Backlash: Disabling the Able? Br. J. of Special Education*, Vol. 14, No. 3, Sept.

Black, D. (1969) *The Educators*. Cresset Press: London.

Black, Professor Paul (1992) *The Shifting Scenery of the National Curriculum*. Presidential Address. Education Section – British Ass. Science Festival. School of Education, University of Southampton.

Bobath, Karel (1980) *The Neurophysiological Basis for the Treatment of Cerebral Palsy*. The Bobath Centre, London.

Bobath, Bertha and Bobath, Karel. (1975) *Motor Development in the the Different Types of Cerebral Palsy*. The Bobath Centre, London.

Bookis, Joan (1990) *Beyond the School Gate: A Study of Disabled Young People Aged 13–19*. Published by RADAR: London.

Booth, T. and Swann, W. (1987) *Including Pupils with Disability*. Open University Press: Milton Keynes.

Bovair, Keith, Upton, Graham (Eds) (1992) *Special Curricula Needs*. David Carpenter, Barry and Fulton Publishers and NASEN: London.

Brisenden, Simon (1992a) *Poems for Perfect People*. SCIL, 6 Northlands Road, Southampton, SO15 2LF.

Brisenden, Simon (1992b) *Body Shopping*. SCIL, 6 North-lands Road, Southampton, SO15 2LF.

Broadhurst, P.L. (1957) 'Emotionality and the Yerkes-Dodson Law.' *Journal of Experimental Psychology*, 54, 345–352.

Brown, A. (1987) *Active Games for Children with Movement Problems*. Paul Chapman Publishers: London.

Butler, Engelbrecht et al (1986) *Physiological Cost Index of Walking for Normal Children and its use as an Indication of Level of Handicap*. Journal of Developmental Medicine and Child Neurology.

Butt, Norman and Scott, Elizabeth (1994) Individual Education Programmes in Secondary Schools. *Support for Learning*, Vol. 9, No. 1.

Caffyn, Rachel and (1992) 'From Special School to Main-Mallet, Dorothy stream: Perspectives of Physically Disabled Pupils.' In Ed Jones, P. R. & Crowley-Bainton, T. *Education and Child Psychology*, Vol. 9, No. 1.

Caplan, D. (1981) 'On the Cerebral Localisation of Linguistic Functions: Logical and Empirical Issues Surrounding Deficit Analysis and Functional Localisation' *Brain and Language*, **14**, 120–137.

Caramazza, A. 'On Drawing Inferences about the Structure of Normal Cognitive Systems from Analysis of Impaired Performance: The Case for Single-Patient Studies.' Brain and Cognition, 5, 41–46.

Caswell, J. and Portsmouth, R. (1989) 'One-to-One.' *The Times Educational Supplement*, 27th January.

CCAM (Charity Communications Service and Marketing) 'A Complete Communications for Non-profit Organisations.' Proprieter: Mick Daws (BSc, AMIPR), 141 Humslet Road, Burntwood, Staffs. WS7 9LF.

CCETSW (Central Council in Social Work) (1991) *Disability Issues: Developing* for Education and Training *Anti-Discriminatory Practice*. Improving Social Work Education & Training – Number Nine CCETSW, Derbyshire House, St. Chad's Street, London, WC1H 8AD.

Charlton, T. & Hunt, (1993) 'Towards pupil's self-image enhancement: The EASI teaching programme.' *Support for Learning*, Col. 8, No. 3, August.

Chu, S. K. H. (1989) 'The Application of Contemporary Treatment Approaches in Occupational Therapy for Children with Cerebral Palsy.' *Br. J. of Occ. Therapy*. Vol. 52, No. 9, September.

Clayton, T. (1989a) 'The Role of Welfare Assistants in Supporting Children with Special Educational Needs in Ordinary Primary Schools', in Evans, R. (ed.) *Special Educational*. Basil Blackwell, Oxford.

Clayton, T. (1989b) 'The Role and Management of Welfare Assistants,' in Bowers, T. (ed.) *Managing Special Needs*. Open University Press: Milton Keynes.

Clayton, T. (1990a) *Welfare Assistants: Are they Equipped for their Role?* Support for Learning, Vol. 5, No. 4, 193–8.

Clayton, T. (1990b) 'The Training Needs of Special Welfare Asssistants: What do Heads, Class Teachers and the Assistants themselves Regard as Important?' *Educational and Child Psychology*, Vol. 7, No. 1, 44–51.

Clayton, T. (1991) *Welfare Assistance: as a Resource to Help with the Education and Management of Children with Special Educational Needs in Ordinary Primary Schools*. Doctoral thesis, Council for National Academic Awards.

Clayton, T. (1992) 'Support for Special Needs.' *Support for Learning*. Vol. 7, No. 4.

Cooper, Deborah (1987) 'Developing Effective Policy Statements: Guidance for College Staff . . .' SKILL, 336 Brixton Road, London, SW9 7AA.

Cooper, Deborah (1992) 'Opening Doors? The Implications of the Further and Higher Education Act 1992.' SKILL, 336 Brixton Road, London, SW9 7AA.

Cooper, Deborah (1993) 'Further Education: Starting Afresh.' *British J. of Special Ed.*, Vol. 20, No. 2.

Cooper, Deborah (1994) An Opportunity for Change: A Practical Guide to In-Service Training for Special Needs Staff in Further Education and Training Establishments. SKILL 336 Brixton Road, London, SW9 7AA.

Coopers & Lybrand (1992) *Within Reach: Access for Disabled Children to Mainstream Education*. National Union of Teachers in association with the Spastics Society.

Cornwall, J. V. (1992) Children with Cerebral Palsy: Exploring their special educational needs. Multi-disciplinary training and awareness project for Local Authorities (1990–1992). The Spastics Society.

Cotton, Esther (1980) *The Basic Motor Pattern*. The Spastics Society. London.

Cratty, Bryant J. (1973) *Intelligence in Action*. Prentice Hall Inc., New Jersey.

CSIE (Centre for 'Action for Inclusion . . . '.

Studies on Integration O'Brien and Forbot with Snow and Hasbury. From CSIE, 415 Edgeworth Road, London, NW2 6NB.

Cummins, R. A. (1988) *The Neurologically-Impaired Child: Doman-Delecato* Technique Re-appraised. Croom Helm: London.

Davies, Michael (1992) 'Assessment of the Special Educational Needs of Children.' Nat. Primary Centre, Special Issues, No. 2, April.

Davies, Michael (1995) 'Beyond Physical Access for Students with Cerebral Palsy: The neurological sequelia.' Article for the *The Psychologist Magazine*. Due to be published at the time of going to press.

Department for Education (1994) *Code of Practice on the Identification and Asssessment of Special Educational Needs*. HMSO: London.

Department of Education and Science (1981) Education Act 1981. HMSO: London.

Department of Education and Science (1987) The National Curriculum 5–16: A Consultation Document. HMSO, London.

DES (1989) *Report: Pupils and Young People with Physical Disabilities*. HMI Inspectors, DES: London.

DES (1989) Circular No. 22/89: *Assessments and Statements of Special Educational Needs: Procedures with the Education, Health and Social Services*. HMSO: London.

Doman, Glenn (1974) *What to Do About Your Brain Injured Child*. Doubleday: New York.

Donkersloot, Paul (1991) 'Humberside Initiative: County Education Service for Physical Disability.' *Head Teacher's Review*, Spring Edition.

Downey, M. E. Kelly, A. V. (1975) *Theory and Practice of and Education*. Harper and Row: London.

Edwards, Alistair D. N. (1990) *Speech Synthesis: Technology for Disabled People*. Paul Chapman Publishing: London.

Employment Service (1993) *Sources of Help: Employing Disability Services Branch People with Disabilities*. Published free by ESDSB (above), DS1. Level 3, Steel City House, c/o Rockingham House, 123 West Street, Sheffield, S1 4ER.

Evans, J. & Lunt, I. (1993) *British Journal of Special Education*, Vol. 20, June.

Fenton, Melissa (1992) *Working Together Towards Independence: Guidelines for Support Staff working together with Children with Physical Disabilities.* Published by RADAR, 25 Mortimer Street, London, W1N 8AB.

Fenton, Melissa (1989) *Passivity to Empowerment: Aand Hughes, Pippa Living Skills Curriculum for People with Disabilities.* RADAR.

Forest, M. & Pearpoint, J. (1991) *Two Roads – Exclusion or Inclusion.* Centre for Integrated Education and Democracy, McGill University Toronto.

Foundastion for Conductive (1989) Report of the Foundation for Education Conductive Ed. Annual Conference. Birmingham 30 June 1989. In – *Speech Therapy in Practice.* Vol. 5, No. 3.

Francis, Dave and Woodcock, Mike. (1975) *People at Work (A Practical. Guide to Organizational Change).* University Associates, California, USA.

Fulcher, G. (1989) *Disabling Policies?* Falmer Press: London.

Fullwood, Deborah and (1986) *Facing The Crowd: Managing Cronin, Peter Other People's Insensitivities to your Disabled Child.* Royal Victorian Institute for the Blind. ISBN 0949390 062

Gage, James R. (1987) 'Pre-operative Planning and Post-operative Evaluation using Clinical Gait Analysis.' *Journal of Development Medicine and Child Neurology.* June.

Gordon, Neil and McKinley, Ian (1990) *Helping Clumsy Children.* Churchill Livingstone: U.K.

Hadley, Roger, Wilkinson, Heather and Rodwell, Graham (1993) *Movement Disabilities and Primary Education: A Pilot Study* Lancaster University.

Halliday, Paula (1989) *Special Needs in Ordinary Schools: Children with Physical Disabilities.* Cassell: London.

Hargreaves, D. H. (1972) *Interpersonal relations and education.* Routledge and Keegan Paul: London.

Hary, Dr Maria and Akos, K. (1988) *Conductive Education.* Routledge: London.

Hary, Dr Maria. (1988) *The Human Principle in Conductive Education.* The Peto Andras Institute: Budapest.

Haskell, Simon H. &Barrett, Elizabeth K. (1977) *The Education of Children with Physical and Neurological Disabilities.* (3rd Ed.) Chapman & Hall: London.

HEFCE (1995) *Access to Higher Education: Students with Special Needs.* A report of the 1993–94 special initiative to encourage widening participation for students with special needs. Higher Education Funding Council, Northavon House, Coldharbour Lane, Bristol, BS16 1QD.

Hegarty, Sean and Moses, Diana. (Eds) (1988) *Developing Expertise: INSET for special educational needs.* NFER-Nelson, Berkshire, England.

Herbert, Martin (1993) *Working with Children and The Children Act.* BPS Books. The British Psychological Society: Leicester.

Heron, J. (1994) Opening Speech at the 1994 S.E.A.L. Conference.

Hill, M. (1991) 'Race and Disability,' in Department of Health and Social Welfare: *Disability – Identity, Sexuality and Relationships. 1991 Readings,* Open University, Milton Keynes.

Hodgkinson, C (1992) Alternative Accreditation: A Study of Some Issues Arising from the Introduction of Unit Accreditation in One LEA. Sheffield University. Unpublished PhD Thesis.

Hornby, Garry (1994) Counselling in Child Disability: Skills for working with Parents. Paul Chapman: London

Horwood, W. (1987) *Skallagrig.* Viking Penguin Books: London.

Howarth, Sylvia (1987) *Effective Intregration.* NFER-Nelson.

Hudson, Liam (1972) *The Cult of the Fact.* Jonathon Cape: London.

Humphreys, K. A. et al (1991) *Unlocking the Evidence: Teacher Assessment.* Published by The University of Northumbria.

I.C.A.C. (1994) Initiative on Communication Aids for Children. Newsletter. Ann Bernadt 336 Brixton Road, London SW9 7AA.

Ingrams, R. (1993) Article from 'The Observer', 21st February.

Jones, Philip R. and Crowley-Bainton, Theresa (1992) *Pyschology and Physical Disability A monograph.* BPS Division of Ed. and Child Psychology. *Educational and Child Psychology* Vol. 9, No. 1.

Jones, J.G. and Hardy,(1989) 'Stress and Cognitive Functioning in Sport.' *Journal of Sport Sciences,* pp. 41–63.

Jones, M. (1993) 'Including Everyone.' *Managing Schools Today* Vol. 3 & 2, Nov/Dec.

Jones, M., Jennings, V. and Levaudel, M. (1992) 'Take a Seat.' *Special Children Magazine* November/December.

Jones, Michael (1993) 'Observing Good Practices.' Part of the work done on SCOPE (formerly The Spastics Society) project with J. Cornwall: Children with Cerebral Palsy: Exploring their Special Needs.

Jones, Philip R. (1992) 'Psychology for Physically Disabled People.' In Ed Jones, P. R. Crowley-Bainton, T. *Education and Child Psychology,* Vol. 9, No. 1.

Jowett, S., Hegarty, S.and Moses, D. (1988) *Joining Forces: A Study of Links between Special and*

Ordinary Schools. NFER-Nelson, Berkshire, England.
Jowsey, Sheila A. (1992) *Can I Play Too? Physical Education for Physically Disabled Children in Mainstream Schools*. David Fulton Publishers: London.
Kanter, Rosabeth Moss (1988) 'Managing Change – The Human Dimension.' *Creativity and Innovation Yearbook* – Volume I. Manchester Business School.
Kelly, A. V. (1990) *The National Curriculum: A Critical Review (1994 Update)*. Paul Chapman Publishing: London.
Kelly, G. A. (1955) *The Psychology of Personal Constructs*. Norton: New York.
Lacey, Penny and Lomas, Jeanette (1993) *Support Services and the Curriculum: A Practical Guide to Collaboration*. David Fulton Publishers: London.
Lamb, Brian and Layzell. Sarah (1994) *Disabled in Britain: A World Apart*. SCOPE (The Spastics Society) 12 Park Crescent, London.
Leeds Department of (1992) Equal Opportunities Policy. Education Leeds City Council, Leeds.
Lefebure, L. M. (1979) 'Achievement Motivation and Casual Attribution in Male and Female Athletes.' *Int. J. of Sport Psych.*, **10**, 31–41.
Leonard, M. (1989) *The 1988 Education Act: A Tactical Guide for Schools*. Blackwell: England.
Lewin, Kurt (1981) *Field Theory in Social Sciences*. Harper & Row: London.
Luria, A. (1966) *Higher Cortical Functions in Man* (translated by Haigh). Tavistock: London.
Luria, A. (1970) *Traumatic Aphasia* (translated by Critchley). Mouton: The Hague.
Mackey, Susan (1989) 'The Use of Computer-Assisted Feedback in a Motor Control Task for Cerebral Palsied Children.' *Physiotherapy*, Vol. 75, No. 3. March.
Male, Judith and Thompson, Claudia (1989) *The Educational Implications of Disability: A Guide for Teachers*. Royal Ass. for Disability and Rehabilitation (RADAR), 25 Mortimer Street, London.
Mandelstam, Michael and Kingsley, Jessica (1990) *How To Get Equipment for Disability* (2nd Edition). Jessica Kingsley, 118 Pentonville Road, London, N1 9JN. (£18.95)
Maras, P. and Brown, R. (1991) 'Mainstream Children's Attitudes to Disability.' Edited version of paper presented to Br. Psych. Soc. Ann. Conference. In Br. Psych. Soc. Education Section Review.
Maras, P. and Brown, R. (1994) 'Children's Attitude to Peers with Learning Difficulties: Effect of Contact in Schools.' Research project. University of Kent and article to *The Psychologist* magazine. Still to be published at time of going to press.
Marlett, N. and Buchner. D. 1987) 'Special education funding for children with severe disabilities in Alberta.' In (ed.) Booth, T. *Including Pupils with Disabilities*. Open University Press: Milton Keynes.
Martens, R. 'Anxiety and Motor Behaviour: A Review.' *Journal of Motor Behaviour*, **3**, 151–179.
Mason, Micheline (1994) 'The Importance of Partnership with Parent'. Transcript of a talk given on 15th June 1994. Unpublished at time of going to press.
Massie, Bert Backflash: Fighting for a New Act.
Masters, R. S. W. (1992) 'Knowledge, Knerves and Know-how: The Role of Explicit Versus Implicit Knowledge in the Breakdown of Complex Motor Skills under Pressure.' *British Journal of Psychology*, Vol. 83. Part 3. August.
MENCAP – Interlink Under 5's Project (1990) *Ordinary Everyday Families. . . A Human Rights Issue*. MENCAP (London Division). 115 Golden Lane, London, EC1Y 0TJ.
Mittler, Peter (1989a) 'Towards Special Training Needs For All?' In Jones, Neville, *Special Educational Needs Review*, Volume 2, Chapter 1 (p. 1), Education and Alienation Series, Falmer Press.
Mittler, Peter (1989b) 'Towards Special Needs Training for All?' in Jones, N. (Ed) *Special Educational Needs Review* Vol. 1. Falmer Press, England.
Mittler, Peter (1992) 'Educational Entitlement in the Nineties.' *British Journal of Special Education*.
Moore, J. (1992) Good Planning is the Key. *British Journal of Special Education* **19**, (1).
Moore, J. and Morrison, N. (1989a) *Someone Else's Problem*. Falmer Press: Sussex.
Morris, J. and Morrison, N. (1989b) 'Progress with Humanity? The Experience of a Disabled Lecturer,' in Booth, T. and Swann, W. *Including Pupils with Disabilities*. Open University Press: Milton Keynes.
Morris, Jenny (1991) *Pride Against Prejudice: Transforming Attitudes to Disability*. The Womens Press.
Morris, Jenny (1992) *Disabled Lives*. BBC Publications, Chief Education Officer, Room 2316 BBC, White City, 201 Wood Lane, London.
Moses, D, Hegarty, S. and Jowett, S. (1988) *Supporting Ordinary Schools: LEA Initiatives*. NFER-Nelson, Berkshire.
NAGM, NAHT, Coopers & Lybrand and SHA (1993) *Working Together*. Available from Nat. Ass. of Gov. and Managers, Coopers & Lybrand Nat. Ass. of Head Teachers and Secondary Heads Ass.

Noonan, J., Barry, J. and Davis, H. (1970) 'Personality determinants in attitudes toward visible disability.' *Journal of Personality*, **38**, 1, 1–15.

North Yorks County Council (1992) Special Education Needs: Education Committee (NYCC) Guidelines for Schools: *Guidelines for Schools – Physically Disabled Pupils*, NYCC.

OFSTED (Office For Standards in Education) (1992) *The Handbook for the Inspection of Schools*. HMSO: London.

Oliver, M. (1989) 'Disability and dependancy: a creation of industrial societies.' In Barton, L. (Ed) *Disability and Dependancy*. Falmer Press: Lewes.

OPCS (Office of Population Census & Surveys) (1988) Surveys of Disabilities in Great Britain. Social Surveys Division.

Orwell, G. (1945) *Animal Farm*. Secker & Warburg: London.

Parkin, Shirley and Padley, Margaret (1989) *Working With Clumsy Children: A Practical Approach for Teachers*. Special Needs Advice and Support, Oakes Park School. Sheffield Education Department.

Paull, Margaret E. (1992) Personality, Attitudes and Self-concept in Physically Disabled Children: A Study using Repertory Grids. *European Journal of Special Needs*, **7**, No. 2. June.

Pimm, Paul (1992) 'Cerebral Palsy: A Non-Progressive Disorder?' In Ed. Jones P. R. and Crowley-Bainton, T. *Education and Child Psychology*, Vol. 9, No. 1.

Prosser, Glyn (1992) Psychological Issues Related to Having Others mediate in your Life. In Jones, P and Crowley-Bainton, T., Psychology and Physical Disability. British Psychological Society, Division of Ed. and Child Psychology, *Educational and Child Psychology*, Vol. 9, No. 1.

Quicke, J. & Winter. C. (1994) 'Labelling and learning: An interactionist perspective', *Support for Learning*, Vol. 9, No. 1, February.

Ralph, S. (1989) 'Images of Disability as Portrayed through the Media.' *Educate*, pp. 10–15, March 1989.

Randall, Robert and Southgate, Jonathon (1980) 'Co-operative and Community Group Dynamics.' Frances Tomlinson: U.K.

Reindal. S. M. (1995) 'Discussing disability – an investigation into theories of disability,' *European Journal of Special Needs Education*, Vol. 10, No. 1, 58–69.

Rieser, R. and Mason, M. (1992) *Disability Equality in the Classroom: A Human Rights Issue*. (Republished version). Disability Equality in Education. 78 Mildmay Grove, London, N1 4PJ.

Rieser, R. (1994a) 'Making, Sense and Nonsense of the Code of Practice'. *New Learning Together Magazine*, Issue No. 2, September

Rieser, R. (1994b) 'An opportunity not to be Missed: 1994 Inclusive School Policies', *New Learning Together Magazine* Issue no. 1, April.

Rosenthal, R. and Jacobson, L. (1968) *Pygmalion in the Classroom*. Holt, Rhinehart and Winston: N.Y.

Russell, P. (Special Education Consortium) (1993) Council for Disabled Children, 8 Wakely Street, London, EC1 7QE.

Rutter, M., Maughan, B., Mortimore, P. and Ouston, J. (1982) *Fifteen Thousand Hours*. Open Books: London.

Salmon, Phillida (1988) *Psychology for Teachers: An Alternative Approach*. Hutchinson: England.

SCIL (Southampton Centre for Independent Living) Publish Simon Brisenden's poems. Proceeds towards a bank of books, videos, etc. Co-ordinator: David Gibson, 6 Northlands Road, Southampton, SO15 2LF.

Scottish Education Council (1990) Opening Doors: Pupils with Physical Disabilities. (The Integration of Children with Physical Disabilities). A project in special educational needs funded by the Scottish Education Council.

Seligman, M. E. P. (1974) 'Depression and learned helplessness.' In Friedman, R. and Katz, M. (Eds) *The Psychology of Depression: Contemporary Theory and Research*. Wiley: New York.

Shakespeare, T. (1994) 'Poor Dear' – 3rd in a series of BBC programmes on disability and charity. BBC Television.

Shallice, Tim (1988) *From Neuropsychology to Mental Structure*. Cambridge University Press: U.K.

SKILL, (National Bureau for Students with Disabilities) (1992) *Further and Higher Education Acts 1992: Students with Disabilities and Learning Difficulties*. SKILL, 336 Brixton Road, London, SW9 7AA.

SKILL (National Bureau for Students with Disabilities) (1992) *Meeting the Personal Care Needs of Physically Disabled Students at College*. SKILL, 336 Brixton Road, London, SW9 7AA.

Stein, J. F. (1985) 'The Control of Movement.' In Coen, C. W. (Ed) *Functions of the Brain*. Clarendon Press; England.

Stendler, C. B., Damrin, D. and Haines, A. C. 'Studies in Co-operation and Competition: I: The Effects of working for Group and Individual Rewards on the Social Climate of Children's Groups.'

Stern, Gerald (1987) 'The Bobath Concept.' *Association of Paediatric Chartered Physiotherapists*,

No. 44, pp. 10–15, August.
Sternberg, R. J. (1984) 'Facets of intelligence.' In Anderson, J. R. and Kosslyn, S. M. (eds). *Tutorials in Learning and Memory: Essays*. W H Freeman, San Franciso.
Sutton, Andrew (1987) 'Teaching for Independence,' Special Education Section, *Teachers Weekly*, 19 October.
Swann, Will (1985) 'Is the integration of children with special needs happening?' *Oxford Review of Education*, **11**, 1, pp. 3–18.
Swann, Will (1991) *Segregation Statistics, English LEAs 1988–91*. Centre for Studies on Integration: London.
Swann, Will (1992) *Segregation Statistics, English LEAs 1988–91*, Centre for Studies on Integration: London.
The Spastics Society (1992) Children with Cerebral Palsy: Exploring their Special Educational Needs. A 2 year project for Local Authorities and multi-disciplinary teams. Consultant: John Cornwall (1990–1992).
The Spastics Society (1994) *Within Reach: Access for Disabled Children to Mainstream Education. (The School Survey)*. SCOPE (formerly The Spastics Society), 12 Park Crescent, London.
Tingle, Myra (1990) *The Motor Impaired Child*. NFER, Nelson, Berkshire: England.
Tomlinson, Sally (1981) *Educational Subnormality: A Study in Decison Making*. Routledge and Keegan Paul: London.
Tomlinson, Sally (1982) The Sociology of Special Education. Routledge and Keegan Paul: London.
Tomlinson, Sally (1985) 'The Expanson of Special Education.' *Oxford Review of Education*, **11**, pp. 157–165.
TUC (Trades Union Congress) (1995) Civil Rights for Disabled People. A TUC statement from the Equal Rights Dep., London. January.
U.D.E.T. (1995) (Understanding Disabilities Educational Trust). All enquiries to the Education Officer, RADAR, 12 City Forum, London, EC1V 8AF (as from 1995).
Vaughan, Mark (1992) 'From Disability to Giftedness.' *Contact*, Autumn Issue.
Vevers, P. (1992) 'Getting in on the Act,' *British Journal of Special Education*, Vol. 19, No. 3.
Vygotsky, Lem Seminovich (1962) *Thought and Language*. Wiley: New York.
Ward, David (1994) 'Brain damage boy caught in education tussle.' *The Guardian*, 12th September.
Warnock Report (1978) Report of the Committee of Enquiry into the Education of Handicapped Children and Young People. Department of Education and Science. HMSO.
Webber, Aileen (1991a) *In-Service: Practical Approaches, Attitudes and Equipment for Staff Working Alongside Students with Physical Disabilities*. Folens Publishers: U.K.
Webber, Aileen (1991b) *Sport and Mobility: For Students with Physical Disabilities*. Folens Publishers: U.K.
Webber, Aileen (1991c) *Living Skills: For Students with Physical Disabilities*. Folens Publishers: U.K.
Webber, Aileen (1991d) Independence and Integration. (Series of 4 books of photocopiable resource materials). Folens Publishers, Albert House, Apex Business Centre, Boscombe Road, Dunstable, LU5 4RL.
Webber, Aileen (1991) Pre-Vocational Skills: For Students with Physical Disabilities. Folens Publishers: U.K.
Wechsler, D. (1958) *The Measurement and Appraisal of Adult Intelligence*. Williams and Wilkins: New York.
Wedell, Klaus (1994) 'Training the Teachers.' *Teaching Today*. Autumn issue.
Weinberg, N. and Sanatana, R., (1978) 'Comic Books: Champions of the Disabled Stereotype,' in *Rehabilitation*, Vol. 89, nos. 11–12, pp. 327–331.
Williams, David (1990) *The Education of Children with Cerebral Palsy with Special Reference to Conductive Education*. David Williams (For Lincolnshire Ed. Authority), St Francis School, Wickenby Crescent, Emine Estate, Lincoln, LN1 3TJ.
Yerkes, R. M. and Dodson, J. D. (1908) 'The relation of strength of stimulus to rapidity of habit formation.' *Journal of Comparative Neurology and Psychology*, **18**, 459–482.
Young, M. F. D. (1979) An Approach to the Study of Curricula as Socially Organised Knowledge. In Young, M. F. D. (ed), *Knowledge and Control*. Collier Macmillan: London.

Index

access, and differentiation 119, 120-4; and entitlement 25-6, 28; to computers 221-33; to curriculum 134-5, 239; to educational buildings 19, 74, 75-6, 89, 103, 111, 121-2, 235, 257; to further and higher education 239-41; to tests 44-5; to transport 70, 236
accountability 21, 37, 38
active learning 158-9
admissions policies 89, 237
affirmative action 239
aided communication 221-2; access devices 222-30
anxiety and physical performance 211-13
assessment 20, 37; access to tests 44-5; and "accounting" activities 128; areas measured 44-5; bureaucratisation of 61; and Code of Practice 78, 95-7, 100-1; "criterion referenced tests" 44, 45; differential 167; holistic approach 116-18; IQ tests 49-50; issues involved 99-100; and national curriculum 26, 27-30, 117-18; normative 43-4, 45; process for disabled students 101-5; standardised tests 44, 102, 118, 134; through teaching (ATT) 101, 102
attitudes to disability 79-80, 174, 255-6
Audit Commission 29, 68, 74

Barnes, Colin 2, 4, 10, 14, 17, 38, 55, 66, 70, 75; *Disabled People in Britain and Discrimination* 39
Barnes, Harry 15, 235
behavioural psychology 26-7, 204-9
Bishop, Michael 55; on attitudes to disability 49
Black, Paul 38, 240-1; on national curriculum 25, 26, 27-8
Bobath treatment 193, 199-210
body language 221-2
Brisenden, Simon 135, 138, 139, 199, 258
bullying 183, 184-5

Canada, funding of special needs provision 29-30
Candoco Dance Company 212
cerebral palsy 41, 173-7, 186-91, 193, 249
choice, by parents 93-4; and collective responsibility 62; denial of 4-5, 7, 62, 214-15; development of 90; and equal opportunity 56; exercised by students 106, 131-3; variation in 172; ways of facilitating 215-20
civil rights legislation 1, 4, 5, 15, 234, 235
Clayton, T. 83, 87
Code of Practice on Identification and Assessment of SENs (1994) 74, 78-9, 94-5, 134, 135, 144, 191, 193-4; on assessment 100-1; for GCSE 194; internal stages 95-7
collective responsibility 62
communication, and disability 34-5; technical aids 223-33
computers 196; communication aids 223-8; Internet 232-3; multi media 230; overlay keyboards 230; voice control 229
Conductive Education 175-6, 193, 199-210, 250
contact teachers 164, 165-6
Cooper, Deborah, on legislation 38-9
Coopers and Lybrand 74, 75
County Education Service for Physical Disability (CESPD) 84-6

Davies, Michael, on personal physical needs 130
Dearing report 28
deficit model of teaching 114, 115, 196
dependency, creation of 70, 165
development, environmental factors 50-1
developmental checklists 32-3
differentiation 65, 89, 102, 118-20; and access 119, 120-4; in assessment 167; and balance 122-3; and breadth 125; and national curriculum 119-20; and relevance 123-4; as shared activity 170
disability, attitudes to 79-80, 174, 255-6;

and communication 34-5; concept of 2, 13-14, 33, 69; and empowerment 252-3; images of 52-3; medical model 3, 6-7, 16-17, 45-8, 50, 69-70, 72-3, 114, 253; social model 50, 70-3
disability equality training 77-8
Disabled People's International (DPI) 253
Disabled Student Allowance (DSA) 168
disabling procedures in schools and colleges 76-8
discrimination 57-8, 70; against women 59; in employment 236; and power structures 58; through lack of awareness 77
Dolman-Delacato treatment 204-9
Donkersloot, P. 84-5
Downey, M.E. and Kelly, A.V., on equality of opportunity 64
Down's Syndrome 41
Dussart, Georges, on dyspraxia 178-86
dyslexia 50-1
dyspraxia 50-1, 178-86, 187-8

Education Act (1944) 16-17
Education Act (1981) 13-14, 20-2,64, 113
Education Act (1993) and Code ofPractice 36-8, 86-7, 88-9
Education Reform Act (1988) (ERA) 24-30, 64, 113
employment discrimination 236
enabling environments 196
enabling technology 221-33
enrichment activities 114, 121, 127
environment, role in development 50-1
equal opportunity 56, 79-81; and disability 56-7; policies for 64, 256-8
eugenics 13, 42-3
evaluation, involvement of disabled students in 93
evaluation *see also* assessment
Evans, J. and Lunt, I., on LMS 29
exclusion 243-8
expectations 79-80, 127; lowering of 124-5

facilities, lack of 234-5
Forest, Marsha and Pearpoint, Jack 243-6, 248, 252
fragmentation of education and therapy 140-3, 160, 248
Francis, Hazel, on assessing individuals 45, 50
functional ability, and structural impairment 50-3
funding 35-6, 48-9, 78, 82, 91
Funding Agencies for Schools (FAS) 29, 237
Further Education Funding Council (FEFC) 239-41
further and higher education 35-6, 38, 107, 138, 164-5, 166-8
Further and Higher Education Acts (1992) 35, 38, 86-7

governors 23-4, 28-9, 89
Grant Maintained (GM) schools 29
groupwork 196-7

Hawking, Steven 212, 223
health authorities 83
health services 96, 97
Herbert, Martin, on Children Act (1989) 32, 33-4
hidden curriculum 112
Hirstle, Liz, experience of disability 173-7
holistic approach 7, 63, 138, 150, 249-50; partnerships 158-9; to assessment 116-18
Howarth, Sheila 82
humanistic psychology 40, 198

identification of "children in need" 31-5
inclusion 72, 243-8; barriers to 73-6, 82, 88; and integration 254-5; policies for 88-94, 110-12
independence skills 105-9, 195
Individual(ised) Education Plans (IEPs) 97-101, 127, 129, 130-1, 134, 170, 193-4
institutionalisation 18
integration 6, 12-13, 22, 58, 71-2, 85, 133, 247; and inclusion254-5; of learning experience148
interactive approach 204-9
IQ tests 49-50
irresponsibility by adults 185-6

Jones, Michael 161-2
Jones, P., on patronising attitudes 60

Kelly, George, "Personal Construct Psychology" 40-1
key workers 148

labelling 51-2, 66-8, 81; and research 41-2, 250-1
language, misuse of 11-12; problems of terminology 251; social meaning 251-2
learning difficulties, and physical disability 68-79, 74-5
Learning Support Centres 107
legislation, anti-discrimination 14-15; Children Act (1989) 19, 31-5, 145; Children and Young Persons Act (1969) 18; Chronically Sick and DisabledPersons Act (1970) 19; civilrights 1, 4, 5, 15, 234, 235; costs of 234; Disabled Persons Act (1986) 22; Education Act (1944) 16-17; Education Act (1981) 13-14, 20-2, 64, 113; Education Act (1986) 23-4; Education Act (1993) and Codeof Practice 36-8, 86-7, 88-9; Education Reform Act (1988) (ERA) 24-30, 64, 113; Further and Higher Education Acts (1992) 35, 38, 86-7; future 238-9; Handicapped Children Act (1970) 18; National Health Service Re-organisation Act (1973) 19; omissions in 235-6; United States 235; Warnock Report 2, 20, 22, 34, 113
Lewin, Kurt, on self-perception 53
litigation, medical 188
local education authorities (LEAs) 28, 192, 237; responsibilities 91; variation in provision 74
local management of schools (LMS) 23, 29, 87, 134, 236-7

Mason, Micheline 191, 192
"mechanisation" of education 61
mediated learning 115-16
medical model of disability 3, 6-7, 16-17, 45-8, 50, 69-70, 72-3, 114, 253
Mittler, Peter 6, 133
Moore, John, on differentiation 122-3
Morris, Jenny, on attitudes to disability 55, 59, 80
Moses, D., Hegarty, S. and Jowett, S. 6, 82, 133
motivation 170, 198, 214
movement and development 195-6, 199-210
Mulligan, Avril, experience of disability 186-91
myths concerning disability 12-14

national curriculum 24-5, 26, 204-9; and assessment 27-30, 117-18; and breadth of learning 26-7; and differentiation 119-20; entitlement to 113; and individual needs 125-30; politically defined 24, 26; supplementing 115, 134-8

OFSTED inspections 6, 7, 91, 117,238
Oliver, M., on dependency 70
one-to-one teaching 196-7
opting out 28
orthofunction 200-1
Owen, Wilfred 11

parents 129, 133; and assessment of special needs 96-7; and Children Act (1989) 34; choice by 93-4; and disabled young adults 171-2; and early development of child 171; experience of disability 51, 173-91; involvement of 23-4, 204-9; partnerships with 148-50, 171; pivotal role 148; recognition of 239
partnership 239
partnerships, barriers to 144-5, 153-8; formation of 140-2; and growth 150-3; importance of 169-70; levels of 145-7; natural 143-4; role of parents 148-50, 171
pastoral care 111-12
paternalism 60
personal, social and health education 135-6, 137
personal and social support 106-9, 121
Peto, Andras, and conductive education 197-8

physiotherapy 147, 193; Bobath treatment 193, 199-211; Conductive Education 175-6, 193, 199-211, 250
Pimm, Paul, on cerebral palsy 41
planning, partnership in 169-70
posture and seating *see also* Bobath treatment; conductive education 104-6
professional cooperation *see also* partnership 193-4, 239, 249-50

quality, monitoring of 36

reading skills 179, 180
research, ethical problems 42; interdisciplinary 249-50; and labelling 41-2, 250-1
resourced schools 84-6
resources, special needs seen in terms of 17, 29
Rieser, Richard, *Disabled History* 10, 87
Rieser, Richard and Mason, Micheline 39, 55, 66, 75, 92
role models 55, 112

SATs (Standard Attainment Targets) 44, 102, 118, 134
Sayer, John, on 1986 Education Act 23-4
SCOPE (formerly Spastics Society) 5, 21, 176; "Curricular Aims for "Schools for Parents"" 149-50; model of partnership 159, 161
segregation of education provision 71-3, 75
selective schools 157
self-concept 53-4, 55-6
self-esteem 53-6, 117, 242, 248; enhancement of 197-9
SENCOs (Special Educational Needs Coordinators) 86-7, 97, 99, 110,161-2, 184
Shakespeare, T., experience of disability 66-7
SKILL (National Bureau for Students with Disabilities) 36, 38-9
Snow, Judith, experience of disability 252
social model of disability 70-3
special needs, collective responsibility for 2; as continuum 22; definition of 38-9; social perspective 13-14
Special Needs Training Consortium 87-8
special needs tribunals 192
specialist schools 159, 161, 176-7, 190, 238
speech, synthetic 224
speech therapy 102, 187-8
sport psychology 194-5, 204-9, 211-13
statements of special needs 29, 102, 183-4, 188, 189-90
support assistants 77-8, 82-3, 85, 104, 121, 128, 161-2
supported education 48
surgical intervention 204-9

teacher-pupil relationships 198, 241
Tomlinson, Sally, on legislation 38
training and research 249-50
transitions, pre-school to school 162-3; primary to secondary 163-4, 165-6; to further/higher education 164-5, 166-8
transport, access to 70, 236

under-5s provision 236, 237-8

Vevers, Paul, on 1981 Education Act 20-1

Warnock Report 2, 20, 22, 34, 113
Webber, Aileen, *Independence and Integration* 107, 108, 115, 122, 131, 216, 218, 219
Wedell, Klaus 116-18
Weinberg, N. and Santana, R., depiction of disability 66
whole school issues, partnership 158-9
whole school policies 72-81, 118
withdrawal from lessons 47-8, 196-7